This book is to be returned on
or before the date stamped below

UNIVERSITY OF PLYMOUTH

ACADEMIC SERVICES
PLYMOUTH LIBRARY
Tel: (0752) 232323
This book is subject to recall if required by another reader
Books may be renewed by phone
CHARGES WILL BE MADE FOR OVERDUE BOOKS

CHARGES WILL BE MADE FOR OVERDUE BOOKS

CORPORATE TAXATION AND INVESTMENT

Corporate Taxation and Investment

The Implications of the 1984 Tax Reform

ELEANOR J. MORGAN
School of Management,
University of Bath

Gower

Published by
Gower Publishing Company Limited,
Gower House, Croft Road, Aldershot, Hants GU11 3HR,
England

Gower Publishing Company,
Old Post Road, Brookfield, Vermont 05036,
USA

British Library Cataloguing in Publication Data

Morgan, Eleanor J.
  Corporate taxation and investment : the
  implications of the 1984 tax reform.
  1. Corporations——Taxation——Great Britain
  I. Title
  336.24'3'0941   HD2753.G7

  ISBN 0-566-05265-2 ✓

Printed and bound in Great Britain by
Biddles Limited, Guildford and King's Lynn

Contents

PART 3 THE FINDINGS

Tables

Preface

The 1984 Budget proposed the most fundamental changes to the system of corporate taxation in the UK for over a decade. These changes, which included the gradual reduction of the corporation tax rate and the phasing out of first year allowances, were seen by the government as reforming some of the worst features of a tax system which had been widely criticised for some years.

There was little disagreement about the need for revising the pre 1984 corporate tax system, but the implications of the new tax provisions, which became fully operational in 1986-87, have been widely disputed. The lack of evidence on which to base an assessment of this major shift in the direction of government policy from a high allowance, high tax to a low allowance, low tax system provided the impetus for the research contained in this volume.

One of the main reasons for introducing the new measures was the effect they were expected to have on firms' investment decisions, so the purpose of this book is to provide evidence about the likely effect of the tax changes at the micro level. It focuses on sixty past investments, which were examined in depth, primarily to see whether different decisions would have been taken had the post 1986 system of allowances and tax rates applied when the investment was being considered.

Part 1 puts the empirical research in context by outlining

the past developments in government policy towards investment incentives and the recent Budget changes. The nature of the present empirical study is then discussed, against the background of previous British studies of the impact of government policy on investment decisions. Part 2 contains the detailed cases. These are individually presented, sector by sector, with foreign multinationals appearing first in each chapter, then UK listed firms and finally private businesses. An overview of the results and their implications for the likely effects of the 1984 reform is provided in Part 3.

The author wishes to acknowledge the support for this study provided by the Equipment Leasing Association, as part of a wider research programme on the effects of the 1984 Budget on corporate taxation and investment, carried out in the School of Management at Bath University. The ELA also encouraged and publicised the work but it must be emphasised that the views expressed in this volume are those of the author alone.

A large number of organisations and individuals participated in the study. I am extremely grateful to them for their cooperation and interest in the research, as well as their permission to publish the detailed cases in an anonymous form.

David O'Loan assisted with the fieldwork enquiries and helped to prepare the original research report, as well as carrying out the detailed calculations of the effects of the tax changes on project returns reported in Chapter 1. I am pleased to record my appreciation and thanks for his valuable contribution. I would also like to express my thanks to Professor Cyril Tomkins for his encouragement and support as the project progressed.

A number of people have helped in typing this work, whom I have thanked individually for their efforts. I am particularly grateful to Elspeth Morrison, for her assistance with the various drafts, particularly in seeing the case studies through their different stages; to Michelle Henley for her help with the tables, and to Hazel Gott for efficiently preparing the final typescript.

PART 1
THE ISSUES

1 Business taxation and investment incentives

DEVELOPMENT OF THE PRE 1984 SYSTEM OF INVESTMENT INCENTIVES

Capital allowances originated from the view that the measurement of business profits earned in any period should take account of the physical capital which was used up in obtaining them. A 'wear and tear' deduction for tax purposes was first introduced in 1878, representing the reduction in value of the plant and machinery used during the year in the course of the business. This wear and tear concept formed the basis of capital allowances until 1945 and resulted in allowances which normally approximated depreciation as calculated for commercial accounting purposes.

The first government measures to stimulate investment in fixed capital through a more generous treatment of investment for tax purposes than would be provided by normal depreciation over the asset's life, were introduced in 1945. The aim of the policy was to encourage re-equipment in manufacturing after the disruption of the war years, and hasten Britain's economic recovery. Fiscal incentives to stimulate investment in manufacturing industry have been continued by successive government since, apart from in the late 1960s when they were replaced by cash grants, and the pre 1984 system of capital allowances embodied both the wear and tear and incentive elements.

3

Over the years, a large number of different systems of tax incentives have been applied to encourage investment, each involving different arrangements and subject to fairly frequent changes in rates, particularly before 1966. These alterations occurred against a background of changes in the overall rates of business taxation, as well as the introduction of a variety of selective regional aids.

Two main fiscal instruments were used to provide the nationally available incentives on selected types of assets, namely initial allowances and investment allowances. Initial allowances enabled firms to write off a relatively large proportion of their expenditure on plant and machinery against pre tax profits in the first year which, in effect, accelerated the depreciation provided by the normal writing down allowances. This also applied to industrial buildings, although the rate allowed was lower in view of their longer average lives. The second main incentive, investment allowances, represented a net addition to the depreciation allowed against tax over and above the actual cost of the asset. In addition, increases in the ordinary writing down allowances for plant and machinery have also been used. A useful summary of the announcement dates of changes in the capital allowances and/or the rates at which the various incentives were applied is given in Melliss and Richardson (1976).

Although these measures were taken partly to compensate for the effects of inflation on the value of existing depreciation allowances, their main aim was to stimulate manufacturing investment by raising post tax rates of return and by leaving firms with more profits after tax to finance their capital expenditure programmes. Doubts about the effectiveness of tax based incentives in encouraging investment led, in 1966, to the abolition of both initial and investment allowances and their replacement by cash grants. Cash grants were abandoned after only four years, however, primarily on the grounds that such grants benefit firms whether or not they are making profits and can therefore result in uneconomic investment, leading to a waste of resources (HMSO, 1970).

Since 1971, investment incentives have again operated through the tax system. Investment allowances were never reintroduced and, instead, accelerated depreciation for tax purposes represented the main policy instrument. Although the incentives became progressively more generous, the system at the time of the 1984 Budget was still operating broadly along the lines established in the early 1970's. In 1972, initial or first year allowances on plant and machinery were increased to 100 per cent and remained at this level until the 1984 Budget changes. Small industrial workshops and new ships similarly qualified for 'free' depreciation. First year allowances on industrial buildings were gradually raised, to reach 75 per cent by 1981. As the main aim of the investment incentives was to encourage manufacturing investment, commercial buildings (which also tend to retain or increase their value) received no allowances and, by the early 1980's, the Green Paper on Corporation Tax identified nine other classes of assets, apart from industrial buildings, receiving allowances between the extremes of 100 per cent and zero allowances (HMSO, 1982).

These investment incentives must be viewed in the context of the taxation of business profits, which has itself been subject to alterations both of system and rate. Until 1965, income tax was charged on the income of companies and unincorporated businesses alike. In 1965, corporation tax was introduced at a uniform rate on all profits of incorporated businesses, whether distributed or not. As shareholders were liable to income tax on the dividends received, this 'classical system' meant that distributed profits were liable to double taxation. The present 'imputation system' was introduced, with effect from April 1973, to prevent this problem. It allows companies to offset advance corporation tax (ACT), paid to satisfy the shareholder's basic rate income tax liability on dividends, against their corporation tax liabilities, but only to the extent that these dividends are paid out of profits which have borne corporation tax.

From 1973-74 until the 1984 Budget changes, the statutory rate of corporation tax was 52 per cent, subject to special tapered provisions for small companies. Corporation tax was (and is) charged on the income and capital gains of companies. As far as trading income is concerned, companies have been able to make a variety of other deductions from their trading incomes, in addition to the allowances on fixed investment, before arriving at their mainstream corporation tax liabilities. Interest payments on debt finance can be deducted, relief is given for trading losses and tax paid abroad and stock relief was first introduced in 1975 to provide relief against tax on the unrealised inflationary gains on stockholdings. Further details of the reliefs which existed prior to 1984 and the provisions for carrying them into different accounting periods appear in the Green Paper on Corporation Tax.

The combination of the selective allowances on fixed investment and the various deductions available before tax liabilities were computed, meant that, by 1984, the system of corporation tax had become very complex in its operation and discriminatory in its effects. Three major factors determining the potential impact of the old system of high allowances and tax rates on firms' investment decisions can be distinguished. First, as discussed earlier, the tax based incentives for investment depended on the type of capital expenditure, with plant and machinery being most favoured. Second, the effect of the tax system depended on the way the investment was financed; dividends could only be partially offset for tax purposes (via the imputation rate of 30 per cent) whereas loan interest was fully deductible. This favoured debt over equity when companies were in a position to benefit from the interest relief, particularly in periods of high nominal interest rates. The preferential treatment accorded to certain suppliers of finance (e.g. tax exempt bodies) was a further source of discriminination on the financing side, as shown by King and Fullerton (1984). Third, it varied with the current and future tax position of the firm undertaking the investment. This third aspect is worth discussing in more detail here.

During the 1970's, the effects of recession and periodic profits crises, together with the increases in allowances and reliefs meant that many companies became 'tax exhausted' because the total deductions for which they were eligible exceeded their historic cost profits. The situation, as it existed by the early 1980's, is highlighted by the official estimates given in the following extract from the Green Paper on Corporation Tax:

> In current circumstances with average company profitability at an unprecedentedly low level and many companies making a loss (certainly after adjustment for inflation), it is estimated that in any year only about 40 per cent of all companies are currently earning sufficient profits, after all tax reliefs and allowances,to pay mainsteam corporation tax. Excluding the North Sea sector, about a third of all home industrial and commercial companies consistently pay mainstream tax, and another third move in and out of liability from year to year. The remaining third rarely or never pay mainstream tax. (HMSO, 1972)

When firms became tax exhausted, any unused allowances, or 'tax losses', could be carried forward to set against profits when future tax liabilities were assessed. This resulted in a substantial overhang of allowances building up. Indeed, according to official estimates from the same source, the accumulated tax losses (excluding those of public corporations) totalled some £30 billion by 1981 and were increasing by £5 billion annually. About one-third of this was attributed to unused stock relief and most of the remainder to unused capital allowances. Many companies were paying dividends out of historic cost profits which had not borne corporation tax and ACT became an additional tax charge on a tax exhausted company, the seriousness of which depended on how long it would be before the company earned taxable profits again. By the late 1970's, the government estimated that total surplus averaged some £600 million annually.

Although tax exhausted companies could carry forward their unused capital allowances, they could be carried forward in nominal terms only, so their real present value to the company depended on the firm's tax horizon and the rate of inflation in the intervening period. For the large number of companies which were in an almost permanent non tax paying position, the only possible way of benefiting from capital allowances was by financing their investment through leasing. The rationale and growth of the financial leasing industry has been fully documented in earlier work (see Tomkins, Lowe and Morgan, 1979). Essentially, leasing provided a mechanism whereby companies earning taxable profits, often the subsidiaries of financial institutions, could purchase the required equipment and pass on a proportion of the benefit from the allowances to the equipment users, the lessees, in the form of reduced rentals. The proportion of tax shelter passed on grew as the leasing industry developed, so that by the late 1970's as much as 90 per cent of the tax benefits was being reflected in the rental payments on some larger leases (Morgan, 1986).

THE 1984 TAX REFORM

Details of the major reform of corporation tax announced in the 1984 Budget are given in Table 1.1. The reform includes a stepped reduction in the statutory rate of corporation tax to 35 per cent (and an immediate reduction in the small companies rate), together with the gradual abolition of initial allowances for investment. Under the new system, the only capital allowances given will be annual writing down allowances and stock relief was abandoned immediately after the 1984 Budget, although unused relief could still be carried forward.

The new tax system is certainly simpler than the one it replaces and less discriminatory in its treatment of fixed investment; the multiplicity of forms of allowances for tax purposes given previously have been reduced to three different types, namely 25 per cent writing down allowances, 4 per cent writing down allowances and zero allowances. Capital allowances on plant and machinery have been brought much nearer to true rates of economic depreciation, but it was intended that they should still on average allow rather faster depreciation than would otherwise be provided for accounting purposes, so retaining some incentive element. The longer write off period resulting from 25 per cent allowances calculated on the annual balance of unrelieved expenditure will particularly affect assets which depreciate over a short period. In recognition of this problem, the 1985 Finance Act introduced depooling provisions, allowing the net cost of short life assets to be fully relieved within five years.

The phased reduction in capital allowances was accompanied by the immediate abolition of stock relief, as it was thought to be 'inappropriate to continue stock relief in a world of falling inflation' (HMSO, 1984). Under the new system, which aligns profits for tax purposes more closely to historic cost profits, the corporate sector is much less protected against inflation than before. The only relief on stock will occur through the deductability of nominal interest rates when debt is used to finance it. The writing down allowances on fixed investment are based on historic costs so inflation, even at 5 per cent, will substantially erode their value. For example, under the new system, 80 per cent of the value of plant and machinery acquired can be written off in the first 6 years of its life if prices remain stable. With 5 per cent inflation, this would take 8 years and with 10 per cent inflation it takes over 15 years. Any erosion in the value of the writing down allowances due to inflation will be particularly noticeable for firms which previously earned sufficient profits to benefit almost immediately from the former first year allowances.

As far as incorporated businesses are concerned, the phased shift from high allowances to low allowances was linked with a move from high to low rates of corporation tax. The proportionate reductions in the tax rates for small companies were less substantial than for those liable to corporate tax at the full rate, (21 per cent compared with 33 per cent) and the marginal tax rate which applies to the band of profits within which the reduced small companies rate is gradually withdrawn, is now less unfavourable, compared with the full rate, than previously.

It is not easy to predict the overall effect of these changes on the tax burden of the corporate sector as a whole because of the variations in individual companies' tax profiles and because any forecasts of tax liabilities depend on the underlying assumptions concerning, for example, future inflation rates, interest rates and growth rates. The Treasury expected the tax reform to have little effect on the total tax liability of the corporate sector in the transitional period of stepped reductions, but anticipated that average tax bills would fall in the longer run with the lower corporate tax rate, as writing down allowances built up.

Table 1.1
Changes to the UK corporation tax system introduced
by the 1984 Budget

---

1. Statutory rates of corporation tax (previously 52%)

Financial year ending	Main rate
31.3.84	50%
31.3.85	45%
31.3.86	40%
31.3.87	35%

Small companies rate reduced from 38% to 30% from financial year ending 31.3.1984 onwards

2. Capital allowances

	Plant & machinery	Industrial buildings
Expenditure incurred	Initial allowances	
Before 14.3.84	100%	75%
On or after 14.3.84	75%	50%
On or after 1.4.85	50%	25%
On or after 1.4.86	Nil	Nil

	Writing down allowances	
On or after 1.4.86	25%	4%
	(reducing balance)	(straight line)

Over the same period, most other capital allowances will be brought into line with these changes

3. Stock relief and clawback abolished from 13.3.84. Unused relief for past periods will continue to run forward

4. ACT can be carried back 6 years to offset against taxable profits (previously 2 years)

5. Double taxation relief on overseas earnings now available as an offset against taxable profits before ACT (previously after)

Source: Treasury Press Release

This view was challenged by Devereux and Mayer (1984) who used a computerised corporate tax model developed at the Institute of Fiscal Studies (Mayer and Morris, 1982) to estimate the differential effect of the 1984 Budget changes, including the transitional arrangements, for average corporation tax rates until 1992. They found that with a constant 7 per cent inflation rate, the average tax burden for their sample of firms would be higher under the new system than if the pre Budget arrangements had remained unaltered, although the difference would lessen after 1986-87.

In contrast, the tax forecasts produced by Levis with Thanassoulas (1985), as part of the current research programme, using the same framework but incorporating different assumptions and studying a different sample of firms, provide support for the Treasury view (Levis and Morgan, 1985). They suggest that, over the long term, if price rises remain at the low levels currently forecast, the rapid build up of writing down allowances is likely to outweigh the loss of stock relief and capital allowances.

Both studies highlight the sensitivity of the new system to inflation and show that the net effects of the new tax regime will be far from uniform across all companies. These studies did not include unincorporated businesses; it is important to note that these will continue to pay tax at personal rather than company rates and receive no compensating benefit from the lower rate of corporation tax, despite the loss of allowances. [1]

In view of the sizeable overhang of allowances which existed by 1984 and the ability of firms to carry unused allowances forward under the new system, the potential effect of tax incentives and the 1984 Budget changes on individual firms will continue to depend on their tax histories. A substantial number are likely to remain tax exhausted into the 1990s and, while some will benefit from lower tax payments, others which were previously tax exhausted or had surplus ACT will move into positions of higher tax payment. In particular, the ability since 1984 to carry back ACT and set it against tax liabilities for up to six years (rather than two years, as previously) has improved the available options and is expected to lead to a more rapid utilisation of surplus ACT.

The theoretical implications of the 1984 Finance Act for individual investment projects can be analysed in terms of the effect it will have on the pre tax returns required if projects are to achieve a given post tax yield. Using the methodology developed by King and Fullerton (1984), the Treasury illustrated the effects of the tax changes by reference to the

returns required from hypothetical investments undertaken by
fully tax paying companies (HMSO, 1984, Appendix 10). Their
illustrations showed the pre tax rate of return needed to yield
a 5 per cent after tax return on investment in specific kinds
of assets at different rates of inflation. The results with an
inflation rate of 5 per cent are reproduced in Table 1.2.

Table 1.2
Required rates of return, old and new systems

a) Debt finance	Plant and machinery	Industrial buildings	Commercial buildings
Old system	-0.2	-0.1	3.2
New system	2.5	2.7	4.1
Change	+2.7	+2.8	+0.9
b) Equity finance			
Old system	2.0	2.2	7.7
New system	3.1	3.4	4.8
Change	+1.1	+1.2	-2.9

Assumptions:
  Plant and machinery depreciates at 10 per cent annually;
  buildings at 3 per cent.
  Lags in tax payment are ignored.
Source: HMSO 1984, Appendix 10.

This table illustrates the subsidy on plant, machinery and
industrial buildings provided by the old tax system, which
allowed an investment yielding less than 5 per cent pre tax to
yield a 5 per cent after tax return to the suppliers of
finance. The figures also highlight the relatively favourable
tax treatment of debt compared with new equity finance prior to
1984. With the higher rates of inflation which existed for
most of the period when the old system was in operation, the
tax subsidy on debt finance would actually have been
substantially higher than is shown here. The comparison
between the old and new systems shows that the discrimination
in favour of investment in plant and machinery is reduced, but
not eliminated, by the tax changes and there is a reduction in
the previous relative tax disadvantage of investment in

commercial buildings. The table also illustrates that debt finance is still favoured for a fully tax paying company, because of its interest deductability, but the lower tax rates mean it is relatively less attractive than before.

The calculations used by the Treasury to explain the effects of the tax changes only relate to fully tax paying companies, although it was noted that the required returns under the pre 1984 system would vary substantially according to the firm's overall tax position. As part of this programme of research, the analysis of the effect of the 1984 Budget changes on required returns has been extended, using King and Fullerton's methodology, to illustrate that the effect of the new tax system on the returns required and marginal effective tax rates depends critically on the firm's tax profile (Levis and Morgan, 1985).

The framework developed by King and Fullerton provides a convenient way of summarising the potential effects of the tax changes on marginal investments, by incorporating both the impact on the cost of capital and the returns from investment. However, it was clear, both from recent empirical studies of capital budgeting techniques (e.g. Pike, 1983) and initial discussions with practitioners, that most capital expenditure decisions are not actually made in the context of a unified calculation of returns and the cost of capital. The theoretical effect of the tax changes on the attractiveness of investment projects was therefore investigated, as a background to the later empirical work, by examining the separate impact of the tax changes on a) the after tax internal rate of return on individual projects and b) the firm's cost of capital.

a) Project returns

Clearly, the investments which benefited most from the shift from a high tax, high allowance system to a system of low taxes and allowances were those made prior to the Budget announcement, which attracted allowances at the old rates (particularly in plant and machinery) but with returns earned after March 1984 being taxed at the reduced corporation tax rates. This effect continued through the two year transitional period of stepped reductions in allowances, providing additional incentives to invest before the tax changes were fully implemented.

The windfall gain to existing investment and the incentive to accelerate investment in plant and equipment to take advantage of temporary high allowances have been illustrated by W Greenwell and Co (1984). As far as the transitional arrangements are concerned, their Monetary Bulletin depicts the substantial potential gains for a company with a 31 March financial year end from bringing investment forward from the first half of 1985-6 into the last half of 1984-5 and, to a lesser extent, from the first half of 1986-7 into the last half of 1985-6. The incentive for companies with a 31 December year end to accelerate investment is also shown; in this case the maximum benefit would have been gained by bringing investment forward into the last quarter of the calender year. Their analysis also illustrates that the potential advantages of accelerating investment by a whole year were much less than could be gained by altering the timing of investment within the year.

The net effects of the tax changes, when fully implemented, on the post tax returns from various types of investment projects were estimated, as part of the present study, under different assumptions about tax rates and inflation. In each case, the procedure was to calculate the real post tax return that a given investment, with a particular post tax return under the old tax system, would have yielded if the investment, with the same implied pre tax cash flow as before, had been evaluated under the post 1986 tax system. The examples concentrate on investments which were eligible in whole or in part for 100 per cent allowances on plant and machinery, as such investments provide the focus of the empirical work reported in later chapters.

The results of this analysis (of which examples are shown in Tables 1.3 and 1.4) demonstrate that the direction and extent of the change in real post tax returns depend on the proportion of expenditure qualifying for 100 per cent allowances, the pre 1984 profitability of the project under the old system, its life, the rate of inflation and the tax band within which the firm making the investment is assumed to lie.

Each of the hypothetical investments yields steady pre tax income flows in real terms, which begin one year after the investment outlay, and the fixed capital is treated as having no disposal value at the end of the project's life. It is assumed that the company undertaking the investment has sufficient tax capacity to benefit fully from the available allowances and both tax relief and payments occur with a one year lag. The 25 per cent reducing balance allowances under the post 1986 system are calculated over a 30 year period for simplicity, but by this time the remaining value of the discounted benefits would be negligible.

Table 1.3a presents results for investments by large firms qualifying fully for 100 per cent allowances under the old system. It illustrates the reduction in real post tax rates of return, after 1986, for projects of varying life and former after tax profitability. In the absence of inflation, a 3 year investment yielding 5 per cent net before the Budget changes, for example, would only yield 2.9 per cent under the new system of lower allowances and tax rates. Even highly profitable plant and machinery projects show a lower return under the new

Table 1.3
Effect of new tax system on real post tax
internal rates of return:
firms paying large company tax rate

a) Plant and machinery 100% of initial outlay

Pre 1984		Internal rate of return (%)				
		5	10	15	20	25
Post 1986						
Life	Inflation (%)					
3 years	0	2.9	6.1	9.6	13.2	17.1
	5	1.3	4.8	8.5	12.4	16.5
5 years	0	3.4	7.1	10.9	14.9	19.1
	5	2.2	6.1	10.2	14.4	18.7
7 years	0	3.7	7.6	11.7	15.8	20.1
	5	2.8	6.9	11.1	15.4	19.8

b) Plant and machinery 50% of initial outlay

Pre 1984		Internal rate of return (%)				
		5	10	15	20	25
Post 1986						
Life	Inflation (%)					
3 years	0	5.0	10.1	15.2	20.2	25.3
	5	3.8	8.9	14.1	19.2	24.3
5 years	0	5.4	10.7	16.0	21.1	26.2
	5	4.3	9.7	14.9	20.1	25.3
7 years	0	5.6	11.0	16.3	21.5	26.6
	5	4.6	10.0	15.3	20.5	25.6

system because, as the discount rate increases, the effect of the 100 per cent allowances (received after only one year) in reducing the gross cash flows needed to yield a given pre 1984 after tax return, continue to outweigh the increasingly heavily discounted benefits of reducing balance allowances stretching into the future and the lower tax rate on the income streams. A 3 year project yielding 25 per cent under the old system, with zero inflation, would give returns of 17.1 per cent under the new system; taking a more extreme example (not shown in the table), a 3 year project previously yielding 75 per cent would now give returns of just over 60 per cent. For any given post tax internal rate of return before the 1984 Budget, the reduction in returns is greater for the shorter life projects. This is because the early receipt of capital allowances under the old system assumes more importance over a shorter period, relative to the tax reduction on the gross income flows. The effect of inflation, even at a modest 5 per cent, is to reduce the post 1986 returns further, particularly at low discount rates, by reducing the real value of the stream of writing down allowances, relative to the 100 per cent allowances, which are received after only one year with little erosion in their value.

Table 1.3b presents results for projects where only half of the outlay is on plant and machinery, with the remainder accounted for by working capital. Stock is assumed to amount to 80 per cent of the net investment in working capital and stock relief is received, with a one year lag, on all the inflationary gains on stockholdings under the pre 1984 system; no such relief is assumed to appply after 1986. These investments show similar or higher returns under the new tax system with zero inflation. This is because the smaller proportion of the initial outlay qualifying for 100 per cent allowances means a higher pre tax cash flow than before is required to yield a given post tax return under the old tax regime; when the after tax return from these pre tax cash flows are looked at under the new system, more benefit than before is derived from the reduction in the tax rate. As before, the longer life projects have the more favourable post tax returns after 1986. The effect of inflation is again to reduce the real return under the new system; this reduction, compared to the results with stable prices, is more marked than before because there is now not only the effect of inflation in reducing the real value of the writing down allowances but also, with the benefit of stock relief under the old system, a smaller pre tax cash flow is required originally to yield a given post tax return.

Table 1.4 presents results calculated using a similar procedure and assumptions to those used in Table 1.3 but, this

time, for firms paying the small companies tax rate. The
returns on investments qualifying fully for 100 per cent
allowances are again reduced under the new tax system, but to a
lesser extent than for the firms paying tax at the full
statutory rates. Unlike the large firms, however, the
investment with outlays split equally between machinery and

Table 1.4
Effect of new tax system on real post tax
internal rates of return:
firms paying small company tax rate

a) Plant and machinery 100% of initial outlay

Pre 1984		Internal rate of return (%)				
		5	10	15	20	25
Post 1986						
Life	Inflation (%)					
3 years	0	3.2	6.7	10.4	14.3	18.3
	5	1.8	5.5	9.5	13.6	17.8
5 years	0	3.6	7.5	11.6	15.7	20.0
	5	2.6	6.7	11.0	15.3	19.7
7 years	0	3.9	8.0	12.2	16.5	20.9
	5	3.1	7.4	11.8	16.2	20.7

b) Plant and machinery 50% of initial outlay

Pre 1984		Internal rate of return (%)				
		5	10	15	20	25
Post 1986						
Life	Inflation (%)					
3 years	0	4.6	9.3	14.0	18.8	23.6
	5	3.4	8.2	13.1	17.9	22.8
5 years	0	4.9	9.7	14.6	19.5	24.4
	5	3.9	8.8	13.8	18.7	23.6
7 years	0	5.0	9.9	14.9	19.8	24.7
	5	4.1	9.1	14.1	19.0	24.0

working capital generally show reduced returns, as a result of
the different tax rates.

Tables 1.3 and 1.4 illustrate the complexity of the
relationship between the returns from given projects under the
old and new tax regimes. One result which consistently emerges
from these comparisons is the lower return on shorter life
projects under the post 1986 allowances and tax rates. It was
the relatively unfavourable effect on short life assets under
the provisions of the 1984 Finance Act which led to the
depooling proposals in the 1985 Budget, allowing such assets to
be fully relieved within five years.

Table 1.5
Effect of depooling provisions on real post tax internal
rates of return of investments with a three year life

Plant and machinery 100% of initial outlay

Pre 1984	Internal rate of return (%)				
	5	10	15	20	25
Post 1986, large company rate					
Inflation 0%					
No depooling	2.9	6.1	9.6	13.2	17.1
With depooling	3.5	7.1	10.9	14.8	18.8
Inflation 5%					
No depooling	1.3	4.8	8.5	12.4	16.5
With depooling	2.2	6.0	9.9	14.0	18.1
Post 1986, small company rate					
Inflation 0%					
No depooling	3.2	6.7	10.4	14.3	18.3
With depooling	3.7	7.6	11.5	15.6	19.7
Inflation 5%					
No depooling	1.8	5.5	9.5	13.6	17.8
With depooling	2.7	6.6	10.7	14.9	19.2

Table 1.5 shows the effect of electing to follow depooling
procedures for investments with a three year life, both for
firms paying the large and small company rates. These results
are for investments qualifying fully for the 25 per cent
reducing balance allowances, where depooling will clearly have

most effect. With depooling, the after tax returns on a three year investment are increased but are still substantially below the pre 1984 levels. Whether firms will elect to follow depooling procedures will partly depend on the managers' perceptions of the administrative costs involved, which may be thought to outweigh the beneficial effect on the after tax returns.

b) Cost of capital

The net effect of the Budget tax changes on the final outcome of such after tax project appraisals will, in theory, also depend on the impact of the tax reform on the firm's cost of capital; this should affect the hurdle against which the internal rate of return is compared. Table 1.6 provides estimates of the cost of debt and new equity finance under the pre 1984 and post 1986 systems for firms in different tax positions. The changes in the overall cost of capital with different gearing ratios are also shown. These examples were based on a simple textbook calculation of the cost of different types of finance, ignoring risk, using assumptions based either on estimates used by firms participating in the research or current macroeconomic data.

Looking first at the fully tax paying companies, the 1984 Budget changes increase the cost of debt, which had been substantially favoured under the pre 1984 tax system because of its interest deductability, as discussed earlier. This will increase the cost of capital, except for firms relying entirely on equity finance. Although debt finance is still favoured it is much less so than previously and this may influence firms' future financial strategies although, of course, a variety of other considerations will also help to determine their future financial mix. These results for fully tax paying companies can be compared with the estimates of project returns in the last section. For example, taking the projects where all the expenditure is on plant and machinery, this rise in the cost of capital, coupled with the fall in real post tax returns, makes such investments less attractive overall.

The cost of capital will also rise for firms with continuing surplus ACT, as they will move to positions of lower tax payment. Under the old system, the maximum credit that could be given to a shareholder on a dividend paid from taxable profits arising from trading income was equal to the standard rate of income tax of 30 per cent, leaving the company with a residual tax liability of 22 per cent. For a company paying the full statutory rate of corporation tax, the residual tax borne by the company, assuming the basic income tax rate had remained unaltered, would be reduced from 22 per cent to 5 per

Table 1.6
Effect of new tax system on cost of capital according to
tax position and gearing

	Pre 1984		Post 1986		Change according to gearing debt (%)		
	Debt	Equity	Debt	Equity	10	33	50
Large firms (%)							
Fully tax paying							
Tax relief	52.0	30.0	35.0	30.0			
Cost of capital	-0.2	6.5	1.5	6.5	+0.17	+0.56	+0.75
ACT surplus							
Tax relief	22.0	0.0	5.0	0.0			
Cost of capital	2.8	8.0	4.5	8.0	+0.17	+0.57	+0.85
ACT surplus to fully tax paying							
Tax relief	22.0	0.0	35.0	30.0			
Cost of capital	2.8	8.0	1.5	6.5	-1.48	-1.43	-1.40
Tax exhausted to fully tax paying							
Tax relief	0.0	0.0	35.0	30.0			
Cost of capital	5.0	8.0	1.5	6.5	-1.70	-2.17	-2.50
Small firms (%)							
Fully tax paying							
Tax relief	38.0	30.0	30.0	30.0			
Cost of capital	1.2	6.5	2.0	6.5	+0.08	+0.27	+0.40

Cost of debt = i(1-t)-p; Cost of equity = d(1-t)+g
where, based on company estimates or current data
   interest rate, i   = 10%
   inflation rate, p   = 5%
   gross dividend yield, d = 5%
   growth, g   = 3%
   tax, t   = (tax relief/100)

cent or, in the case of a small company, would give the
shareholders credit for the whole of the firm's tax liability.
This fall in the effective rate of tax payment would again

lead, in theory, to an increase in the hurdle rates applied to investment.

Although some firms will apparently face stiffer hurdles in investment appraisal than under the old tax system, the effect is far from uniform across all firms, owing to the differences in their tax profiles. Some firms are likely to stay tax exhausted into the 1990's, because of their substantial accumulated tax losses, and their after tax cost of capital will be unaffected. Others are likely to face a heavier tax burden, as a result of the new tax regime. The improved provision since 1984 for carrying back ACT is expected to lead to a more rapid utilisation of surplus ACT and the less generous allowances will broaden the tax base by bringing currently tax exhausted firms into the tax net. Table 1.6 illustrates the fall in the cost of capital in such cases.

----

[1] The reduction in the standard rate of income tax from 30 per cent to 29 per cent in the 1986 Budget occurred after this study was complete and is therefore ignored throughout.

2 Assessing the impact of investment incentives

PREVIOUS STUDIES

A number of empirical studies have examined the impact of government investment incentives on investment expenditure both in Britain and other countries. The studies can be divided into two main types, namely those adopting an econometric modelling approach, which are based largely on published data, and surveys of investment behaviour, carried out by questioning those responsible for making investment decisions. Only a very small minority of studies have combined the two approaches. The econometric research has generally used aggregate data to estimate the impact of tax incentives on investment in the economy as a whole, while the surveys have been more concerned with establishing their effects on individual firm's investment decisions.

Compared with the number of econometric studies of the determinants of aggregate investment and its tax sensitivity which have been carried out recently, there have been relatively few recent surveys of the effect of fiscal incentives at the micro level. The small number of British studies, which were based on questionnaire and interview data and published in the 1960's, indicated that many firms felt their investment had not been in any way affected by the tax incentives available at the time. Among these were studies by the FBI (1960), Hart and Prussman (1964), Corner and Williams (1965) and George (1968), all of which were primarily based on postal questionnaires.

The survey carried out by the FBI in 1957 included questions on firms' reactions to changes in initial and investment allowances since 1951. 369 of the 1595 respondents (23 per cent) claimed that their investment decisions had been 'materially affected' by favourable changes in allowances and 230 (14 per cent) had been so affected by unfavourable changes, with little difference in the replies from firms of different sizes. However, the nature of these effects, whether on the scale of investment or its timing, was not probed.

In the course of Hart and Prussman's survey of the 1954-63 period, businesses were asked 'Have investment allowances for plant and machinery (for taxation purposes) at any time proved to be an inducement to your concern to replace (or add to) plant and machinery?'. Responses to this question suggested more widespread sensitivity to tax incentives, with 42 of the 116 respondents (36 per cent) answering affirmatively. Approximately the same period was covered in the more detailed survey by Corner and Williams, but only 33 of the 181 firms replying to their enquiry had actually accelerated the timing of new plant and equipment because of improvements in initial allowances; the same number claimed to have reacted in this way to changes in investment allowances. 13 had postponed the introduction of new plant and equipment due to unfavourable tax changes in the period but none had abandoned projects for this reason.

A rather more influential role for fiscal incentives emerged from George's (1968) study of large retailing firms. 35 of the 84 respondents said that investment allowances were a significant influence on their investment decisions; only 7, however, quoted instances in response to a request to do so. All the examples given referred to the purchase and replacement of cash registers or the earlier replacement of vehicles, suggesting that views on the general impact of investment incentives could not easily be linked to major capital expenditures on particular projects.

Earlier research based on detailed case studies has also suggested that many business people see tax based incentives as playing a relatively small or insignificant role in their investment policies. For example, McKintosh's (1963) in depth investigations revealed that investment decisions were not generally very tax sensitive, but firms under strict financial constraints appeared to respond most, a finding supported by Corner and Williams' later study; in contrast with other studies, McKintosh's work also suggested that small firms were more sensitive to fiscal incentives because of their more limited access to funds.

Ten years later, Rockley (1973), in a questionnaire and interview study of the investment policies and practices of 69 UK firms, again concluded that tax incentives were of little importance to company planners when they formulated past investment programmes. The state of demand for the firm's products and need for replacement investment were most frequently cited as the main determinants of corporate capital spending. Reductions in the tax rate were not found to have had a very powerful influence on corporate investment and Rockley concluded that this was because firms commonly evaluated investment proposals on a pre tax basis, had no idea how to assess the cost of capital and did not appreciate its post tax implications. A more recent survey of capital budgeting techniques by Pike (1983) suggests that, although large firms are becoming more sophisticated in their appraisal techniques, highly developed evaluation systems are still far from universal.

The influence of tax based incentives on the investment policies of individual firms would be expected to depend, among other things, on the precise nature of the incentives available at the time and how often they had been changed in the recent past, as well as on the prevailing economic climate. One of the suggested reasons for many firms' apparent lack of tax sensitivity, as revealed in the early investigations, was the frequency with which incentives had been altered during the periods studied. In view of this, a recent survey of UK firms by Alam and Stafford (1985), after more than a decade of relative stability in the allowance system, is of particular interest.

Their study was based on a postal questionnaire and concentrated on listed manufacturing firms. Just less than half of the 249 respondents claimed to take tax into account when calculating the rate of return on investment outlays, while expected profits, sales and the general economic conditions were usually regarded as more important than tax in the determination of their company's investment. This research did not attempt to interpret the responses of individual firms in the light of their financial and tax position, as would have been possible using published accounting data, and the conclusion that large companies are more responsive to tax advantages than 'small' firms appears questionable, given both the nature of the sample and the authors' consideration of only a few of the various ways in which tax potentially affects investment decisions.

Despite the differences in the nature of the samples, the

periods studied and survey techniques used, these and other questionnaire and interview studies in the UK (see Lund, 1976, for a more comprehensive review of the earlier work), in common with similar research in the USA, suggest a fairly modest role for fiscal incentives in the actual decision making processes of individual firms. Some of the later evidence from studies based on the econometric approach, however, indicates that the incentives may have been a rather more effective policy instrument in Britain than earlier survey work suggests (e.g. Feldstein and Flemming, 1971, and Boatwright and Eaton, 1972). Overall, though, the results of the econometric research are very mixed, leading Hay and Morris to conclude from their detailed review of the determinants aggregate investment:

> Overall it seems clear that tax policy does have an effect but that the magnitude of impact in the past and even more the forecast effect of tax and incentive changes is extremely uncertain. (Hay and Morris, 1979, p.408)

There are, of course, various reasons why similar results from the two types of studies should not necessarily be expected, as discussed in an early article by Eisner (1957) and more recently by Lund (1976). In particular, the determinants of investment in individual projects or by individual firms, as seen through fieldwork, may differ from the determinants of fixed investment in the economy identified by econometric analyses because some factors which are important in individual decisions will 'wash out' in the aggregate. For example, one firm may be investing in new technology to cut cost and improve quality but, if the resulting increase in sales merely represents an increase in this firm's share at the expense of another, investment in the sector as a whole may be unaffected. As noted earlier, widespread tax exhaustion is an important influence which may have reduced the recent importance of tax in many firms' investment decisions; this will also tend to be averaged out in the aggregate statistics.

In essence, the two approaches to the study of investment are complementary and both are being pursued in the wider programme of research of which this forms part. The unique role of micro economic studies, such as the one reported here, is to establish what role tax considerations actually play in business investment decisions and to identify any particular types of firms and investments which are especially responsive to fiscal incentives.

RESEARCH DESIGN

Introduction

In view of the likely differential effects of tax based incentives generally and the 1984 proposals, in particular, this book was based on in depth case studies using semi structured interviews, so that the influence of tax on investment in different circumstances could be examined in detail. Much more information was obtained by this method than would have been possible through a postal questionnaire and the resulting interview data, including copies of investment proposals and evaluations, were interpreted in the light of accounting information.

The research dealt mainly with past investment decisions because reliable data about future investment intentions at the firm level are difficult to obtain, and their sensitivity to alternative tax assumptions would be virtually impossible to analyse. Earlier studies have shown how difficult it is for businessmen to isolate the various factors which affected past investment decisions in the abstract so, although the survey did investigate the determinants of the firms' total capital expenditure programmes, it focused on the analysis of specific decisions taken between 1979 and March 1984.

The projects selected were ones which had been eligible, in whole or in part, for 100 per cent allowances, usually on plant and machinery, under the pre 1984 tax system. The main issue dealt with in each of the cases was whether the approval, scale or timing of the project had been so dependent on the pre 1984 fiscal environment, that a different decision would have been taken if the post 1986 tax system of 25 per cent allowances and tax rates had existed at the time the investment was approved.

A copy of the questionnaire used as the basis for semi structured interviews, which were carried out between January and September 1985, is available from the author on request. This gives the detailed questions on which conclusions about the likely sensitivity of the investment projects to the new tax regime were based. It also shows the additional information collected concerning, for example, the effect of the transitional arrangements, the likely impact of depooling procedures, the importance of government grants, future leasing intentions and the outcome of the project studied, where sufficient time had elapsed for this to be assessed.

Sample and data

The sample was drawn from seven diverse sectors, namely data processing, electronic components, non energy extraction, mechanical handling, pharmaceuticals, printing and road haulage, so that possible intersectoral differences in the impact of the 1984 Finance Act could be explored. Substantial investment took place in all these sectors between 1979 and 1984 but other characteristics varied, particularly with respect to the size distribution of firms, the importance of foreign multinationals, the nature of the technology involved, the length of asset lives and overall profitability and growth.

Electronic components and data processing were selected primarily on account of the rapid technological changes in the sector and recent high growth rates. The pharmaceuticals industry was chosen to represent speciality chemicals; this relatively profitable sector is dominated by a few large firms, with heavy multinational involvement and large investment programmes. Both mechanical handling and commercial printing were badly hit by recession and had generally low profits in the 1979-84 period; firms in these sectors are typically fairly small in size but, whereas new technology has been diffusing rapidly for some years in the printing industry, firms in mechanical handling have been fairly slow to modernise. Non energy extraction is a capital intensive activity in which asset lives are typically long. It is dominated by large vertically integrated groups and has been relatively profitable, despite the effects of recession. Finally, the road haulage sector includes many small firms, profit margins are generally low and the lives of the main assets (vehicles) are fairly short.

A stratified sample of firms was selected within each sector by size, ownership type and tax position. The firms were identified primarily by using Kompass and the relevant accounting data. Approximately one-third of the companies approached agreed to participate in interviews, a fairly typical response rate in this type of fieldwork. The only sector with a particularly low response was road haulage, where the managers were often 'too stretched' to help, especially in the smallest firms. Other reasons for a negative response included recent takeovers, closures and changes of personnel. In general, however, there was no evidence of any important differences between the characteristics of the surviving non respondents and those of the respondents.

Altogether 56 firms were studied; 24 were UK listed firms, 19 were privately owned (including 2 sole traders) and the remainder were foreign multinationals. Table 2.1 classifies the sample by sector and size of employment in the parent company or group as a whole. Just over half had more than 5000 employees, but smaller firms were also well represented and 10 firms with less than 100 employees were included in the sample.

Table 2.1
Distribution of firms by employment size and sector

Sector	Number in size class				Total number of firms
	1-99	100-499	500-4999	5000+	
Data processing	1	1	3	4	9
Electronic components	1	2	2	3*	8
Mechanical handling	2*	–	1	4	7
Non energy extraction	1*	1	–	5	7
Pharmaceuticals	–	–	–	8	8
Printing	1	2	3	2	8
Road haulage	4*	1	1	3	9
Total	10	7	10	29	56

*includes one firm where two cases were analysed

Table 2.2 shows the main feature of the parent or group's UK tax position in the period preceding the investment studied. 5 small firms were effectively paying tax at personal rates, including the 2 unincorporated businesses and 3 owner managed private firms, where the profits were taken as the owner's salary. Of the remaining 51 firms, only 15 were paying substantial mainstream corporation tax, reflecting the low average rates of tax payment and tax exhaustion of many companies during the period.

Nearly half of the interviews were with financial directors, although the owner and/or managing director usually participated in small firms. Where foreign multinationals were concerned, the interviews had to be carried out with the UK affiliate rather than at head office; in the case of UK groups, the interviewees were almost equally divided between the holding companies and operating subsidiaries, with the contact point depending on the degree of autonomy exercised by the subsidiaries in their investment decisions.

A topic list was generally sent in advance of the interviews, outlining the main areas to be covered and asking for details

27

Table 2.2

Distribution of firms by employment size and tax position

Tax category	Number of firms in size class				Total number of firms
	1-99	100-499	500-4999	5000+	
Low taxable profits or losses before accelerated capital allowances	3*	4	7	8*	22
Significant surplus advance corporation tax	-	-	-	7	7
Mainstream corporation tax significantly reduced by accelerated capital allowances	1*	3	1	2	7
Substantial mainstream corporation tax paid	1	-	2	12	15
Profits taxed at personal rates	5*	-	-	-	5
Total	10	7	10	29	56

*includes one firm where two cases were analysed

of a specific investment programme or project for which orders had been placed between the beginning of 1979 and 13 March 1984. 52 firms supplied details of one investment, whereas 4 provided information about two separately identified projects, resulting in a total of 60 cases. 16 of the investments were pre selected for discussion by the interviewee; they were usually the firm's most recent pre March 1984 investment. The remaining cases were chosen after discussion, either at random or according to the availability of suitable data. Although the selection of investment decisions taken early in the target period would have been preferable in terms of assessing the outcome of the investment, there was often a trade off between this and the interviewee's recall of the detail; on balance, it was decided to concentrate on the more recent projects.

Table 2.3 shows the size of the projects studied in different sectors in terms of their budgeted capital cost. More than one-third cost over £1 million, of which four cost over £20 million. The remainder were almost evenly divided between projects costing less than £100,000 and those between £100,000 and £1 million. Over half were expansionary investments which required increased sales to be successful and 17 were financed, at least partly, by leasing. Most of the interviews took place in the South of England, the Midlands and South Wales but the investment projects themselves were dispersed throughout the country.

Table 2.3
Distribution of projects by capital cost and sector

| Sector | Number in size class | | | | Total number of projects |
	Less than £100k	£100k–£1m	£1–5m	£5m	
Data processing	3	3	2	1	9
Electronic components	2	4	–	3	9
Mechanical handling	4	3	1	–	8
Non energy extraction	2	2	4	–	8
Pharmaceuticals	1	2	1	4	8
Printing	1	3	3	1	8
Road haulage	6	–	2	2	10
Total	19	17	13	11	60

Methods of analysis

The analysis divided the possible effects of the pre 1984 system of allowances and corporation tax rates into two types, namely direct and indirect effects. Direct effects refer to the influence of capital allowances and tax rates on the actual evaluation of the returns from the project or its effects on the overall tax charge; these must have been considered at some stage in the decision process for it to be possible for tax to have had a direct influence on the investment decision. In contrast, indirect effects of taxation may impinge on the financial and strategic environment in which the decisions were taken; these need not have been directly perceived by the decision makers, in the context of the specific project, to have had an influence on its acceptance. These possible types of influence and the methods of assessing their importance in the analysis of particular cases will now be considered in more detail.

A) Direct effects

1) Project returns. For tax to have directly influenced quantified project returns, projects must either have been assessed on a post tax basis or have included lease rentals, in which case the benefits of capital allowances may have been partially reflected in the assumed costs of leasing. Where tax was found to have been taken into account in evaluating the project, either through post tax appraisal or the inclusion of lease rentals, the tax sensitivity of the decision was examined to see whether it might have been different if taken in the post 1986 environment.

When a copy of the proposal was available, the original evaluation was reworked to estimate the effect the post 1986 tax system would have had, if similar evaluation procedures had been adopted but reflecting the new tax rules. If the project had been evaluated as an outright purchase, the same assumptions about the timing and treatment of the tax flows were used in the reappraisal as in the original calculations, but the post 1986 corporation tax rates and writing down allowances were applied rather than the pre 1984 provisions, taking into account possible changes in the firm's tax profile. If leasing costs had been built into the analysis, the sensitivity of the returns to the likely rise in leasing costs under a system of 25 per cent reducing balance allowances was assessed. When the original calculations were not released, the conclusions about the effect of the post 1986 tax regime on project returns were based on an examination of the tax position of the firm, the relationship of the expected returns to the firm's targets and other characteristics of the investment established at the interview.

2) Overall tax charge. Another possible direct effect of tax on project decisions could stem from concern about the effect of the investment on the amount of tax paid and/or reported This might be especially important where an investment was seen as instrumental in reducing marginal tax rates, either because the income was taxed at personal rates or because it would fall beneath a small company tax threshold as a result of the capital allowances received.

Where investments were either not formally evaluated or were appraised pre tax, despite an overall current or expected tax paying position, attention could still have focused on the effect on total tax payments, particularly in the case of year end investments. Even when the appraisal was carried out on a post tax basis, taking into account the time value of the tax cash flows, the effect on total tax payments could have been a consideration, especially in a public company reporting post tax earnings per share.

Some individuals might simply have an aversion to tax payments, leading to tax driven behaviour which might not have occurred under the post 1986 tax regime, given the differences in tax shelter provided by the two systems. The research attempted to identify whether this attitude existed in the specific cases, as well as probing, for example, the sequence of tax planning (if any) in the decision, the timing of the investment relative to the accounting year end and the possible effect of the investment on tax paid and reported under the different tax systems, in the light of the company's tax position and policy towards deferred tax provisions.

B) Indirect effects

1) Cost of capital. One of the effects of a reduced corporation tax rate is to increase, in post tax terms, the relative cost of servicing debt finance compared with the cost in dividends of servicing equity capital. In theory, such a tax induced rise in hurdle rates could result in some projects being rejected which would have gone ahead in earlier years. As Chapter 1 shows, the effect is likely to vary between companies due to differences in financial structure and the effective rate of tax payment. It will also vary according to the role the firm's cost of capital actually plays in the determination of its investment programmes. The effect of any change in the cost of capital due to the 1984 Finance Act was assessed in each case to establish the net result of any tax sensitivity on the relationship between calculated returns and firms' targets and the possible implications of this for project acceptance.

2) Liquidity. The system of corporation tax could have an indirect effect on investment decisions through its influence on a firm's ability to fund particular projects and programmes of investment. This 'liquidity effect' on after tax earnings could reflect both the level of past tax payments and, where firms had made significant use of lease finance, the possible reduction in financing costs below the normal cost of borrowing due to some of the benefits of tax shelter being passed on by lessors.

The cumulative effect of the pre 1984 tax system on company liquidity by the time of the investment was compared, as far as possible, with what might have occurred if the post 1986 tax rules had applied instead (assuming that stock relief or an equivalent relief on stock appreciation had still been available). Accounting data was obtained for several years preceding the investment, as well as details of the types of investment expenditure and use of lease finance.

The effect on mainstream corporation tax payments under the pre 1984 system vis-a-vis the post 1986 system was measured at holding company level, by setting the effect of less attractive capital allowances and the lower tax rate against the higher (usually 52 per cent) rate on taxable profits and the more generous allowances, taking the background of ACT, overseas taxation and the firm's profit position into account. The results were then checked against the interviewee's views on the matter. Where a firm was found to have relied heavily on lease finance, the effects on the balance sheet of a reduction in the tax advantages of lease finance (such as might be expected under the post 1986 tax system) were also examined and discussed at the interviews.

The measurement of possible changes in past tax payments under the new system of corporation tax, like the recalculation of project returns, was based on the static assumption that tax changes would not have affected other aspects of behaviour. Some of the possible changes in behaviour which could have affected liquidity were explored, as far as possible, in the interviews. Where there seemed to have been some liquidity advantage to the company or group from the pre 1984 system, particular care was taken to probe the importance of the actual investment studied and the likelihood of its approval being dependent on the additional liquidity generated. Questions were asked, for example, about the role of finance as a possible constraint on investment and whether any deferred tax provision, raised as a result of the 1984 Finance Act, had significantly affected the firm's ability to borrow.

3) Sector attractiveness. At a more strategic level, another possible indirect effect of the change in the corporate tax system is to alter the attractions of investing in different sectors, by changing their relative after tax profitability. Differences in the likely impact of tax on the firm's profits in different sectors (due for example to their growth rates or capital intensities) under the old and new tax systems might have affected the attractiveness of investment in various areas, particularly for new entrants and diversified firms. The impact of tax on industrial buyers could theoretically have affected demand forecasts, while perceived differences in the scope for tax shifting could have altered returns expected from individual investments. From the point of view of

multinationals taking a more global view of investment opportunities, the incentive to invest in the UK compared with other countries could have been changed.

These potential effects on sector attractiveness were pursued as far as possible at the interviews, although it was recognised that the available evidence would be extremely limited, partly because of the short length of time which had elapsed since the tax changes were announced and also because of the predominantly financial interests of some of the interviewees.

PART 2
THE CASES

3 Data processing and office equipment

This sector was defined in accordance with group 330 of the 1980 Standard Industrial Classification (SIC) and consists of computer equipment, including computer subassemblies and peripheral equipment, as well as a wide range of electronic and non electronic office equipment. According to official statistics, the sector as a whole accounted for sales of over £1.8 billion in 1983 and had more than 40,200 employees, with net capital investment in plant and machinery of £66.8 million. Sales of office equipment by domestic producers have declined substantially in recent years and the fieldwork concentrated primarily on the rapidly growing and relatively profitable manufacture of data processing equipment, which is responsible for most of the activity in this sector.

The sector as a whole, both in Britain and internationally, is dominated by large multinational firms competing worldwide and three of the nine firms studied were multinationals. The USA is predominant in the world market for data processing equipment and accounts for all the top five firms, with no British firm and only one European firm featuring in the top ten. IBM is the clear market leader and, in 1984, its revenues exceeded the combined turnover of the world's next 22 largest computer companies, with its share of various product areas ranging from an estimated 74 per cent in the mainframe market to 30 per cent in manufactured systems.

Although the industry is highly concentrated, it fragmented into a series of increasingly specialised market niches with the advent of micros in the 1970's, and this fragmentation of the market has allowed many small companies to survive. The high rate of technical change has meant that smaller firms had the flexibility and, initially, the competitive advantage over the existing large firms in newer product areas. This advantage is now lessening as the large firms have become more aggressive in their fight for market share and as each change in technology is increasingly linked to a move towards integrated systems and services. The current emphasis is on providing a package to solve all user requirements, with networks the main growth market.

Rivalry in the industry is increasingly intense and competition takes place both on price grounds, with discounting common, and non price grounds. Heavy R and D expenditures, an emphasis on marketing, joint ventures and low cost automated manufacture have become important aspects of policy in the larger firms. Many of the components used in assembly operations are bought in to reduce costs and hardware assembly has increasingly shifted overseas, where local wages significantly undercut those of UK assemblers. Imports of the data processing equipment itself have become more important over the last five years, sourced from the USA, the Far East and Western Europe, leading to a growing balance of payments deficit in these products.

A high proportion of the investment in the UK by data processing firms is in human resources rather than manufacturing plant and equipment and this, together with relatively high profit and growth rates and the maintenance of 100 per cent allowances on scientific research facilities, made it seem likely that the sector as a whole would benefit from the 1984 Finance Act, despite the possible effect on customer demand for its high technology, short life products. Some of the projects examined in other sectors involved investment in data processing facilities and there is evidence of these being regarded as an overhead expense, with an unquantifiable payback, and any formal appraisal being based solely on an evaluation of the possible alternative equipment.

CASES

Case 1

This UK subsidiary of a major US corporation first invested in manufacturing in Britain in the 1950's and has maintained a significant presence since. 6 per cent of the corporation's employees work in the UK, accounting for about 5 per cent of its worldwide turnover of approximately £4 billion in 1983. The group and all its subsidiaries are involved in the design, engineering, manufacture and marketing of electronic equipment and data processing installations.

The UK company has a sound balance sheet, with investment in stocks and debtors more than double that in fixed assets. This, together with net lending to group companies, is financed by a mixture of retained earnings and short term bank borrowing. The UK company has been paying high mainstream corporation tax for some years and would probably have paid slightly less under the tax system proposed by the 1984 Finance Act. The group operate a tight monitoring system over subsidiary companies and divisions, using post tax discounted paybacks to evaluate investment proposals. The UK corporate treasurer and the UK finance director helped with this study; specific questions on the individual project were also referred to the divisional management which had sponsored it to the group's US headquarters.

The specific project discussed was the extension and re-equipping of an existing UK manufacturing unit to produce an updated version of the product already produced there. Capital expenditure of £3 million was involved, two-thirds on plant and machinery. The proposal was put forward by the manufacturing unit on the realisation that the size of the existing plant was no longer adequate for a viable operation. The decision, as far as the unit was concerned, was one of 'step-up or close down'. As far as the corporation was concerned, however, the normal expectation that the unit which develops a new product will also produce it, is secondary to securing a rational and profitable worldwide production pattern.

During 1982, the corporation's head office was convinced that the proposed new product would be viable, but the question of where to produce it had still to be decided. The UK manufacturing unit took the initiative and obtained a package of grants worth over half the capital cost of the project, including maximum regional development grants. The proposal, with the grants and accelerated capital allowances included, was approved in early 1983 and the installation began the same year. The design of the machine has been changed since its inception but is still considered promising. As with most product development, the risk of being technically bettered by competitors remains, but it is estimated that 100 new jobs will be associated with the project and 150 jobs safeguarded.

The parent evaluated the proposal using a discounted payback analysis. Both grants receivable and accelerated capital allowances were shown in the cash flows. The main requirement was a fast payback, which is understandable in view of the risks involved in this high technology sector. The estimated payback was less than three years, due mainly to the attractive grants. The influence of the accelerated capital allowances was said to be 'not important' and those interviewed were quite certain that the grants had been 'absolutely the winning feature'. The company's finance executives explained that the corporate philosophy is against being tax driven. Investment outside the USA is seen as being made to obtain a return which is paid via dividends, ultimately suffering tax at the US rates. Grants therefore increase operating income and net after tax income, while tax incentives tend only to change the timing and location of tax payments.

The interviewees were convinced that the grant incentive had been important to the project's approval and that the tax incentives of accelerated capital allowances had a lesser effect. This appears an acceptable analysis, given the size of the grant incentive and the corporation's worldwide tax situation. Although the inclusion of the accelerated tax allowances in the cash flow must have had some influence on the payback, it seems reasonable to accept that the cash grants were very important and far outweighed the tax effect of accelerated capital allowances. Leasing was not considered as part of the proposal and the effect on reported earnings of potentially permanent timing differences would not have been shown in the all important US tax charge.

The UK company probably paid slightly more tax under the 52 per cent rate, despite accelerated capital allowances, than it would have under a 35 per cent rate with little acceleration of writing down allowances, so no liquidity advantage was conferred by the pre 1984 tax system. As far as the effect of tax incentives on the attractiveness of investing in this industry and on the UK as a manufacturing location is concerned, the company's finance director was of the clear opinion that such decisions were not dependant on UK tax considerations and that conditions in the UK industry would not change significantly as a result of the 1984 Finance Act, particularly for a company exporting a high proportion of its UK manufactured output.

It appears that this project involved a product that the group wished to develop but the location of the manufacturing unit in the UK was dependent upon grant incentives. The size of the grant and the importance of US taxation meant that the direct effects of accelerated capital allowances were not critical to the decision. There appears to have been no influence via indirect effects of the tax system through enhanced liquidity (rather the reverse, due to the high tax rate) while sector attractiveness has not been significantly affected, and the corporation's target project returns would not be altered by UK tax changes.

Although maintaining a policy of making strategic rather than tax driven investment decisions, this company was at the forefront in using the opportunities presented by the transitional tax arrangements. Some factory expansion was slightly accelerated and some capital equipment from the company's parent was brought into the UK before 31 March 1985. However, this acceleration was relatively small and limited by the strict adherence to corporate budgets. The main effect occurred through the company's sales policy. A sales conference was organised to impress on the sales force the advantages for customers of buying a machine before 31 March 1985, which would result in a 'discount' through the tax system of up to 16 per cent, depending upon individual circumstances. In a few cases, the customers were persuaded to buy a more powerful machine before 31 March for a similar post tax cost as an intended purchase after that date, but the main effect was to persuade them to accelerate purchases by as much as £20 million in total.

The company does not anticipate future plans will be significantly influenced by changes to regional grant rules. Investment in the UK is expected to continue, with equipment still being purchased outright, except for the use of fleet management facilities to finance its large vehicle requirements.

Case 2

This UK holding company is a subsidiary of a US multinational enterprise with a worldwide turnover of well over $10 billion. The group is organised into large marketing areas, with specialised manufacturing units in different countries within each area supplying the distribution needs of the whole area. The group's UK companies account for around 3.5 per cent of worldwide turnover and half the UK sales, with much more than half of the UK output being exported.

The group and its subsidiaries invest in the context of a planning cycle whereby broad strategies flow out of the corporation's well defined goals and the management's perception of the future business environment. These strategies are refined into specific operating 'commitments' whereby managers commit themselves to, rather than simply forecast, a financially defined outcome. Capital investment within the plan is closely examined just prior to commitment and actual results are monitored carefully against the operating plans. The company has been investing heavily in the UK for some years and foresees a similar level of capital expenditure for the rest of the decade. Despite the initial and first year allowances claimed on capital expenditure, the company has paid mainstream corporation tax on its considerable profits at effective rates of between 40 and 50 per cent in recent years.

The interviewees were a senior manager responsible for treasury planning, including project appraisal, and one of his assistants, a qualified accountant mainly responsible for corporate planning and project evaluation. They emphasised firstly, that there was no shortage of good projects and secondly, that it was corporate practice to provide long term employment. Much investment was therefore geared to enabling existing employees to increase output and work done without recourse to temporary staff, for whom no future long term employment could be guaranteed.

The specific project was a clear example of the corporate policy of equipping employees to achieve greater results, involving the provision of an advanced network of workstations linking employees in the company's marketing and service divisions to each other, to the production and supply departments and to the large corporate database. The project, which mainly used the company's own products, had a capital cost well in excess of £5 million and was begun early in 1984. The project arose from the recognition that networks constituted a very important future market. There was therefore a strong unquantified strategic motive to demonstrate within the company the successful use of such a network as an example to potential customers. After its inclusion in strategic proposals in early 1983 and a limited pilot trial, the investment was evaluated by looking at the costs and benefits of implementing the network throughout the company. The resulting payback was within 'guidelines' which, although not rigidly laid down were important in that 'most projects recommended to senior management by the treasury studies department tend to be in that area'.

The effect of this particular project will be to generate more output from the same number of people, raising the capital-labour ratio considerably in the distribution and service functions. During 1984, the first year of the project, the productivity benefits were modest and it was too early to judge whether the higher yields for 1985 and beyond would be achieved. In time, progress in accordance with the operating plan would be taken to indicate that expectations had been met while large variances would be carefully investigated.

The payback calculation looked at the effect on profit and loss before depreciation but after interest. The taxation system affected the calculation to the extent that tax cash flows, reflecting first year allowances and a 52 per cent tax rate, changed the interest costs of the project. This would have been a much smaller effect than a crude post tax cash flow payback would have shown but, in view of the proximity of the calculated coefficient to the upper limit of the guidelines, the question 'what if, under the post 1986 tax system, the early tax cash flows had been less favourable, giving rise to higher interest costs and pushing the payback beyond x years?' was raised. Both interviewees were sure that the response would not have been to cancel or postpone the project but that operating managers would have been asked to 'commit' additional productivity benefits to bring the payback to an acceptable level. In fact, the initial figures showed a satisfactory payback, so there had been 'a sigh of relief' and the plan had gone ahead without the need to renegotiate operating commitments.

Both interviewees doubted if capital allowances had ever changed priority between projects. Although the company had an active tax department reporting to the treasury planning manager, its contribution tended to occur after the commercial decisions had been taken. In this case, the direct effect on the project return had been slight due to the revenue, rather than cash, definition of payback. Even the possibility of this slight effect altering the perceived attractiveness of the project seems remote, as additional commitments would have been sought to bring the return within the company's usual limits. Leasing was not considered as a possible source of finance and there would have been no worthwhile reporting effect on current taxation to a US corporation providing in full for deferred tax.

Indirectly, this company's liquidity would have been considerably improved if the 1984 Finance Act proposals had applied in the past and its distribution policy had remained the same. However, it is unlikely this additional liquidity would have increased investment by the UK company because strategic considerations and management resources, rather than financial constraints, appear to have determined the extent of capital investment. As the main quantitative criterion used for assessing projects is a payback guideline set at a level which implies a return well in excess of the cost of capital, it is unlikely that the UK taxation environment could have influenced investment through its effect on the cost of finance. The senior interviewee was also adamant that UK tax considerations, under the pre 1984 system would not have altered the parent's commitment to the sector, or to the UK, although he was of the opinion that the UK 'has become a very attractive location' following the reduction in the tax rate.

Much of the company's recent investment in the UK has been similar to the specific case above. Although both interviewees believed that tax had been of little significance to project attractiveness and priority, they explained that timing would sometimes be altered slightly to take advantage of tax rules. This had been particularly true of the transition to lower first year allowances. The company had advanced over £4 million of capital expenditure into the 1984 financial year, as well as accelerating expenditure within 1985 to fall before 31 March. Although intended to be a timing adjustment only, the senior interviewee believed that this may be a permanent once and for all increase in investment.

The company was still looking at the 1985 Budget's depooling rules, which seemed attractive for equipment leased to customers and the turnover of internally produced equipment. Regional development incentives had influenced location decisions in the UK to some extent, but the company assessed these within the context of the many characteristics which it looked for in an investment location. Some investment had been accelerated to fall prior to the November 1985 rule changes for regional development grants, but the effect had been merely to add impetus to strategically worthwhile investment which would otherwise have been made in the future.

Case 3

This UK subsidiary of a North American group was incorporated in 1981. The group designs, manufactures and sells word processing and other office automation equipment and has recently placed increasing emphasis on providing compatible hardware and software to operate as networks. The group employs over 1,700 people, 250 of whom work in the UK, generating a turnover of more than £15 million. The group's main manufacturing sites are in North America and continental Europe but considerable value is added in the UK, mainly by designing sophisticated systems to meet individual customer's needs.

The company's investment in the UK is concentrated on providing employees with the capacity to add value to its products and is financed mainly by equity and loans provided by the parent. Heavy setting up costs resulted in tax losses which had still not been exhausted by the end of 1984. The company has used lease finance, particularly for buildings and vehicles, but has not attempted to sell and lease back its own capitalised products, which form quite a high proportion of investment in plant and machinery. The interviewee was the UK company's finance director, a chartered accountant who had joined the company in 1981. The UK management submits capital investment plans to the parent company and the proposals, which would generally have been included at an earlier stage in the budgeting process in broad terms, are normally approved at group level.

The investment discussed was the acquisition of an IBM computer to form the basis of the company's system of management and financial accounting. The previous 'archaic' system relied heavily on manual procedures and expensive leased lines to the group's mainframe computer in North America. With an anticipated increase in throughput of 30 per cent annually, the finance director believed that there had to be a better way of organising the company's own data processing. During 1982, a proposal was made to obtain an IBM machine which was compatible with the group's own peripheral equipment and the capital cost of £65,000 was included in the 1983 annual budget. The detailed proposals, including a financial evaluation, were sent to group headquarters in February 1983, where two specialist departments reviewed and approved them. The computer was then leased and installed in May 1983. The installation, judged informally, has met the expectations of its sponsors and utilisation has increased with 16 screens now linked up to the system. No redundancies resulted from the investment, although the number of staff would probably have increased if the old system had been retained.

The financial appraisal evaluated the potential revenue savings which would be achieved by installing an in-house computer facility, instead of continuing the existing sytem. This showed that the investment would have a pre tax payback of less than two years, in addition to the other intangible benefits of better management information and an in-house application of the type the company was trying to sell outside. The project looked profitable and relatively risk free and the interviewee 'didn't even have to look at taxation'. There appears to have been no direct impact on the attractiveness of this investment project from the pre 1984 tax system vis-a-vis that proposed in the 1984 Finance Act. A pre tax evaluation supported the proposal and leasing was not considered. There would also have been no noticeable impact on the short term reported tax charge of a company with significant tax losses brought forward.

Indirectly, the pre 1984 tax system had contributed little to

the ability of the company to invest by mid 1983.   The amount
of tax based leasing, and therefore accumulated interest
savings, had been small in relation to capital employed.   The
criteria for accepting the project was not related to the post
tax cost of capital. The need for fast paybacks depended on
the likelihood of technological obsolescence and would not have
differed had the tax system in 1983 been that proposed by the
1984 Finance Act.   As an international company where tax
planning is carried out at group level, the UK finance director
believed that the parent's management took national tax systems
into account when assessing investment outside its home
country.   However, in his view, the 1984 Finance Act, and the
government policies generally, had 'made the UK a more
attractive location in which to be profitable'.   This might in
future lead the group to increase its investment in the UK,
particularly in software development.   The interviewee's
opinion, that the 1983 computer investment would still have
gone ahead under the new tax system, appears to be supported by
the high pre tax return from the investment and the weakness of
indirect mechanisms, which did not seem to have enhanced this
group's ability and willingness to invest in the UK.

    The company had not accelerated any of its own investment to
take advantage of the stepped reduction in first year
allowances and had noticed only a small impact on customers'
purchases. No deferred tax provision had to be raised as a
result of the 1984 Finance Act so its gearing was not adversely
affected.   Investment in the existing business will continue
to be dictated largely by the demands of the market place, with
typically short paybacks being required due to the risk of
obsolescence.

Case 4

Throughout the 1973-84 period , this publicly quoted UK group
was active in the development, manufacture and marketing of
computer systems and networks, including peripheral equipment
and applications software. Group turnover has been over £500
million since 1978, of which a substantial proportion has been
in the UK. Group sales dropped in real terms during 1980-82
and no profits were earned taking these years together.
Gearing increased sharply as a result and very significant UK
tax losses arose.   While gearing was reduced to below 30 per
cent by 1983, tax losses had still not been exhausted at the
end of 1984. The group used to 'lease to the limit', but the
effect on gearing and finance costs led to a change in policy
and little plant and equipment is now leased.

    The interviewee was the senior manager responsible for coordinating the capital budgeting and decision making process, acting as secretary to the two main committees responsible for the group's investment direction. He stressed that by far most important investment decisions concerned product development and, in these, the broad aim was to concentrate on areas suitable to the group's strengths and likely to show good growth and returns. Once a major product development was launched, capital expenditure tended to follow on as a fairly minor part of wider expenditure covering development, marketing and the build up of trading to a profitable level.

In the last two years, the group has invested at a level of around 1.5 times its annual depreciation, yet less than 20 per cent of this has been in manufacturing. A significant proportion of capital expenditure, particularly for development, sales and servicing, is on equipment produced in-house. Another factor affecting the direction and level of investment has been the group's financial situation, which has resulted in capital rationing and further increased the importance of strategic considerations when deciding between projects. The project examined in detail is a good example of the relatively minor place of capital investment in the commitment required to develop a new product. This decision concerned the development of an updated model of an important peripheral device. Plant and equipment costs were £2.2 million but the projected cash flows showed total outflows of nearly £25 million before the beginning of net inflows.

Late in 1978, a strategic working party identified the need for an updated model of a successful device launched some years previously. A broad definition of the product was reached by early 1980 and the following year saw the compilation of a detailed development proposal, including comprehensive sections on technical, marketing and financial matters. By the time the two main group committees examined the final proposals, the strategic considerations had become very significant. The proposal stated that the updated model was long overdue and current poor market penetration could endanger the sales of mainframe computers if an up to date peripheral was not developed soon. The project was approved in April 1981 and has now been completed, thereby filling the gap in the product range. The manufacture of the new model used existing facilities, with the addition of some specialised equipment, but created no extra employment.

The group has had a sophisticated approach to investment decisions for some time and this is still evolving. For more recent investment, the capital and development expenditure has been sanctioned for the next year's need only and a well designed method of presenting previous forecasts and results sets future forecasts in perspective. The interviewee referred drily to the 'bow-wave effect' by which profits and positive cash flows always seemed to stay just one step in the future. However, the final approval of this investment decision covered all future expenditure. The financial evaluation forecast the effect of the project on turnover (over £600 million) and reported profit before tax (over £100 million), as well as the net present value of cash flows at a discount rate of 15 per cent (over £30 million, positive). This was by no means a 'hurdle' rate but provided some guide to the decision makers in allocating scarce funds. The evaluation was entirely pre tax and did not consider the leasing option in arriving at profit or cash figures.

The urgent strategic factors would have been very important in the approval of this project in preference to competing proposals. The decision to go ahead with the project was not directly affected by taxation considerations in any way. The evaluation was pre tax due to the group's tax losses; leasing was out of favour with the group and not considered as a financing option, and the capital expenditure would have had no effect on reported taxation and therefore earnings per share.

Indirectly, the group's trading had not given rise to significant UK mainstream taxation, particularly since 1980, so there would have been little liquidity benefit from the pre 1984 tax system compared with the post 1986 system. The existence of capital rationing meant that there was no effective hurdle rate which could have been influenced by the tax system to the indirect advantage of marginal projects. The interviewee found it impossible to say whether the tax system affected the attractions of investment within the sector but the company's major competitors already had a substantial presence within the UK, a situation which was unlikely to change much following the 1984 Finance Act. This representative decision, involving over £2 million in capital expenditure and much more in terms of overall cash outlays, does not appear to have been significantly affected by the pre 1984 tax incentives. The existence of substantial tax losses, strict capital rationing and overriding strategic considerations together neutralised any possible direct or indirect effects of tax incentives.

The group announced cuts in employment in 1985, as part of a major investment programme aimed at reducing costs to a competitive level through more efficient manufacturing techniques. At the same time, the group is tapping additional sources of funds and future investment seems likely to be directed towards less strategic cost saving projects, which were squeezed out in the period of severest capital rationing.

During the period before the transition from 75 to 50 per cent first year allowances, the group's ability to capitalise its own equipment has been limited by the demand from customers, who seemed very aware of the significance of the 31 March 1985 deadline. Any major investment in outside equipment has been limited by the group's tight financial targets. The impact of first year allowances on demand in the data processing sector, and possibly on the naturally fast speed of investment by competitors, appears the only conceivable way the tax system could have impinged on this group's capital investment behaviour in the last five years.

Case 5

This company manufactures, sells and services computer systems. Its turnover has exceeded £10 million for a number of years and, until late 1984, it was ultimately controlled by a major UK owned public group. The ultimate holding company has a turnover from diversified activities of nearly £1 billion and gearing is approximately 60 per cent. Capital expenditure in the company has been at a modest level for some time, reflecting the large number of bought in subassemblies, and over half the capital investment has normally been in equipment rented to customers.

Following a difficult period in the late 1970's and flat profit performance since then, the company has generated no taxable profits for many years. In some recent years, fresh tax losses have been generated, principally by stock relief, and these were surrendered to group companies. The ultimate holding company paid mainstream corporation tax at the full marginal rate until 1983, when rising foreign earnings and dividends resulted in surplus ACT. The finance director and the chief accountant of the company assisted with this case study. Capital investments over £50,000 were referred to the immediate holding company, which had authority to approve all the company's recent capital investment.

The project was the most significant capital purchase in the company for several years, namely the main unit of a computer aided design (CAD) system which cost £220,000, and comprised 70 per cent of the expenditure on non rental equipment in the year to 31 March 1984. The unit was bought to update the existing design equipment, which would otherwise have required eight of the company's own machines to bring it up to an acceptable standard. The project was sponsored, very soon after his arrival, by the technical director who joined the company in January 1983. A submission to the immediate parent board was made by March 1983, following approval by the company's own board. This was supported by a pre tax payback calculation showing a return in approximately 2 years, which compared to a guidline maximum of of 3 years. In addition to this favourable payback, the interviewees felt that the technical director's strong personality, backing his first investment request, made it virtually impossible for the board to refuse what he judged to be an important piece of equipment. The submission was successful and the equipment delivered in June 1983. The machine was financed by leasing but this was not part of the original decision. The machine has performed satisfactorily, without altering employment, but no formal post investment audit has been carried out.

The financial evaluation compared the cost of buying the new machine with the savings obtained from not having to commit eight of the company's own products to the design team. The method of financing was not addressed until after the decision was taken, so the payback looked at how quickly pre tax savings would recoup the full capital cost of the machinery. Such an evaluation clearly did not attempt to bring in the effect of first year allowances on the project, or include the rate of taxation. As the lease option was not decided upon until after the decision was taken, the effect of capital allowances on finance costs was neither evaluated nor considered. The chief accountant explained that, in the context of declining UK taxable capacity, the group had 'no shortage of capital allowances' so it is extremely unlikely that the effect of additional capital allowances on the reported tax charge for the following year would have influenced the decision. The interviewees' opinion, that first year allowances had no significant direct incentive effect on the decision to acquire this equipment, seems fully justified.

Indirectly, the ultimate holding company would probably have suffered only very slightly, if at all, had the tax system proposed in the 1984 Finance Act been in operation since the mid 1970's, but with relief for inflationary stock increases. The lack of any significant liquidity impact makes it highly unlikely that this investment would have been constrained by possible funding difficulties, had the tax system proposed by the 1984 Finance Act been in force. The ultimate holding company has recently restructured its electronics division and sold off this company to its management. The initiative for these decisions began before the 1984 Budget and reflected concern over previous and future profitability rather than tax efficiency, at a time when the group's marginal tax rate on UK profits had fallen to 22 per cent. The electronics division, and this company in particular, would have generated relatively less capital allowances than the ultimate holding company's other main activities, namely construction, transport, industrial services and leisure, so the pre 1984 tax system is unlikely to have made investment in the computer division more attractive vis-a-vis other group activities than otherwise.

Since the 1984 Budget, no attempt had been made by the group to alter the payback criteria used as a guideline in judging investment proposals. It is therefore very unlikely that any indirect mechanism of liquidity, sector attractiveness or cost of capital could have altered the decision to acquire this CAD equipment, particularly in view of the strong unquantifiable factor whereby a new technical man was making his first request for important equipment from those who had recently appointed him.

The firm's other recent investment has mainly been for replacement purposes and was not tax sensitive, even in respect of timing. No efforts were made to advance capital expenditure prior to March 1985, but the company has noted a very strong shift during the transitional period away from renting machines towards buying (from 80 per cent rental to 25 per cent) which it attributes mainly to the effect of the 1984 Budget on customers. The company still has more than adequate manufacturing capacity and does not foresee substantial capital investment in the near future.

Case 6

This company is engaged in the design, manufacture and sale of computer systems and is a subsidiary of a broadly based UK public group with a successful growth record. Group turnover is over £100 million and borrowings are small in relation to shareholders' funds. The company was formed in 1982 and grew rapidly to achieve sales in excess of £10 million in the year to 31 March 1984. The financial controller explained that the rapid expansion had meant the company 'dragging in infrastructure on a needs basis'. As each stage of the company's business plan was realised, the capital expenditure necessary to maintain expansion had been triggered. The company had submitted its capital expenditure 'wish list' in late 1983 for the following financial year and this had been agreed in full, reflecting the potential of the company perceived by the group when other subsidiaries' investment was being rationed. The group has recently been paying full mainstream corporation tax, after modest benefits from stock relief and accelerated capital allowances and full utilisation of ACT.

The project examined was one taken at random from the capital expenditure files. On establishing its UK manufacturing base, the company had built the shell of the main building and equipped part of it for production. The business plan allowed for capacity to be extended as the company' sales expanded by contracting out, until the level of demand proved permanent enough to take on staff on a long term basis. This not only reduced the risk of undesirable 'hiring and firing' but also provided an additional period of consideration before investing in new production facilities. The company's annual turnover was doubling during 1983-84, and this project, proposed in late 1983 as part of the annual budget, was to fit out part of the existing building to allow its use for production purposes.

The project was not evaluated in a formal framework; the cost was £29,000, productive capacity would be greatly enhanced and the 'margin currently being made on UK produced items (was) approximately 50 per cent'. The group board agreed the capital budget, including this project, and the company's managing and finance directors approved the detailed proposals in January 1984. The fitting out of the building commenced early in the financial year. This is a good example of a small investment in infrastructure which was essential before larger investments could go ahead. It is typical of this company's capital spending in that it was wholly needs related within a carefully thought out business plan, in which the rapidly increasing turnover provided both a physical pressure and an indicator of likely profitability. It was also typical in that it was not leased.

The interviewee was of the opinion that tax had not critically affected this investment decision, either in the short term or when setting up the company and establishing the business plan, although at that time the potential flow of dividends back to the group holding company from the new business was an important criterion. This benefit to the group was realised at a faster rate under the old tax system than it would have been under the new rules. Accelerated capital allowances postponed the payment of tax on 83 per cent of pre tax profits in this subsidiary's first two years of trading. Under the new system, capital allowances would not have exceeded depreciation, giving rise to a substantial tax charge in only the second year of operation. In view of the high growth potential for the products this company makes and the relatively low capital intensity of its manufacturing processes in relation to some of the group's other activities, it is unlikely that the pre 1984 tax system had critically added to the attractiveness of investment in this sector when the group decided to invest in the company. However, it was thought likely that the short term attractions of similar startups may be reduced by the tax changes.

The group's recent taxation burden, examined over the last five years, would not have been significantly higher under the tax system proposed by the 1984 Finance Act, so the ability to invest was not enhanced under the existing system. Another indirect mechanism, the effect of taxation on the group's perceived post tax cost of capital, would have been negligible, vis-a-vis the post 1986 system, due to the low gearing the group enjoys. There appears also to have been no direct consideration of the effect of tax on this investment, either through a post tax financial evaluation or through tax based leasing. The effect of capital expenditure on the reported tax charge, if significant, would have impinged on other, less favoured, group activities rather than this subsidiary. The interviewee's view, that the tax system was not critical to this investment therefore appears correct. The interviewee explained that a pre tax payback evaluation was normally made, for larger projects, with discounted cash flow techniques only used when a large project had a payback of beyond two years. The group assesses its subsidiaries in terms of profit before taxation and its capital approval forms do not specify any prescribed means of financial evaluation and justification.

The company had tried to advance capital expenditure into the period up to 31 March 1985 but financial constraints meant the net result was probably to accelerate only £30,000 of expenditure, mainly on the company's own products. The interviewee felt that the 1985 Budget proposal on short lived assets would apply to a significant number of the company's capital assets, particularly own products capitalised, but would be 'messy to control'. The company has been granted government aid for software development. The possibility of siting in a regional development area was considered when the factory was set up but it was decided that the advantages of being near other similar firms, with easier access to a suitable labour force, outweighed the incentives for choosing a grant aided site.

Case 7

The main activity of this UK group is the design, manufacture and marketing of computer peripherals, although it also supplies related goods and services. The group has over 1500 employees and reached a turnover of more than £70 million by 1984. Its turnover has grown rapidly in the last five years, especially overseas, and earnings from abroad accounted for just over half total turnover in 1984. The group made very substantial losses in the early 1980's, mainly as the result of the large startup costs associated with a major new activity. Although the group has gradually moved into profitability since

1982, no mainstream corporation tax has yet been paid and the size of losses carried forward means that the group is unlikely to pay tax for some considerable time. In view of the tax position, it has been group policy to finance capital investment through leasing wherever possible and, in the five years to 1984, nearly £3 million of equipment (excluding cars) was leased. Reliance on lease finance is expected to continue, until the tax advantages lessen as the group moves into a fully tax paying position.

The group finance director helped with these enquiries and provided the financial calculations on which a specific investment decision was based to illustrate the usual group procedures for investment appraisal, as well as the negligible effect he felt the changes in the tax system would have on the group's investment programmes. The project was the installation of a CAD facility costing nearly £1 million. The need for this general purpose design facility was first identified in the engineering department, where the investment was regarded as essential to maintain a competitive design function. The proposal gained the support of group management as it would clearly increase revenue by allowing more rapid introduction of new products, as well as slightly reducing the number of draughtsmen required.

The investment was appraised as an outright purchase assuming that a £60,000 grant would be received, that the full benefit of the first year allowances would be gained and mainstream corporation tax paid at the 52 per cent marginal rate. The return from the investment was taken as the additional revenue resulting from a three month reduction in product launch times and the expected manpower savings were not included in the calculation. Even so, the project had a post tax payback of 1.75 years and the internal rate of return was well in excess of 75 per cent.

The group does not have any specific guidelines against which investments are assessed and the finance director explained that, in his experience, all projects reaching this stage of evaluation showed returns of over 40 per cent; the revenue projections often proved over optimistic but the calculations were used more to justify a project to which management were already fairly committed than to act as a screening device.

Although the anticipated government grant was not actually obtained, the project was approved at the end of 1983 and installed soon afterwards. The equipment is now being used in product design and has already reduced lead times, although the group is not yet deriving the full benefit from all the facilities it offers, owing to the time and training needed to learn to use it fully. The investment was not regarded as risky and is expected eventually to lead to a 100 per cent improvement in productivity in the design function. Although it is hoped that the equipment will have a useful life of more than 10 years and the returns were appraised over 8 years, it is being written off over 5 years because of the risk of technological obsolescence.

The finance director was firmly of the opinion that the investment would still have gone ahead if the post 1986 system of allowances and corporate tax rates had applied at the time. All the available evidence support this view. Although the investment was leased, it was evaluated as an outright purchase on a post tax basis, in line with usual group procedure. The calculated internal rate of return was extremely high and, under the post 1986 tax system, the project would still have shown very high returns and a rapid payback, given the underlying assumptions about the additional revenue which would be generated by three month shorter lead times. In any case, the commitment to this investment rested less on the results of the financial appraisal, which appears to have been used to justify the investment in the final stages of decision making, than on the earlier recognition that the investment was necessary to stay competitive in the design function; the financial director explained that 'it gets to the point when investment in equipment like this is as essential as the draughtsman having a pencil in his toolkit'. The effect of this investment on reported after tax earnings would not have been a consideration in view of the group's tax position.

An examination of the likely indirect effects of the two different tax regimes on this investment also suggests that it would have gone ahead under either system. The heavy net trading losses over the four year period prior to the investment had a far more important effect in reducing tax payments than did the benefits of any first year allowances gained. In addition, the amount of leasing carried out by the end of 1983 was insufficient for the accumulated tax based interest saving to have affected the balance sheet significantly. It therefore seems very unlikely that the effect of the pre 1984 tax allowances on liquidity would have been a material influence on the group's ability to fund the investment. The financial director did not regard the group as being in a capital rationing position and said engineering time was the scarce resource in carrying out the group's investment programmes rather than any cash constraint.

While no hurdle rates were used to assess the projected returns, the internal rate of return was far higher than any conceivable group cost of capital under either the pre 1984 or post 1986 tax regime. As far as the effect of the changes in corporate taxation on the attractiveness of investing in this industry is concerned, the only possible effect was seen as operating via the influence on customer demand. This influence was regarded as negligible compared with other factors, particularly in view of the importance of overseas earnings, and certainly would not have altered the decision to go ahead with the 'essential' design facility. It seems safe to conclude on the basis of the above analysis that this investment would have been unaffected if the post 1986 changes in the corporate tax system had been operative when the proposal was being considered.

Although the specific project studied did not receive government funding, the group has received very substantial government support in the past and this has been an essential element in its development. During the first year of the transitional arrangements, there was an attempt to accelerate investment but the amount of investment brought forward was small. The financial director explained that the management 'would not override technical and commercial considerations for a small financial gain'. They did consider speeding up one significant investment but found further engineering work was needed which they decided not to rush, despite the potential tax savings this would have brought.

Case 8

This UK company designs, manufactures and sells microcomputers and related devices. It has a turnover in excess of £5 million and recently became publicly quoted, after a short period of rapid growth. The move to a broader product range, with in-house hard tooling, accompanied the flotation. The company did not invest heavily in fixed assets until then, as its earlier growth had been less rapid, less profitable and based on a product with a high proportion of bought in parts. The company paid virtually no mainstream corporation tax in its earlier years due to a combination of stock relief and mixed profitability. In the financial year ending in 1982, the rapid growth in turnover and profit gave rise to a sizeable tax liability. In the next financial year, even larger profits meant potentially higher tax liabilities. By this stage, the reported taxation charge had become a significant issue at board level.

The investment decision discussed with the company chairman was the acquisition, in 1983, of automated and semi automated machinery for the production of two new products designed by the company. The total cost of the equipment was £359,000, of which part was leased. The need to increase manufacturing capacity significantly had been identified late in 1982, when rapidly growing turnover had put existing capacity under great pressure. The management's strategy crystallised into plans to expand production, working capital and product range. These plans were not based on any formal financial evaluation as they were felt to be clearly justified by the very high margins and rapidly growing market which the company was then enjoying. The flotation of the company in 1983 raised welcome additional finance but the transition from design to production of the new lines began to lag behind schedule and there was great difficulty in finding the right site to expand factory capacity.

As the end of the company's 1983 financial year approached, the directors were irreversibly committed to developing and manufacturing the new products, despite ominous market signals and development difficulties, with the demand for the major existing product rapidly declining. Although the siting of a new factory had barely been agreed, it was decided to buy the new machinery early and house it in the company's existing premises. The major motive in accelerating this purchase was to benefit from first year allowances. It was recognised that this would significantly reduce the reported tax charge by giving rise to timing differences, which a rapidly growing company need not provide as deferred taxation. The company succeeded in reporting a tax charge amounting to 25 per cent of reported pre tax profits, compared to a forecast tax charge of 41 per cent.

Events quickly turned against the company thereafter. The new products were brought to manufacture much later than anticipated. The remainder of the manufacturing capability, which had not been purchased prior to the end of the financial year, was acquired several months later and was leased in view of a rapidly deteriorating cash flow. Even when production was finally achieved, sales fell short of expectations. Expensive stocks had been built up in anticipation of high sales and these remained on the storeroom shelves, while their prices tumbled. The new factory was completed, but the company now did not need two factories; amid heavy trading losses, the company closed down its original manufacturing site and has struggled to remain in business since then.

The interviewee was of the opinion that the taxation incentives incorporated in the pre 1984 system had played no part in the decision to expand manufacturing capacity, except in so far as they persuaded the company to accelerate the purchase of part of the plant and machinery for the expansion. Tax had not entered the assessment of the desirability of the investment, leasing was not considered when placing the early orders and consideration of reported post tax earnings had only affected the timing of part of the investment. Indirectly, the company's ability to fund investment had not been significantly enhanced as a result of the pre 1984 tax system compared with the post 1986 system. The attractiveness of investment in the microcomputer sector owed little to the tax system at that time, in view of the expected high growth and high margins which dictated the investment. This company did not refer to the cost of capital to evaluate decisions so the tax system would not have altered any hurdles applied in appraising investments.

The interviewee was asked whether the tax incentive to bring some capital expenditure forward had prejudiced the company's chances of avoiding the subsequent losses, by reducing the time in which forecasts might have been reassessed. In view of the slowdown in sales of its main product, the company regarded the investment in new products, and therefore new machinery, as essential. Over optimistic market forecasts were seen as the main problem leading to costly overbuying of stocks and the commitment to a second factory, which would not have been set up if actual demand had been correctly anticipated. The acceleration of the purchase of some of the equipment had not, in the chairman's view, prevented a full appraisal which might have averted some of the losses. The company's investment is now constrained by cash flow pressures and restricted to the bare minimum. The effect of the 1984 Budget on future taxation and financing policies has not been assessed, in view of the substantial tax losses available in the short term.

Case 9

This private company employs less than 20 people and generates a turnover in excess of £0.5 million. The company designs and manufactures specialised word processing systems with considerable reliance on bought in components and subassemblies. Additional finance is currently being sought to enable expansion of manufacturing capacity as, until 1985, investment in plant and equipment was limited by cash constraints. The company incurred trading losses in its infancy and has not had to pay mainstream corporation tax to date. Despite this, the company had made no use of leasing to finance plant and machinery. The interviewee was the director responsible for manufacturing and finance and a co-owner of the company.

The main source of value added in this company arises from design and development effort and the most recent sizeable investment which the interviewee could identify was the purchase, in the 1982-83 financial year, of a piece of electronic test equipment costing £1,300. The previous equipment had belonged to the manufacturing director personally and had ceased to function acceptably. The equipment was essential to the testing of the company's product and the board agreed to its purchase without any formal financial evaluation. The equipment has been very heavily used since installation and has performed 'very well'.

The interviewee was of the opinion that taxation considerations had played no part at all in the decision and all the evidence supports this view. As far as possible direct effects are concerned, the absence of any post tax evaluation reflected the essential nature of the investment, as well as the fact that first year allowances had no financial impact; there was no consideration of leasing and the effect on the reported tax charge would have been negligible, given the losses brought forward.

Indirectly, the tax system would not affect the post tax profits and hence liquidity of a company making little capital investment and with trading losses brought forward since its early years. The tax rate could not have influenced the target return for projects, as no such target existed. The interviewee found it difficult to say whether the pre 1984 tax system had affected the attractiveness of investment in this sector. However, he did point out that in the case of small companies such as his, it is technological discovery which tends to induce startup, rather than the post tax evaluation of the attractiveness of investing in the sector.

The transitional arrangements had persuaded a number of the company's commercial customers to insist on deliveries prior to 31 March 1985. This was in addition to the normal concern of government departments to ensure that deliveries fell into their 'correct' budget year. The company had once applied for and obtained grant assistance for a development project, amounting to 33 per cent of qualifying costs. Despite the cash benefit of the grant, the interviewee believed it was 'very questionable if the executive time spent in applying is worthwhile to a small business' and thought the company would not want to repeat the experience.

4 Electronic components

BACKGROUND

This sector covers a very diverse range of products which are usually divided according to their function into active components, such as valves, tubes and semiconductors, and passive components including capacitors, connectors and printed circuit boards. Component manufacturers vary greatly in size and range from the subsidiaries of foreign owned multinationals and large, often diversified, UK companies to the very many small independent specialists. Foreign multinationals have a significant presence, especially in the production of active components, and 4 of the 15 leading producers of electronic components are foreign owned, all of them featuring among the top 5 firms in the sector.

Large firms are particularly important in the production of active components, as very sizeable capital outlays are required for both R and D and investment in plant and equipment, and there are significant economies of scale in production. Timely product development is regarded as crucial for success in manufacturing many active components and large sums are required for effective marketing. In contrast, the smaller firms tend to be concentrated in the less technologically advanced, relatively labour intensive areas of passive component manufacture although here, too, there is a trend to greater volume and a higher degree of capital intensity in some products, which is putting increasing pressure on smaller firms.

There have been substantial variations in performance in different product areas but the industry as a whole experienced rapid growth in output between 1979 and 1984, despite a setback in 1981 and more recently. Profitability was generally higher than in other sectors of manufacturing, although some of the smaller firms in less rapidly growing areas were badly hit by recession. Productivity has increased due to investment in more capital intensive techniques, learning effects and the shift from the production of components to the assembly and/or distribution of imported components, which has resulted in a decline in employment despite the output growth. Imports have been growing faster than exports and between 1979 and 1984, the balance of trade in this sector deteriorated sharply.

The intensifying foreign competition in what is regarded as a key area of manufacturing has led to a variety of government schemes to assist the components industry, both by encouraging foreign firms to locate in the UK and by improving the competitiveness of UK firms through various grants, such as the Microelectronics Industry Support Scheme, and other aids. While the interviews were in progress, the industry was suffering from a sharp downturn, especially in mass market semiconductor devices, with low demand and excess capacity leading to reduced product prices. Although UK companies are not generally heavily engaged in semiconductor production and attention is usually confined to specialist niches, most major firms have been affected by a slowdown in growth and the increased competition in user markets.

CASES

Case 10

This UK company is a subsidiary of a large foreign multinational enterprise with worldwide turnover in excess of £1 billion. The division of which this subsidiary is a member has manufacturing facilities in developed economies throughout the world and is a world leader in high quality variations of a particular passive electronic component. The subsidiary now has a turnover of more than £20 million and has been investing heavily, with capital expenditure over the last four years of twice the depreciation charged during the period, financed mainly by retained earnings, bank borrowings and inter group credit.

Although earning pre tax profits of over £5 million during the last four years, this company has generated tax losses in

61

two of those years, due to stock relief and accelerated capital allowances. Such losses are surrendered to group companies for full consideration and the net charge to corporation tax in these four years, ignoring prior year adjustments, was £32,000, although a recent reduction in the group's UK taxable capacity may still result in some first year allowances being disclaimed. The interviewee was the acting financial controller; he and his staff are responsible for both initial screening and the final financial evaluation of all projects, including ones referred for approval at group level.

The project was chosen at random from files of approved projects. It concerned the establishment of UK manufacturing capacity for the production of a product which had previously been developed and manufactured in the group's home country. The UK demand for this product was one of the fastest growing sectors of the company's market and a UK manufacturing facility was regarded as 'a highly important project'. The creation of such capacity involved the purchase of plant and machinery costing over £500,000, which could be accommodated within existing buildings. The project was originally suggested by the engineering and marketing departments of the UK company; after screening on the basis of likely financial viability, a thorough evaluation was carried out early in 1983; this was approved in April 1983 by group headquarters and the capital expenditure was virtually complete before the end of the year.

The company has a flexible manufacturing workforce and constantly changing product emphasis. Some of the existing workforce were involved in the additional production but this project probably also contributed towards a modest rise in the company's manufacturing employment. The investment increased the value added to this component in the UK, which was specifically for the UK market. The project was financed by an expansion of bank borrowing and/or inter group indebtedness rather than by a distinct package; the plant and machinery was purchased outright and 100 per cent capital allowances were shown in the company's initial tax computations.

The main evaluation of the project was based on thorough study by the engineering, production and marketing sections of the company, which resulted in clearly documented comments and projections. This process was completed within five weeks and was fast by the company's normal standards. The results were then passed to the management accounting section where the projections were summarised into financial statements and key ratios were calculated, principally the post tax internal rate of return and the post tax payback. First year allowances were treated as being 'sold' to areas of the company or group with taxable capacity one year after the outlay occurred, giving rise to tax inflows in the cash flow projections.

The internal rate of return was calculated to be between 25 and 30 per cent and the payback period was less than 4 years. The proposal was accepted by the group's headquarters, although the interviewee did not know what hurdle rates, if any, were used. An important strength of the company's procedures for identifying and evaluating investments is the emphasis on using a thorough initial study of the proposed investment by the operating sections as a basis for the full financial analysis.

This project's direct sensitivity to the pre 1984 tax system vis-a-vis that proposed by the 1984 Finance Act apppears to be negligible. The internal rate of return recalculated under the new system would have been above that calculated under the old system and the payback would have been unchanged. Leasing was not considered and the availability of first year allowances would not have affected the parent's tax charge, due to the requirement in the parent's home base to provide in full for deferred taxation.

The interviewee completely dismissed the idea that the effect of past first year and initial allowances on liquidity had indirectly enabled some investment which otherwise would not have taken place. The company's ability to fund capital investment from retentions had, due to the group's arms length policy of paying for group relief, benefited considerably from first year and initial allowances, although the UK group, as a whole, would not have been at such a relative advantage under the pre 1984 system. The company's deferred tax provision amounts to approximately twice annual post tax profits and the interviewee was convinced that this would 'absolutely not' affect the ability of the company and the group to finance worthwhile investment. This provision was probably in excess of the net effect of the pre 1984 tax system vis-a-vis that proposed by the 1984 Finance Act, so it appears that funds generated by tax savings were not critical in this case.

An indirect effect through the change of hurdle rates against which projects are judged is not very likely for a foreign based group, especially since projects of this size are examined outside the UK in relation to the group's worldwide criteria. The interviewee was not able to comment on whether the change in the tax system would affect the relative attractiveness of investment in this sector. However, the business of this company is a core activity which the group undertakes worldwide, so the UK tax changes are only likely to affect the relative attractiveness of the UK vis-a-vis other locations. The company serves the local market rather than being part of a global production network and over 80 per cent of the company's sales are in the UK. Such locally orientated manufacturing subsidiaries are less likely than export orientated units to be affected by changes in the relative attractiveness of the tax regime compared with other countries. It is particularly true of this project, which was specifically intended to serve a growing UK market niche.

The project was said to be fairly representative of the expansionary investments undertaken by the company in recent years. The high return is not unusual. The interviewee explained the use of payback as being readily understandable by managers with non financial backgrounds who may initiate potential projects. By having a guide in financial terms which they can roughly calculate, attention can be concentrated on those possibilities which are financially promising and wasted effort on 'non-starters' avoided. The transitional arrangements for reducing first year allowances and tax rates had been recognised by the company as potentially advantageous and the management had tried to encourage speedy implementation of agreed proposals. However, the interviewee pointed out that 'speed is essential anyway' in a high technology environment, and he expected the net effect to be slight.

Case 11

This UK subsidiary of a Californian based semiconductor company accounted for over a fifth of the group's worldwide turnover, with sales of £18 million in 1984. The company built and expanded its European base in a UK assisted region during the 1970's, with particular emphasis on three specialised niches in the integrated circuits market, and UK and EEC grant aid had a great effect on the decision to stay and expand. However, the withdrawal of regional development status in 1980 and the downturn in the world semiconductor industry caused the cancellation of a major additional facility, which had reached an advanced stage of planning and would have involved a further 100 jobs.

Since then, major investment in the UK facility has mainly involved building up the design and engineering section to serve European market needs, particularly in telecommunications. In 1984, the UK company still accounted for 13 per cent of worldwide manufacturing capacity and employed 243 people. It is funded by retained earnings with parental support through the inter company account for components supplied from the USA.

Following heavy investment and rapid growth up to 1980, the

recession pushed the company into two years of trading losses when investment was only just equal to historical depreciation. However, the parent group as a whole remained in profit in these two years and, over the period 1979-83, its gearing never rose above 20 per cent. The UK company's trading losses in 1981 and 1982 eliminated the 1980 taxation liability and covered a substantial part of its 1984 profit. Thus, when the specific investment project was being examined (1981-82), there was an abundance of tax losses for the near future.

The group's European financial controller, who is based at the UK manufacturing unit, assisted in this study. He had a thorough knowledge of the company's business, its investment history and the outlook of its parent. In his view, the group was dominated by technical rather than financial managers, with major decisions always being referred to California.

The specific project concerned the purchase of a large advanced CAD system to provide in-house capacity for designing and testing sophisticated large scale integrated micro circuits. Until the end of 1981, the checking and correction of chip layouts had to be done at the parent's California location, which extended lead times in the design of new products for the European market. The increase in design work in the UK had exacerbated the inefficiency of this system of cross Atlantic checking and rechecking, and both the senior UK technical management and the US parent realised that they needed to either improve the capability and efficiency of the UK design effort or close it down.

The UK managing director made enquiries about the Microelectronic Industry Support Programme (MISP) and found that it was likely that a grant would be given on the machine. He telephoned the US chief executive who was already aware of the need and they agreed that, if the application for a grant was successful, the UK design team could have the system. In the grant application it was made very plain that the US parent would not sanction the purchase unless a grant was forthcoming and this appears to have been the case. However, the reverse was also true; if the grant was awarded, the parent would be committed to buy the machine or lose considerable credibility in Britain, particularly in view of the important project cancelled earlier.

There was no financial evaluation apart from obtaining a quotation for a month old repossessed CAD system which represented the latest state of the art. Total budgeted cost was £121,000 and the grant sought was £38,850. The grant was received and the order for the machine placed almost immediately, in January 1982. It was installed in the same year and the company are pleased with the machine, which has a faster design speed than expected.

As the payoff from development equipment is difficult to define and evaluate accurately, it is not necessarily cavalier to proceed without a financial justification of such a project. The industry is dependent on accurate technical judgements and on fast response times and the interviewee stressed that it was not unusual, in the UK company, for no financial assessment to be made of cost savings or paybacks related to investment in capital equipment. An example of a factor which would have been extremely difficult to quantify in this instance was the effect the introduction of new technology might have in persuading existing, highly skilled employees to stay with the company.

One certainty about the decision is that no prior thought was given to capital allowances. These were not even mentioned before the decision was taken and were only discussed after the order was placed, which is understandable, in view of the large tax losses which had just arisen. There was also no discussion of the part leasing could possibly have played in reducing the financing cost.

Indirectly, the UK company would have suffered slightly rather than gained from the pre 1984 system vis-a-vis that proposed in the 1984 Finance Act. Although before 1980, and the subsequent net trading losses, there were modest accelerated capital allowances of £400,000 (35 per cent thereof being £140,000), £2-3 million of taxable profits had arisen (a 17 per cent reduction in the corporation tax rate would have saved £340,000-£500,000). Therefore the company would probably have paid £200,000-£360,000 less under the post 1986 system during the years up to 1983, more than offsetting any gains obtained later by leasing, but this would not have significantly affected the ability to finance investment.

The possibility of UK tax changes affecting a US corporation's hurdle rate is remote. Although long familiar with discounted cash flow techniques, these have not often been applied to R and D investment within the company, although formal evaluation procedures have recently been clearly laid down. It is therefore extremely unlikely that, under another tax regime, this decision would have been affected by having a different target to meet.

The possible effect of a different tax system on the attractiveness of this sector of industry was thought negligible by the company's European financial controller. He explained that the sector is dominated by technical people who rarely understand tax implications and that most decisions are either overwhelmingly market driven or non quantifiable in their effects, such as the CAD machine just discussed. The importance of speed is considerable and, in this, the first year allowance system was seen as merely suiting a sector where major investment is normally carried out early as technically possible.

Regarding the attractiveness of the UK as a potential investment location following the change in tax system, the interviewee distinguished between the replacement and updating of existing facilities, as in the case studied (which would probably remain unaffected), and the potential expansion of European operations in the UK. In his view, the parent's management tended to look for the best total package of incentives when investing outside the US. He saw the abolition of first year allowances as outweighing the benefit of a lower tax rate because the former had previously reduced the US investment required in a major facility abroad, while the group's European distribution system made it possible to take profit in a country with reasonably low corporate tax rates.

The investment discussed was representative of the company's capital expenditure in that it was heavily dependent on grants and introduced advanced technology to the UK subsidiary. As a machine for design rather than manufacturing, it also reflects the change of emphasis since the 1980 recession began; indeed the company's latest major capital acquisition was a computer to complement the CAD system. This computer, which was installed in mid March 1985, was deliberately purchased prior to the fall in first year allowances from 75 to 50 per cent. This deadline added urgency to the negotiations with the parent company and the effort to complete the purchase. Despite its tax losses, the company has not leased on any significant scale and does not plan to lease in the future. Budgeted capital expenditure for 1985 has now returned to well above annual depreciation and the manufacturing facility is operating at a high degree of capacity utilisation.

Cases 12 and 13

These two cases were provided by a major UK quoted manufacturing group with turnover well in excess of £100 million. The group has a substantial electronic components division, making various devices for sale to third parties and for supply to the group's other divisions, which are largely based on electronic technology. The group paid virtually no mainstream corporation tax from 1973 until recently, due to stock relief, some trading losses and accelerated capital allowances. ACT, which had been written off annually up to 1982, was utilised fully in the ensuing two years.

Investment in buildings, plant and equipment has been growing rapidly since 1979, in line with expansion of turnover and sustained growth in trading profits. The group relied heavily on leasing for off balance sheet finance in the 1970's.   In recent years, the group's much improved gearing and the return to mainstream corporation tax payment have meant that leasing is normally used only for certain grant assisted projects, where a carefully designed lease can ensure a very attractive cash flow profile. The interviewee was the group finance director,a member of the board which considers all significant investments. The group's capital investment tends to be broadly defined, several years in advance, through a strategic planning discipline. In examining major investment proposals, the group's key financial criterion is the pre tax return on assets employed.

Project 12. This decision concerned the purchase, fitting out and equipping of an additional factory for the group's important electronic components division. The building was purchased outright for just over £1 million, and fully fitted out and partially equipped with leased plant for a further £4.6 million. The decision was considered and taken during 1982 and implemented in 1983. The request for the additional capacity was triggered by the realisation that the original factory, established to manufacture a particular product range, could not cope with the demand, which was much higher than anticipated and was expected to continue to outstrip existing capacity.   At least two new jobs were created when the factory was opened and the subsequent demand has justified the decision to expand. The electronic component division's net profit was static during the year of implementation, reflecting the initial costs, but increased by 60 per cent in the following year.

The financial evaluation of the project presented to the board in June 1982 weighed the increased fixed and working capital costs against the revenue generated by a 50 per cent increase in turnover. The key criterion was the undiscounted pre tax return on capital employed by the division. The projections showed a small dip during the initial year followed by a rise to 2 per cent above the returns previously being achieved and 3 per cent above the group's target. A marginal analysis was also performed, on a discounted post tax basis, and showed an internal rate of return of over 20 per cent and a discounted payback of under 4 years.

The board initially approved the project, which had gross

capital costs of £4.8 million, subject to obtaining an expected grant. In November 1982, the project sponsors reported that the grant would be given and requested an additional £0.8 million capital expenditure, mainly to fit the whole building out to the exacting standard required in readiness for this and future expansion. The increased sum of £5.6 million was then approved.

There was no direct incentive from the pre 1984 tax system for this project, although grant assistance clearly played a significant part. The project decision was primarily based on pre tax criteria and, although the bulk of capital expenditure was afterwards leased, the appraisal assumed an outright purchase. The effect of first year allowances on the secondary, post tax criteria would not have been significant to the decision, as the tax advantages vis-a-vis the system proposed in the 1984 Finance Act would probably have raised the internal rate of return by less than 2 per cent, and this would still have given a return under the new system well above any conceivable cost of capital. The group's finance director was firmly of the opinion that neither the tax effect on the project nor any effect on the reported tax charge, had been significant to the decision.

Project 13. An earlier investment decision, taken in 1980, concerned a purpose built factory, with a capital cost of approximately £5 million, for contracted development and manufacture in a highly specialised field of electronics. The investment was triggered by negotiations with a major customer for a long term contract to develop and manufacture a new generation of specialised electronic equipment. The customer doubted whether the group's present resources were adequate, so the board approved the commissioning of a purpose built factory to provide the visible capability   to carry out the contract. The group's financial director pointed out that much capital investment in long term development and contract work was made on such initiatives from major customers.

The costs of the expansion of capacity were evaluated against the benefits of the contract and a satisfactory pre tax return on capital employed was projected. The factory was leased in view of an attractive offer from a non-taxable body to build it, as specified, and lease it to the group. The attractiveness of the lease option owed nothing to the tax allowances but reflected the value placed by the lessor on the employment generated by the construction and   subsequent use of the building.

Taken at a time when the group still had considerable tax losses and surplus ACT, the finance director's view, that 'tax

didn't enter into the decision', appears correct as regards any
direct consideration of tax incentives.   Under the post 1986
tax system, a similar tax horizon would still have been
projected.   After the building was commissioned, the customer
who had requested the additional resources cancelled the
contract.   The group decided not to break its contract for the
factory and the building was completed, leased to the group and
gradually filled with several activities, including the
manufacture of passive electronic components.

The differential effect of the pre 1984 tax system on the
group's liquidity, through the postponement of tax liabilities
and interest savings via leasing, appears to have been slight
prior to these investments.   Even in the unlikely event that
none of the recorded timing differences had occurred, the
additional mainstream tax paid up to 1983 would have been less
than one per cent of shareholders' funds while the group's
leasing, until then, had not been at particularly keen rates.
In view of this muted effect and the way gearing had already
improved, it seems unlikely that the tax system indirectly
provided funds critical to either of the above projects.

The group's key target criterion is still a pre tax return
on capital employed and the 1984 Finance Act has not brought a
change in this.   The finance director viewed the effect of the
legislation on a typical discounted cash payback, a secondary
measure, as requiring the group to 'get used to' the higher
figures rather than rejecting investments which would
previously have been accepted.   The attractiveness of
investment in electronic components to this group is dependent
on technological breakthroughs and the resulting customer
demand, and has not been based on relative tax treatment,
particularly following 10 years of tax exhaustion.

The interviewee took care to point out that the effect of the
1984 Finance Act on the group was limited by the high
proportion of investment which still qualifies for 100 per cent
scientific research allowances.   Looking far ahead, the group
had only judged it necessary to provide for a small proportion
of the potential deferred tax liability which had accumulated
up to 1984. Although slightly affecting some balance sheet
gearing ratios, this had not made financing more difficult or
more expensive. The group had accelerated a recent £5 million
factory purchase to fall before the reduction in industrial
building allowances from 31   March 1985. There had been
little major acceleration apart from this, owing to the long
lead times for specialised plant, and there was absolutely no
question of trying to undertake capital expenditure which had
not been previously approved on the normal commercial and
financial grounds.

This company, with manufacturing interests in both bulk and customised electronic components, is part of the high technology interests of a major publicly quoted group, with worldwide turnover of £2 billion and a strong balance sheet. Recently both the group and the company have been concentrating their substantial investment in areas with the most potential for profitable growth. The custom built side is seen as the most attractive sector in this company's case, and it already has a good reputation for technical innovation in certain customised components.

The company, which currently has a turnover in excess of £3 million and over 200 employees, was taken over by the group in 1983 and, until then, had paid virtually no mainstream corporation tax. Since the takeover, the group's tax position has become the relevant fiscal environment for the company. The group has written off large amounts of ACT in recent years mainly due to its substantial overseas earnings and, as a result, has tended to favour some use of leasing in financing capital expenditure. Since acquisition, the company has had access to the group's financial resources for capital projects and all investment decisions, above a specified limit, have to be confirmed by the divisional board responsible for the group's high technology companies and ventures.

The project discussed with the financial controller was the major expansion of the company's manufacturing capacity in its customised product division, which was the only major pre March 1984 investment since the company was taken over. An initial investment in manufacturing had been made some time earlier and this facility was rapidly moving towards full capacity, particularly in the light of a new product opportunity. The project was being discussed in the second half of 1983 and the group had built the likely expenditure into their acquisition calculations.

The formal proposal was submitted to the divisional board in February 1984 and approved shortly afterwards. Capital expenditure was just over £300,000, with £49,000 of the total being spent on internal building work. The project added 10 new jobs to the manufacturing side of the business and increased the company's export potential considerably. Although still at an early stage, the project is going according to plan, and is seen as less risky than the establishment of the manufacturing facility which it is designed to expand.

The financial evaluation of the project showed all the cash

flows generated by the project over a seven year period and these were evaluated using discounting techniques. The taxation flows were estimated in line with the group's stepped tax horizon, anticipating the future move to a full 52 per cent marginal tax rate. The net present value of the cash flows, at the group's usual and quite high round figure hurdle, was postive and very substantial, while the internal rate of return was calculated to be 19 per cent above the even higher round figure target expected of projects in high technology fields. A sensitivity analysis showed the project still comfortably within the relevant criteria and the interviewee indicated that a project with returns below the target criteria would be unlikely to go ahead.

The project cash flows were recalculated as part of this research, assuming a marginal tax rate of 35 per cent, which the group would almost certainly have faced if the post 1986 tax system had applied since 1973. The effect on the net present value was negligible and although the internal rate of return fell slightly, it was still 15 per cent above the target figure.

The project would have been well above the post tax target return for the division under the pre 1984 or the post 1986 tax system; the possibility of leasing was only considered after the decision to go ahead was taken and the equipment was actually purchased outright; the surplus ACT in the group meant the effect on reported after tax earnings of any accelerated capital allowances would have been negligible, even if the divisional board had considered such a factor. These points lead to the conclusion that the pre 1984 system of allowances and tax rates did not represent a significant direct incentive to this project, compared to the post 1986 model.

Indirectly, the ability of a group with very low gearing to carry out investment would not have been significantly enhanced by the pre 1984 tax system, especially as millions of pounds of ACT were unutilised for many years under that system. For the same reason, the group's cost of capital is likely to fall rather than rise in the long term and no change has yet been proposed to the targets which projects must meet. It is therefore unlikely that any investments would have been rejected due to different targets under the system proposed by the 1984 Finance Act and this one would certainly still have gone ahead.

The other potential indirect effect on the investment decision is through its influence on the attractiveness of investment in this sector. The group's ACT position had reduced the tax benefit of operating in capital intensive sectors and its other main activities are at least as capital intensive as this one. It therefore seems most unlikely that, under a post 1986 tax system, the group's commitment to this company and this investment decision would have been significantly different.

The interviewee regarded virtually all the company's capital expenditure as having a strategic purpose and did not think the tax changes would greatly influence investment policy. The transitional arrangements had only induced the company to accelerate the purchase of a modest amount of office equipment. Although the group's use of leasing had been quite significant in the past, the interviewee knew of no decision to alter the group financing policies significantly in the near future but emphasised that financing was a decision taken centrally, after operating companies had made commitments to purchase capital equipment.

Case 15

This UK public company is engaged in the design, development and manufacture of a particular type of active electronic device. It has manufacturing facilities both in Britain and abroad, employing over 1000 people in the UK. As a result of high R and D and start up costs, the company has experienced large trading losses and has only been able to benefit from capital allowances indirectly by leasing. Even with its heavy reliance on leasing, there has been a continual shortage of investment funds. The company has been investing substantial sums, but the speed of investment has been reduced by the funding constraints and some major planned investments have been scaled down as a result.

The project discussed with the corporate treasurer was the building of a factory in a regional development area to bring the final assembly and packaging of its electronic components in-house. This major investment, which cost over £5 million, was to be financed by leasing the plant and machinery, with the building being sold and leased back. The investment decision was taken in early 1984 and orders placed immediately after the formal approval.

The prime aim of the investment was to reduce the company's dependence on subcontractors; this strategic move was felt necessary because future growth in production was expected to make the reliable placing of the assembly and packaging contracts increasingly difficult. The possibility of siting the factory abroad was considered, but this was found to offer little by way of quantifiable cost advantages compared with the proposed UK site in a regional development area. The decision to build the factory in the UK was mainly based on the likely synergy from carrying out the final assembly stage near to the design and production facilities and the expected reduction in lead times, together with concern about the risk of political instability in possible overseas locations. The construction of the factory has not been completed, so it is impossible to comment on the success of the investment.

The investment was appraised by examining the projected cash flows over a five year period to determine the undiscounted payback and the internal rate of return. The impact on the unit cost of the components and the profit and loss account was also assessed. There was a three year payback, with the building being treated as bought, and the internal rate of return was well above the notional cost of capital hurdle. As the company is in a capital rationing position, the returns from this project were then compared with alternative investment opportunities. The returns appeared relatively low, but the importance attached to non quantifiable strategic factors meant that the project was given priority over competing investments.

All suitable items of plant and machinery were leased, in line with the usual company policy, and the cost of lease finance was considered in carrying out the appraisal. The effective interest rate on lease finance was estimated to be zero, mainly because of the regional development grant passed to the lessor, accounting for about two-thirds of the reduction on usual borrowing costs, but also because of the benefits of tax shelter passed to the lessor, responsible for one-third of the reduction.

The interviewee stated that the decision to go ahead on this project would not have been affected if the post 1986 tax system had applied at the time. The pre 1984 tax system certainly appears to have had no direct bearing on the decision to undertake the investment. The firm would not have been able to derive any immediate benefit from capital allowances and did not expect to be earning taxable profits for some time. Although lease finance allowed some benefit from first year allowances, the interviewee specifically stated that this was largely irrelevant, both because the returns from the project were well above the firm's cost of capital and because of the importance of strategic considerations in the selection of this project.

As far as the indirect effects of the pre 1984 tax system are concerned, it is possible that the firm's ability to finance the project at the time could have been partly dependent on past tax savings enjoyed indirectly through leasing. The company has extremely high gearing and between 1980 and 1984 had financed a large part of its fixed assets through leasing at an effective interest rate well below the typical cost of normal borrowing. In profit and loss terms, the saving involved amounted to approximately £2 million by the end of 1983, of which one-third probably derived from accelerated capital allowances. Had this been reflected in lower shareholders' funds, the company's balance sheet would have appeared even further stretched. However, it is extremely difficult to say whether the company would have been prevented from making this important capital investment in the absence of accelerated capital allowances; certainly the interviewee thought it unlikely. The other indirect mechanisms, namely the effect of the tax system on calculated cost of capital or sector attractiveness, would probably not have had a significant effect in view of the extent of capital rationing and the technological drive behind the company's development.

The investment involved the final stage of component manufactore, which is a relatively mature process technologically. However, the interviewee explained that in this industry, most projects depend on 'catching a technological wave' which, if successful, yield very high returns, making the reduction in finance costs through capital allowances insignificant to the results of project evaluations. Technological circumstances and the availability of cash were described as the vital ingredients in most of this firm's decisions and the tax changes were not seen as affecting the attractiveness of investment in the sector.

Investment has been accelerated in the transitional period, primarily to take advantage of regional development grants before the 1985 deadline, and has been financed as far as possible through leasing. The interviewee expects the firm to continue leasing during 1985 but to review its leasing policy as the tax paying horizon moves nearer, in the light of the changing tax treatment of capital expenditure.

Case 16

From its formation in 1980 until well after the 1984 Budget, this company was jointly owned by two large electronics groups. It was originally set up on the initiative of a dynamic technologist, who persuaded one of the companies to give a loss making activity a chance as an 'independent' small concern. The company, which employed less than 100 people, had a turnover in excess of £3 million by 1984. It produces standard and custom components for professional and consumer products and has invested heavily in plant and machinery, particularly after a large injection of capital by its parents in 1982-83. The company made little cumulative profit until March 1984 but the trend was very favourable, with current profits cancelling out previous losses. One of the joint owners was a foreign company so there was no attempt to pass on tax losses, which were carried forward within the company instead.

The investment discussed with the financial controller was chosen at random from the files of successful investment applications in 1983-84. It is typical of much of the company's investment, which is usually made to ensure the required output levels can be reached and the desired product quality maintained. This project concerned the purchase of a piece of production equipment with a more accurate capability than the existing process.

The impetus for the investment came from the production department where a particular process was causing 'a consistent loss which averages 2-4 per cent of production' and 'occasional catastrophic problems which severely reduce the yield of a limited number of batches'. The suggested solution was a piece of equipment costing £20,000, with installation costs estimated at £1,000. The sponsoring engineer calculated that 'if only 75 percent of this problem is solved there would be a payback of 9 months at most'. The departmental manager quickly completed an investment application and the company's managing director approved the purchase almost immediately in December 1983. The installation was completed before March 1984 and has successfully dealt with the problems of inaccuracy and excessive losses.

The estimated 6-9 month payback was based purely on the costs of reworking and replacing defective products and did not take taxation or interest into consideration. There was, therefore, no quantification of the capital allowance incentive. The company did little leasing at that point, so the possible attractions of this form of finance did not arise in anyone's mind. The effect of obtaining first year allowances on the reported tax charge could not have been significant in view of large tax losses brought forward. The interviewee's opinion that, once the company had embarked on its business plan, investment was dependent solely on the technical and market momentum and impervious to direct tax incentives appears fully justified in this case.

The possible indirect effect of the pre 1984 tax system on the company's ability to invest was negligible; given its low profitability, no tax would have been paid under either tax system. The effect on any post tax cost of capital calculation would have been very small, in view of its low gearing, and probably irrelevant as its investment appraisal procedures excluded tax. However, when the decision to set up the company in the UK was taken, consideration would have been given to the tax incentives; the available first year allowances meant no tax would be paid during the crucial early years of high investment, thus reducing the external finance necessary to support the initial growth phase. It was difficult for the interviewee to say just how important this factor was in persuading the two investors to set up the company in the UK but he thought that cash grants under the MISP scheme had been 'a very powerful influence, much more so than any taxation incentives'. The many business considerations and the more significant grant incentives for setting up in the UK undoubtedly reduced the relative importance of tax considerations. The interviewee suspected that the taxation aspects had simply made the choice of the UK more comfortable, rather than actually tipping the balance.

The company was not able to accelerate any significant investment into the period of 75 percent first year allowances up to 31 March 1985, due mainly to a reluctance to spend part of the 1985-86 budget which had not yet been approved. In total, only £10,000-20,000 of capital expenditure has been brought forward from the following period as a result of the 1984 Budget.

Case 17

This privately owned company, with a turnover below £3 million, was established in 1970 by an executive who left a large electronics group to start manufacturing a high precision passive component and later a specialised hybrid component. The company was set up with grant assistance in a rural assisted area and grew quickly and profitably until 1979. Trading profits were then depressed until mid 1983, mainly due to recessionary forces which were exacerbated by problems in a subsidiary acquired in 1979. Since 1977, manufactured output has been sold through a marketing company owned jointly by the senior management of the main company.

The company continued to invest throughout the early 1980's both in expanding capacity and improving the quality of output. Capital expenditure typically amounted to three times the annual depreciation charge and was financed by retained profits, bank borrowing and hire purchase. The executive interviewed was the finance director, a chartered accountant who is part of the very close-knit management team and responsible for the financial aspects of investment decisions and their execution. The company has not paid any mainstream corporation tax since 1980, which led to taxation being described by him as 'not a problem'. The demand for the company's products has been expanding rapidly in recent years and, with a lower growth in overhead costs, has enabled the return on shareholders' funds in the latest financial year to reach 30 per cent, compared with 14 per cent the previous year.

The investment was a major decision taken before the 1984 Budget to expand manufacturing capacity significantly over the three year period 1984-86, at a capital cost of approximately £700,000 and a £300,000 working capital requirement. The decision was triggered by rising pressure on the marketing side as demand for the company's components outstripped capacity, resulting in lengthening order books and increased lead times. The longer lead times were such as to threaten future customer loyalty and the entire management team recognised the need for expansion. The major restraint was financial and, after the technical questions had been settled, the finance director drew up a three year budget incorporating the capital expenditure and working capital requirements of the expansion. This showed that the company should be able to support the project without stretching borrowed funds beyond what was likely to be acceptable to the bank. On the basis of the overwhelming commercial necessity and this financial ability, the company committed itself to the project.

A formal grant application was prepared and submitted in January 1984. This was approved in June 1984 for an amount equivalent to 24 per cent of the capital expenditure and the project went ahead very quickly. Some expenditure was accelerated into the period prior to 31 March 1985 and as buildings became vacant, they were bought instead of building new ones. The project, although still at an early stage, has already increased capacity and it is expected that an additional 46 jobs will be created in the company within three years.

The project evaluation, which concentrated on the company's ability to fund the investment, was based on the unquantified judgement that the expansion was commercially vital and would further increase profitability. It was hoped that the main part of capital expenditure would be financed by bank borrowing but hire purchase was an additional option. Taxation was not taken into the three year budgets in the expectation that the company would continue to pay no mainstream corporation tax, partly as a result of previous first year allowances but mainly as a consequence of lower profits during the recession.

The finance director's view that tax 'was not a problem'

prior to March 1984, appears justified. The circumstances of the company meant that first year allowances were not explicitly considered when the decision to go ahead with the project was taken, neither in respect of the effect of taxation on project returns, nor through leasing, nor as a means of reducing the company's tax charge. Indirectly, the past liquidity and the perceived future liquidity of the company had benefited to some extent, probably by about £35,000, from the pre 1984 tax system vis-a-vis the system proposed by the 1984 Finance Act. However, this represents only 4 per cent of shareholders' funds or 10 per cent of borrowings and would not have been essential to the company's ability to carry out the vital expansion. The company, given the relatively long life of its main assets (depreciated at 15 per cent on a reducing balance basis), has not provided for deferred taxation on accumulated timing differences and its ability to support borrowing has not therefore been impaired by the new rules in the short term.

On the question of whether the tax changes would alter the attractiveness of investment in the electronic components sector, the finance director's opinion was that 'the motivators in this industry are not accountants, they tend not to understand taxation and will go on motivating regardless of taxation changes'. In the context of a private company specialising in niche markets, this appears a particularly plausible analysis. The company does not use a cost of capital hurdle, so it is not likely that the 1984 Finance Act rules would have lead to a higher return being demanded from this project, particularly since finance, rather than inadequate potential returns, has been the main constraint on investment.

Although it is very unlikely that this project was dependent on the first year allowance incentives, the finance director regards the 1984 Finance Act as 'making tax an issue again'. The abolition of first year allowances and the company's own increased profitability has made a tax payment in the year to mid 1985 a possibility. Before 1979, the company had occasionally looked round in the third quarter of what seemed profitable years to determine whether there was any qualifying capital expenditure which could be brought forward to shelter such profits. This would have been regarded as particularly worthwhile if the potential profit would otherwise have been taxed at marginal rates of over 50 per cent. The interviewee was convinced that the favourable liquidity effect of the pre 1984 tax system, which would have arisen mainly in the 1970's, would not have been essential to fund any of the company's past capital investment. Efforts had been made to accelerate capital expenditure into the period prior to 31 March 1985, including some parts of this major expansionary project.

Grant assistance was an essential part of the original decision to locate the company where it is today. Since then, the availability of regional development grants would have helped liquidity considerably and thus assisted further expansion. In the case of this project, it was felt worthwhile to apply for a grant rather than go ahead immediately without it but the approval procedure undoubtedly delayed the start of the project by a few months, at a time when the market conditions were very favourable for immediate investment. The risks of technological obsolesence are relatively low in this project; however, in an industry where the speed of product development and of the move into manufacturing often needs to be extremely fast, this delaying effect of grant assistance contrasts with the potential effect of first year allowances in reinforcing the commercial need for early investment.

Case 18

This privately owned company was set up in the 1930's to manufacture a product for the electrical industry and later diversified into a specialised field of electronic components. It is still directed by a member of the founder's family and supplies custom built components to customers worldwide, having made steady sustainable growth in this area its goal, rather than seeking to enter the high volume market. Current turnover is less than £10 million per annum.

The interviewee was the finance director and company secretary, who had a long experience of the company. He explained that the company has fluctuated between modest trading profits and modest trading losses since 1978, although the current trend is more encouraging. As a result of occasional trading losses and stock relief, the company has paid no mainstream corporation tax since 1978. Although accelerated capital allowances have assisted in eliminating taxable profits, the company's capital expenditure has been relatively low, due to high gearing and to recessionary pressure on markets. Investment in recent years has tended to be of a replacement or cost saving nature, with an emphasis on reducing unit labour costs in order to remain competitive. It is company policy to fund investment from unsecured bank borrowings rather than lease. The company's relatively low profitability and an overdraft ceiling mean that investment projects have often been delayed, pending the availability of funds.

The chosen project was the new computer purchased shortly before the 1984 Budget for use in accounting, stock control, production monitoring, order and sales administration and the production of management information. The decision to buy the machine was taken in two parts. The suppliers of the company's previous computer, bought in 1977, had given notice in 1982 that they could not renew its service contract. During the company's regular review of capital expenditure, the executive directors examined the possibility of buying a computer capable of doing more than the traditional accounting functions performed by the existing machine. The finance director realised that such an investment was hard to justify financially on a payback basis. He preferred to regard it as an overhead and let the question be one of whether the executive directors could persuade themselves, and the full board, that a new computer was a worthwhile investment. Both the executive and the board did agree, in late 1982, to buy the new machine but only when funds allowed.

A local government official contacted the company secretary early in 1983 and informed him about the availability of selective financial assistance for projects which would protect employment. Following this unsolicited encouragement, the company grouped four fairly disparate capital items together as a loosely defined project 'necessary to improve overall production methods ... thereby safeguarding as many employment places as possible'. An offer of selective financial assistance was made in mid 1983, amounting to 26 per cent of the proposed capital expenditure on top of normal regional development grants. The company accepted the offer and went ahead soon afterwards with all four investments: the computer, a small piece of test equipment, a smaller piece of manufacturing equipment and the remodelling of the company's storage areas. Of these, only the last was brought forward to a major degree by the selective financial assistance and the benefits of this reorganised storage have been considerable. It is difficult to isolate the effects of the grant on employment but the company was recently able to report a larger workforce than it had forecast would be likely, even taking the grants into consideration. The purchase of the computer did not displace any employees but new clerical jobs would probably have arisen without the additional data processing capability. The company is generally pleased with the performance of the new computer. A more recent application for assistance has also been accepted to expand and improve part of the manufacturing process 'to safeguard existing employment'.

At no time, neither during the initial decision to acquire the computer nor when acceptance of selective financial assistance committed the company to making the investment, were the tax incentives of capital allowances considered. The proposed investment was not evaluated on a post tax basis, leasing was not considered and the horizon for the next likely payment of mainstream corporation tax was several years away. This means there was definitely no direct effect on the project from the pre 1984 tax system.

Indirectly, the company had benefited to a very limited extent from capital allowances over the years, as its capital expenditure profile had not been very different from the level of depreciation. No mainstream tax had been paid for six years, due mainly to low profitability and stock relief. It seems unlikely that the pre 1984 system of first year allowances signficantly reduced the tax bills of the company vis-a-vis its probable position under a post 1986 system. As the investment was not assessed with reference to a hurdle based on any cost of capital calculation, there is little chance that a different tax system would have changed the criteria for assessing projects in the company. Being a small stable company utterly committed to a specialist niche in electronic components, it seems inconceivable that any impact of the tax system on perceived sector attractiveness would have influenced the firm's recent investment in components. The interviewee's opinion that taxation had played no part in this investment decision appears completely valid.

The interviewee said that 'tax considerations have never been a material factor in any company I have worked for'. He had, in the past, varied the timing of some minor capital expenditure slightly for tax reasons but would not be taking significant advantage of the March 1985 threshold. He believed that regional selective aid only forms an effective incentive for new jobs when an outside company is induced to set up a new facility in a development area; after being in the assisted area for some time, grants in his view become less vital in relation to commercial considerations. The company had moved its manufacturing to the present location in the 1950's because it was refused permission to expand in London, rather than in response to an attractive grant package. The head office function left London to join the rest of the operation in the early 1970's in order to reduce costs, not because of the grant incentives. The finance director appeared to have a logical and unemotional view of taxation; tax seems not to have had a major influence on this firm's investment decisions, including those taken in a climate of capital rationing.

5 Mechanical handling equipment

BACKGROUND

This sector of the engineering industry produces a wide range of materials handling equipment, such as conveyors, cranes, lifts, hoists and fork lift trucks, to meet a diversity of end user requirements. The definition of the industry used for sample selection was in accordance with activity level 3255 of the 1980 SIC, which excludes equipment used primarily in agriculture, extraction, earthmoving and construction, despite a certain degree of overlap in function. According to official statistics, the total value of UK manufacturing classified to this sector was well over £1 billion in 1984 and the great majority was sold in the home market.

The largest customers are in manufacturing, especially the engineering and process industries, although the transport and distributive sectors are also important end users. The performance of the mechanical handling industry is of particular significance to the economy as a whole. Government studies have estimated that as much as 15 per cent of GNP can be attributed to the cost of handling and other researchers have concluded that up to two-thirds of all industrial costs are due to handling, when all such operations in the production and distributive process are considered. This means that small percentage cuts in handling costs can yield very substantial savings for end users (NEDO, 1983).

Many companies in the mechanical handling sector are small, cater almost exclusively to the home market, and have traditionally specialised in a narrowly defined product area (e.g. cases 24 and 25), so their profits, investment and tax position have reflected performance in that area alone. Larger companies with mechanical handling subsidiaries tend to be more diversified, with substantial interests in other sectors and worldwide. These have begun to offer complete systems to meet all their customer's mechanical handling requirements (e.g. cases 19 and 21), and the provision of integrated systems is seen as a future growth market. Foreign multinationals also play an important part in some product areas, the production of fork life trucks for example, often manufacturing parts in high volume in different locations for subsequent assembly and minor modifications in customer markets (e.g. case 19).

The fortunes of the different subsectors of the mechanical handling industry have varied considerably in recent years. Some traditional products have been adversely affected by structural changes in demand; for example, the re-equipping of ports for container traffic has had a severe effect on manufacturers of heavy dockside cranes and long term trends away from high rise buildings have had an important impact on the lift industry. Foreign competition has also become more important in some sectors, such as fork lift trucks, where the Japanese have been particularly successful in penetrating the UK market.

More generally, there is a clear relationship between changes in mechanical handling equipment and cyclical fluctuations in total user investment, with an especially marked fall in sales in 1981, from which the industry is only recently recovering. As a producer of capital equipment catering mainly to the British market, any indirect effects of the 1984 tax reform on customer demand would be particularly important, and there is evidence of customers accelerating their orders for tax reasons during the transitional period.

CASES

Case 19

This company, which sells over £30 million of mechanical handling equipment in Britain, is wholly owned by a large foreign industrial and commercial group. Heavy manufacturing is carried out abroad but the UK company is responsible for a considerable amount of design, assembly and modification work on its basic equipment range, as well as acting as a contractor in the building of material handling systems. Recent net investment in fixed assets (mainly in premises and equipment for hire) has been approximately double annual depreciation as a result of strong sales growth.

The parent group has, in the past, regarded increasing turnover as the UK company's primary target. This has been reflected in low margins and profitability. The company has not paid mainstream corporation tax in the past five years and had substantial tax losses carried forward at the end of the 1984 financial year. As a further result of aiming for growth in the volume of sales, the company has been highly geared for many years. The company has made considerable use of back to back leasing to finance its hire fleet but its own capital expenditure has not all been financed in this way, with land and buildings being bought outright mainly to strengthen the balance sheet. The company secretary, who assisted with the study, had an excellent knowledge of the company and the group through his role as senior financial executive and as secretary to the board. A majority of the board are nominated by the parent group and this board must approve all capital expenditure in excess of £10,000.

The project concerned the building of a new purpose built regional workshop centre, incorporating works, stores, maintenance, service, sales and administrative functions and costing over £500,000. The main strategic purposes of the project were to replace two existing facilities which were 'at saturation point', to improve workshop facilities for customer services and to provide premises more in keeping with the company's image. The idea was conceived early in 1983 and the group nominees on the board agreed in principle to the investment, but at a different location, on the basis of a proposal made in May 1983. The alternative site was chosen and approved later in the year and bought early in 1984. The building contract was completed two months later and work finished early in 1985. Although at too early a stage for a formal post investment audit, the building appears to be fulfilling the promises of its proposal. The move led to the planned loss of one job.

The financial appraisal included in the proposal was based on the comparison of annual revenue and costs at 1983 prices with and without the project. The cost calculation was mainly concerned with the financing, depreciation and establishment costs of the new building vis-a-vis the rent and establishment costs of the existing sites. The additional cost was compared with that part of the increase in revenue which was expected to result from the better premises. This comparison showed the level of incremental annual revenue would exceed incremental annual costs within two years. The interviewee explained that even where expected financial returns were reasonable, the approval of major capital expenditure projects was largely determined by the immediate direction of a subtle tide of accommodation and intransigence on the part of the group's board nominees. This project had been proposed when the foreign directors were felt likely to be sympathetic and their attitude, as much as the result of the financial appraisal, was seen by the company secretary as vital to the approval.

The decision makers did not take the corporation tax system directly into consideration when making this decision. The financial analysis was entirely pre tax, the assets were to be bought outright rather than leased and no account was taken of any possible effect of accelerated capital allowances on post tax earnings. Given the large tax losses available and the decision, for balance sheet purposes, to own the buildings themselves, there was no cause for tax aspects to be evaluated. Before finalising the plans for the building, the company obtained advice from its auditors in November 1983 on how to ensure that the maximum possible expenditure qualified for industrial building allowances, but this was merely to improve a far future position rather than to capture benefits necessary to the decision.

The pre 1984 tax system also appears not have had a significant indirect effect on the decision. Low profitability meant that accelerated capital allowances had increased rather than created tax losses; under the system proposed by the 1984 Finance Act, the company would almost certainly have paid little or no tax, so it did not gain significantly in liquidity terms from the pre 1984 system. It is also unlikely that the pre 1984 tax system had resulted in an artificially low hurdle rate for project acceptance. The target which existed was set by the foreign parent group and was not altered following the 1984 Finance Act; in any case, this project was not judged against the internal rate of return so set. As the parent's purpose in investing in the UK was to achieve sales volume with little book profit, it is very unlikely that tax considerations affected the perceived attractiveness of investment in this sector.

This investment is typical of major non fleet capital expenditure by the company in recent years, being mainly spent on premises with a view to making improvments in the modification and service facilities for customers, which are seen as being vital to continued success. The company had accelerated virtually none of its own capital expenditure during the first year of the transitional tax arrangements, but it had noticed more pressure for delivery from customers than usual. The company does not expect to alter its investment behaviour as a result of the 1984 Finance Act but recognises that both customers' attitudes to hiring vis-a-vis buying, and the attractiveness of back to back leases for its own fleet hire assets, may change.

Case 20

This company is a subsidiary of a major UK publicly owned group with well over 50,000 employees and interests in several capital intensive sectors of varying maturity. The group, which has paid heavy mainstream corporation tax for many years, maintains only minimal treasury and taxation functions centrally, allowing operating subsidiaries a large degree of autonomy in capital expenditure decisions, treasury management and day to day running. The group as a whole has substantial cash resources and has not suffered any capital rationing in recent years. Divisions and subsidiaries report their results and are judged on a pre tax basis, giving them an incentive only to undertake investments which improve their pre tax return on assets employed. The subsidiary's turnover is in excess of £20 million and over the last four years investment has been 'spartan', including only essential capital expenditure such as replacement of ageing assets or the acquisition of equipment to fulfil particular contracts. The group as a whole does not lease capital equipment.

The specific investment, discussed with the finance director of the subsidiary, was the purchase early in 1984, prior to the Budget, of a paint booth to spray paint its mechanical handling equipment in a purpose built, controlled environment. The initiative for the investment came from the works department and the request was justified on three main grounds. Firstly, the paint booth would improve health and safety arrangements for the company's employees; secondly, it would allow an improvement in the finishing quality, of which there had been complaints in the past, and thirdly, it would enable the company to cope efficiently with bigger units which were becoming an increasingly significant part of its business. The £70,000 investment was approved by the company's finance director and managing director with reference to sub group headquarters. The paint booth has worked 'extremely well' since it was installed, accomplishing the tasks for which it was bought, as well as receiving favourable comment from existing and potential customers viewing the company's works.

The need for this asset was considered so clear cut by the senior decision takers that it was felt unnecessary to quantify the benefits in financial terms. Where a larger sum is involved or a less obvious need is being met, the company normally looks at the pre tax payback in relation to capital cost. This criterion is preferred because few variables are involved in its calculation, it provides a clear yardstick to measure actual performance against, making it difficult for sponsors to 'wriggle off the hook' if things go badly, and it is easily understood by the many non accountants throughout the group.

The finance director firmly believed that tax considerations 'should not be allowed to cloud commercial decisions'. The proper place for such considerations was, in his opinion, when the choice of financing was being made, either of the investment itself or of the company as a whole. He maintained that such an attitude, followed throughout the group, had served well and contributed to the relative strength of its various businesses. There does not appear to have been any direct consideration of first year allowances in this decision. There was no evaluation of the effect of taxation on the investment return, leasing was not considered and the group's policy of fully providing for deferred taxation, combined with the attitude of the company's decision makers, was against considering any reporting advantage through a reduced tax charge.

Indirectly, the old tax system has undoubtedly placed a heavier burden on the group than that which it would have suffered under the system proposed in the 1984 Finance Act. However, the existence of large liquid reserves suggests that no additional investment of any significance would have taken place given the extra cash, and certainly this specific project would not have been affected. The use of a pre tax payback criterion for project appraisal virtually removes any possibility that the tax system influenced the investment by impinging on calculated cost of capital. As the group has extremely low gearing, the effect of the lower tax rate on its post tax cost of capital would be less than a quarter of one per cent on a conventional textbook calculation.

Whether the changes in capital allowances and tax rates will alter the group's perception of sector attractiveness is difficult to judge. The group's liquidity would enable it to move into less capital intensive areas anyway without imposing constraints on activity in traditional areas. The relatively stable level of capital expenditure in the company means that the post tax return on assets should increase under the new system, making it very unlikely that disinvestment or restrictions on capital expenditure would be considered. It therefore seems most unlikely that this investment was dependent on the pre 1984 tax system vis-a-vis that proposed in the 1984 Finance Act.

The above investment is typical of the majority of this
company's capital expenditure, which is in contract related
investment and the replacement of ageing assets essential to
safety or production, and therefore insensitive to tax
considerations. The group's small central tax function could
'always use first year allowances', but no specific
instructions or advice to maximise the benefit of capital
allowances had ever been issued to operating companies. It was
thought that tax, particularly during the transitional period
of stepped reductions in capital allowances, would probably not
have given rise to more than very minor acceleration of smaller
projects, in view of the long lead times for most major
investment.

Case 21

This company makes specialised mechanical handling systems to
individual customer's requirements mainly in the United
Kingdom. A member of a UK publicly quoted group with turnover
in excess of £1 billion, the company itself has recently been
earning profits of more than £5 million per annum on a
turnover of over £30 million. Both the company and the parent
group have invested steadily in capital equipment in recent
years, with the company concentrating on the reduction of unit
costs by using more capital intensive techniques and
integrating its design, production and other functions. The
group has paid very substantial mainstream corporation tax for
many years and, prior to the 1984 Budget, had maintained a full
deferred taxation reserve. The company has a considerable
degree of autonomy and is judged in terms of operating profit,
with short term cash forecasting on a monthly basis providing
early warnings of potential changes in profitability. The
company has been a cash generator for many years which has
further increased its autonomy in capital expenditure
decisions, although all items above a certain value must be
ratified by a group official.

The specific investment examined with the company's finance
director was the purchase of a computer controlled press
costing £38,500. This machine is typical of new equipment
being deployed as part of the company's strategy of integrating
its processes and reducing unit costs. The initiative for the
investment came from the production engineering department but,
even as the idea was being discussed, the company had 'half an
eye' on its potential as part of an integrated computer network
linking design engineering, inventory control and machining.
The equipment was included in the company's 1983-84 budget but
was not specifically requested until a formal proposal was made
in December 1983. This proposal included an explanation of the

machine's purpose and a pre tax payback calculation which was well within the normal range for acceptable projects.

The proposal was 'rubber stamped' at group level on 4 January 1984 and an order placed very soon thereafter. The machine is thought to have a physical life of at least 10 years, although it may be technically superceded before that. Although no post investment audit has been made, the expected savings in terms of labour reduction appear to have been achieved, as well as an improvement in quality. Such savings were quite clearly attainable at the outset and the finance director judged the investment to be practically risk free.

The financial evaluation consisted of a calculation of the pre tax payback. The payoff was the saving of labour costs, which was the most readily quantifiable benefit of the investment. The interviewee emphasised that the most significant consideration given to the investment was by the production engineering department. Here the technical feasibility of installing such a machine would have been examined against information collected through constant monitoring of current technical research, developments by competitors and similar experiences within the group. Considerable energy would also have gone into obtaining the most attractive quotation for the machine.

The interviewee believed that tax had not played any direct part in persuading the company or the group to make this capital investment. As a pre tax financial evaluation was used, leasing finance was not considered and any possible effect on the group's reported tax charge did not concern either the company directors or the group official who 'rubber stamped' (within one working day) the recommendation of the company's managing director, this view seems totally correct.

Indirectly, the group's liquidity would have been even stronger had the tax system proposed by the 1984 Finance Act been in force in the past, and dividend policy unchanged. The group has given no indication that projects should now meet more stringent payback criteria, which is not surprising as the group's theoretical post tax cost of capital (calculated as part of this research using a conventional textbook model) would have increased by only a quarter of one per cent as a result of the changes in corporation tax. The group's commitment to investment in this company or sector is unlikely to be affected by tax considerations as it has a similar capital intensity to the group's main activities and the parent, in the interviewee's opinion 'makes every effort to make a success of every part of the group'. It therefore also appears extremely unlikely that the pre 1984 tax system

indirectly influenced the company's decision to purchase this
machine.

The finance director did not believe any of the company's
investments to be tax sensitive, although some capital gains
were occasionally routed through the company to take advantage
of previous capital losses. The company had examined the 1984
Budget and it was thought that the group generally would be
better off as a result of the changes. The transitional
arrangements did not induce the company or its customers to
accelerate capital programmes, due mainly to the long lead
times involved in both producing the company's customised
product and in its own capital expenditure programmes. The
company had benefited in the past from technology grants and
regarded these as useful, but not essential, to its
investments. Looking outwards, the company believes few of its
competitors have invested significantly in recent years and it
hopes to continue its profitable manufacturing operations on
the basis of a growing cost advantage.

Case 22

This quoted, UK based, contracting and manufacturing group
operates worldwide. Total group turnover is in excess of £1
billion, although there has been little real growth in sales
since the late 1970's. The group's capital investment, net of
disposal proceeds, has been less than current cost depreciation
for each of the last four years, reflecting real capital
disinvestment, while numbers employed have fallen considerably.
At the end of 1983, the group's current cost gearing was less
than 20 per cent after netting substantial liquid assets
against borrowings. The group began paying UK corporation tax
at the full marginal rate again in 1982, finally utilising all
surplus ACT previously written off, although considerable tax
losses remained in certain group companies in the UK and
abroad.

One of the interviewees was the group's financial controller.
He thought that the pre 1984 tax system had assisted capital
investment but that the group's procedures did not enable such
incentives to be visibly significant. Operating companies were
required to justify large investment decisions on 'commercial'
and cash flow grounds, on the basis of pre tax returns. The
group's senior management did not explicitly encourage
investment or approve marginal projects because of the effect
of the associated tax incentives on the group's cash flow or
reported earnings. Despite this, the interviewee believed that
the group's senior decision makers were conscious of the tax
treatment of capital expenditure and this had created a

'climate which was favourable to capital investment proposals', thereby encouraging their sponsorship.

A specific investment was discussed with the accountant of the group's UK subsidiary, which specialises in the manufacture of specialised mechanical handling equipment. The £303,000 investment was in three machine tools needed to meet the quality specifications of a major contract in 1983. The decision was evaluated pre tax on a stand alone basis, ignoring the effect of losing the contract if the machines were not purchased. The calculated return, while modest, would have been enough to sustain interest charges at the UK rates existing at the time so this highly strategic investment was promptly approved by the group's headquarters.

There was no visible direct influence on the attractiveness of this project from the pre 1984 tax system. There was a pre tax evaluation, leasing was not considered and there was no explicit discussion or evaluation of the impact on the group's reported tax charge. Although this does not rule out the influence of the tax incentives on the internal 'climate', it is very unlikely that such a strategically important project would have been turned down had the tax system proposed by the 1984 Finance Act been in force.

Similarly, no indirect influence on the group's ability or willingness to undertake this investment can be discerned. The group's UK tax payments would not have been significantly different under the tax system proposed by the 1984 Finance Act, so the ability to fund this project was not in any way related to previous savings due to capital allowances. The absence of a post tax cost of capital target makes it unlikely that, under the proposed tax system, the return required from marginal projects would have been sufficiently increased to have affected this investment. It is also unlikely, given the relatively high capital intensity of nearly all the group's activities, and the fact that most capital expenditure is bought for specific contracts, that tax considerations have significantly affected the group's perception of the relative attractiveness of capital investment in the mechanical handling sector. Overall, the pre 1984 tax system appears not to have had any tangible direct or indirect effect on this investment decision. However, it was thought to have affected the 'climate' facing capital investment requests, which had been more favourable than is likely under the system proposed by the 1984 Finance Act.

The group has benefited from grant aid from time to time and this is seen as a more tangible and significant investment incentive than favourable tax treatment. The group did accelerate UK capital investment in 1985, but mainly with an eye to the changes in UK regional development grants, and only projects which could easily be brought into the period before 31 March 1985 were accelerated for tax reasons. The 'impractical' depooling provisions in the 1985 Finance Act were being considered and a policy document is to be issued before 1 April 1986.

Case 23

The core business of this unquoted group is in the materials handling sector. The group has a turnover in excess of £100 million and a strong balance sheet. Recession and over capacity in the sector has halved the level of orders since the late 1970's and led to very careful capital investment policies.Net direct investment was below depreciation and at a level less than half the 1978-79 peaks in each of the four years up to 1984. The group has not paid significant mainstream corporation tax since the early 1970's, despite the reversing of accelerated capital allowances in recent years, due mainly to the level of stock relief in relation to profits hit by recession. The group treasurer, who is also a main board director, and the company secretary participated in this study. They both stressed the highly competitive nature of the sector and the importance of technical quality, responsive management and after sales service in competing successfully.

In the tight investment climate of the four years prior to the 1984 Budget, few major investment projects had been sanctioned and investment had been mainly geared to the replacement of ageing assets, the reduction of works cost and improving productivity. The specific investment discussed was typical of this climate and involved the outlay of £400,000 on computer controlled machine tools, to replace older and less sophisticated plant in the machine shop of the group's major subsidiary. The replacement had already been delayed with the onset of the 1980 recession but, by 1982, the existing plant was becoming more expensive to maintain and run and there were also fears that the technical quality of the final products might decline relative to competitors.

The investment proposal outlined the considerable technical advantages of the investment and the cost savings were presented in terms of reduced running costs and extra productivity but not enumerated in a specific framework. In any case, the group has no centrally laid down hurdle rate against which returns on capital investments can be measured. As usual in this group, taxation was not considered when the capital expenditure request was presented to the group board for approval, and no consideration was given at that stage to the method of finance. The group board approved the investment on the basis of the technical and cost saving details presented to it and the corporate treasurer then addressed the question of taxation and financing. He decided the lease purchase of the equipment would be the most tax efficient form of finance, particularly if the acquisition date was brought forward to just before the end of March 1983. This was done, advancing the project implementation by three to four months from the timing originally envisaged, purely for tax reasons.

Indirectly, the group's liquidity undoubtedly benefited from first year capital allowances and little mainstream tax was paid even during the pre recessionary late 1970's. However, the recent low levels of capital investment have allowed the accumulated timing differences to reduce, in a climate where stock relief and rationalisation costs have absorbed the reversing timing differences. The group has raised a deferred taxation provision amounting to around 40 per cent of the tax which could potentially be paid on accumulated accelerated capital allowances. The amount provided has had no significant effect on the strength of the balance sheet and has not interfered at all with borrowing. The full potential provision represents the maximum by which the group might have benefited via the pre 1984 system vis-a-vis the post 1986 system, less the effect of a 17 per cent lower rate on any tax which was paid. The probable benefit represents only 7 to 8 per cent of total capital and reserves and would not have affected the liquidity or gearing of the group very significantly.

The low level of capital expenditure during the 1980's has been due to a deliberate policy of reducing capacity and was in no way related to illiquidity. The absence of any central hurdle means that past investment is unlikely to have been sensitive to taxation through a cost of capital criteria, while the core nature of its materials handling business means that the group would not consider investing or disinvesting in the sector on the basis of sectoral tax characteristics.

It seems that the initial investment decision was not dependant, either directly or indirectly, on the pre 1984 tax system vis-a-vis the post 1986 model but that subsequently the investment was accelerated by a few months primarily for tax reasons. Although no regular post investments audits are carried out, the interviewees thought that this investment had been a success. It has been fully utilised, has allowed a useful reorganisation of the machine shop and enabled the company to build more technical quality into the product investment. It did not suffer from being accelerated.

Both the interviewees and the group's chairman in his annual report viewed the 1984 Finance Act as detrimental to the group, through its likely effect on the future demand for materials handling equipment. The group's tax position has required careful planning since the 1984 Budget and £1.5 million expenditure on service vans was accelerated to fall before the end of March 1985. The interviewees noted in real boost to orders up to March 1985, made more noticeable by a very heavy fall following the reduction of capital allowances to 50 per cent, which was attributed to the acceleration of purchases for tax reasons by some customers.

The 1985 Budget proposal for depooling short life assets was thought more relevant to customers using their equipment on more than one shift in heavy industries than to the firm itself. The interviewees thought some depooling would take place within the group but they were very aware of the additional administration which this would involve.

Case 24

This private, owner-managed company has 12 employees and manufactures specialised components for a widely used type of mechanical handling system. The company's turnover is around £250,000 and has been rising in recent years. Most capital investment tends to be in machinery designed and built by the company itself. A very small part of the company's total capital expenditure of approximately £20,000 per year is leased, typically office equipment. The company's owner, who helped with this case study, expressed clear views on both investment strategy and taxation. He is unwilling to commit resources to capital investment until the demand has actually materialised and the potential investment promises a cost-effective improvement in the way the company is coping with the heavier pressure.

Taxation is regarded as 'purely a liability' which should not affect business decisions. The company does not pay corporation tax but declares taxable profits as director's remuneration. Such 'profits' have been regularly earned in recent years but the taxable income of the owner has not reached the higher personal tax bands. The owner was convinced that the pre 1984 tax system had not resulted in significantly different tax outflows from the business than would have occurred under the system proposed by the 1984 Finance Act and that any difference would not have been sufficient to have affected the ability to make capital investments.

In 1983, the company designed and began to build an improved

metal rolling machine for its own use. The capitalised value
of the machine was approximately £10,000. The impetus for the
decision came from increased demand, which the company was
meeting in 'less efficient ways'. The owner judged that to
improve on the existing rolling machine would benefit product
quality,as well as permit greater output to be produced more
cost effectively. The machine was completed in 1984 and there
has been 'no question that the investment was not worthwhile'.
The possibility of sale and lease back was not considered and
the expenditure was financed from the company's own mixture of
retained earnings and bank borrowings. The owner did not
believe a financial evaluation was necessary to the decision
and did not consider the tax advantages of capital expenditure
in deciding to go ahead. The capacity pressure was already
apparent and he was confident that the development would
succeed.

The evidence supports the interviewee's opinion that the pre
1984 tax system did not in any way contribute to this capital
expenditure decision. Capacity pressure provided the incentive
to develop the new machine and the evaluation of the investment
ignored the post tax returns, the possibility of leasing and
the effect on short term tax payments. The ability to invest
in this machine had not, in his opinion, been dependent on a
particular set of taxation rules (which seems a reasonable
judgement given a steady and spartan investment history). The
company's view of what constituted an acceptable investment,
including the attractiveness of investment in this sector, had
nothing to do with taxation, being ultimately dependent on the
technical and marketing judgement of its owner.

The company's auditors keep the owner informed of changes in
tax legislation, but he had not tried to take advantage of the
stepped reduction in first year allowances in 1985. He regards
the 1984 Finance Act as 'academic' to the future of his
business and the effect on its future tax burden as dependent
on the impact of other, more important, influences on profit.

Cases 25 and 26

This owner-managed private company, which manufactures heavy
mechanical handling equipment, grew continuously over the 20
years before 1979, by which time it employed 45 people and had
a turnover in excess of £350,000. The owner explained that,
during this period of growth and more recently, it has been
this policy to take only a modest salary from the business; any
profits have been reinvested in fixed and working capital. He
does not believe in leasing and the company's fixed assets have
been financed by retained earnings, together with borrowings

from the bank, with which the company had an excellent long term relationship. The company has not paid any significant corporation tax since 1969, mainly as a result of accelerated capital allowances throughout years of real growth and high inflation.

Demand for the company's products and expertise practically disappeared in the recession of the early 1980's; investment in plant and machinery fell to a very low level and there were substantial redundancies. Survival was due largely to an imaginative investment of the company's resources in building an estate of small industrial workshops. By mid 1985, with only 8 employees and turnover around £140,000, the company is beginning to see some signs of an increasing order book. The investments examined in detail were the last major investment in plant and equipment made by the company prior to the recession, and the investment in industrial workshops.

Project 25. This decision involved the purchase of 2 foreign built milling machines, at a cost of £24,000, to increase the workshop's capabilities following success in gaining 2 contracts, each for 4 heavy cranes. The customer, a very large metal processing business, eventually planned to install 7 arrays of 4 cranes each, so further contracts were anticipated. At the same time, the election of the Conservative Government in May 1979, with a specific call for industry to re-equip, was seen as providing additional encouragement to the investment decision.

As future utilisation and profitability were thought unlikely to be a problem, the decision concentrated mainly on the choice of machines. The company's owner did not bring corporation tax into any evaluation of project returns and did not believe that first year allowances made any difference to the decision, in view of the strong demand pressure. Soon after the order for the milling machines was placed, the metal processing customer cancelled (with compensation) the second order of 4 cranes and indicated that the 5 planned arrays would not be required. Other business dried up and, when the milling machines arrived, they remained practically idle for 2 or 3 years. Much of the older equipment was scrapped, enabling the company to move into an old workshop which it had planned to demolish. The newer factory premises, which had already been altered to accommodate the anticipated work, were rented to another user.

The company's owner was convinced that this decision would have gone ahead under the tax system proposed by the 1984 Finance Act. Tax could have had no direct effect in the absence of a post tax evaluation of project returns, any consideration of leasing and any thought to the effect of capital expenditure on reported profits. However, it is clear that the company's growth had indirectly been greatly helped by accelerated capital allowances, which removed all tax liabilities from 1969 onwards, freeing funds for expansion.

While there undoubtedly was such a 'liquidity' benefit, the company would probably have managed to borrow the £24,000 necessary to finance this demand led project irrespective of the earlier benefits of postponed taxation, particularly as instalment credit had been available when necessary in the past to finance plant and machinery. In the absence of such benefits, with tax payable at 30 per cent on part of profits, the company would probably have forgone previous, more marginal, investments or would have had higher gearing by 1979.

It therefore appears unlikely that the indirect liquidity benefit, though strong, was strong enough to have been essential to this important capacity led investment decision. Other indirect mechanisms, namely the effect of tax on a cost of capital hurdle or the attractiveness of investment in this sector, are unlikely to have been significant to a small company with unsophisticated investment appraisal techniques carrying out an activity based on its owner's engineering background rather than considerations of relative tax treatment.

Project 26. This case concerns the construction of a £375,000 estate of 10 small industrial units on land the company already owned, adjacent to its existing premises. Planning took place in 1980-81 and the premises began to be occupied in 1981-82. It was the first such development in the town, but this accommodated rather than dictated the investment.

The main impetus for the investment was the recession, which had resulted in a virtual cessation of work in the company's traditional engineering markets. Although staff had been drastically reduced to eight, it was necessary to find some work to enable the workshop to remain open at all. The owner hit on the idea of using the engineering expertise of the company to build a small industrial estate. It was clear that such an investment would have to be funded mainly by borrowings and that these would have to be serviced and repaid out of the income from the workshops, as the company's own resources were needed to survive the recession.

The company's owner did some rough calculations and then looked with his accountants at the likely future pattern of income, debt interest and repayments. It appeared just feasible to repay the variable rate borrowing over 10 years by 10 rising instalments. This would mean no immediate return to the company in terms of cash flow but would, hopefully, leave an unencumbered industrial estate on the company's balance sheet after a period of 10 years and result in 'paid' work prior to then. The company's bankers reviewed the projections and granted the loan. The industrial estate was built, principally by the company's workshop, with some subcontractors employed for roofing and specialised installations. The units were let as they became available and the company has just suceeded in meeting the first three repayments, despite the high nominal interest rates of recent years.

The owner was convinced that without the benefit of industrial building allowances (100 per cent was actually obtained due to the special rules for small workshops), the project would not have been possible. The allowances postponed the Schedule A taxation on rental income which would have been payable if writing down allowances of only 4 per cent per annum had been given. The surplus of net income over interest charges was all needed to meet the repayment schedule of the loan. Had taxation, even at 30 per cent, been charged on this surplus, it would not have been possible to meet a realistic repayment schedule. The company and the bank directly considered the effect of the capital allowances on the project's cash flows and these were critical to the decision to undertake the investment. Under the tax system proposed by the 1984 Finance Act, this investment could not have gone ahead, even on a smaller scale.

In addition to the direct consideration of the effect of pre 1984 tax incentives on the project's cash flows, the company's financial position had benefited from the previous complete postponement of corporation tax. By improving existing liquidity and gearing ratios, this probably made it easier to raise the new borrowings. It is difficult to say whether this indirect effect was also critical to the company's ability to make the investment but it is likely that the direct effects dominated.

The owner was not particularly averse to paying tax and the importance of the pre 1984 tax system to his investment plans derived from the effect it had in allowing this small, capital intensive business to reinvest surpluses generated without deduction of corporation tax. The untaxed surpluses not only provided more funds for future investment but, as in case 26, enhanced the company's ability to make investments financed by borrowings, which could be serviced and repaid out of future untaxed earnings. The company has never received any grant aid and did not accelerate any capital expenditure to take advantage of the higher allowances available up to 31 March 1985.

6 Non energy extraction

BACKGROUND

A wide range of non fuel materials are extracted in the UK, including the low value, high bulk minerals of sand and gravel, limestone and igneous rock, generally known as aggregates; various other non metallic substances, and relatively small quantities of metal ores and minerals. Most of the firms studied in this chapter are engaged in the extraction of aggregates, which is the main activity, by volume, in the sector. The production of aggregates is dominated by large, vertically integrated groups, with downstream interests in building materials and construction, for example, based on their extracted raw materials. There are also a large number of very small firms which, although unable to reap economies of scale, are able to compete due to the localised nature of their markets.

A significant proportion of investment in this sector has been in the acquisition of additional reserves close to users as well as in the extension of existing workings. This is despite the requirement to depreciate, for tax purposes, the cost of capital expenditure on the exploration, development and purchase of mineral rights over the whole period in which a mine generates income, a system which has for a long time been generally perceived as inadequate. New proposals (Inland Revenue, 1985) would bring mineral depletion allowances more into line with capital allowances generally, allowing qualifying expenditure to be written off at 25 per cent as soon as it is incurred, provided that a mining trade has begun.

The sales of the UK aggregates industry are heavily dependent on the home market, and particularly on investment in the domestic construction industry. From a peak in 1973, construction output in real terms fell 23 per cent by 1981 and sales of aggregates also fell to a low in 1981, when the volume sold was 29 per cent below the 1973 level. However, the position has since improved (BACMI, 1985). The industry's comparatively healthy state, despite market conditions, is mainly due to improvements in productivity.

The fixed assets in this industry generally have a relatively long life but, as demand has been fairly static, much of the investment in plant and machinery has been in replacing worn out or obsolete machinery with more modern equipment, thereby increasing productivity. Between 1979 and 1983, employment fell by nearly 25 per cent, according to industry sources, while in the same period output per head increased by nearly 40 per cent. Performance in overseas markets has often been more buoyant than in the UK and some diversified firms with significant overseas earnings from their subsidiaries abroad have had substantial surplus ACT (e.g. cases 28 and 29).

CASES

Case 27

This case concerns one of a group of businesses in the UK with substantial interests in non energy extraction. The UK group employs over 500 people and is a wholly owned subsidiary of a foreign based group. The UK companies are organised on a divisional and geographical basis with a strong emphasis on local autonomy. Poor UK trading results in recent years have imposed financial restraints on the UK group and the value of total investment has been similar to the depreciation charge. The poor profitability has resulted in little mainstream corporation tax being paid, although optimism about future profits repeatedly postponed any consideration of leasing as a tax efficient means of financing.

The specific investment, examined with the finance director of the holding company, was in the replacement of £1 million of crushing equipment at one of the group's UK workings. The investment was triggered in 1982 by local management, who were concerned that the existing equipment was worn out and unreliable, threatening the company's position in the local market. The need was made known to a divisional director who encouraged the submission of a project proposal.

The proposal, including a five year financial evaluation, was drawn up early in 1983 and anticipated a reduction in unit cost and increased output, with no expansion of employment. This was submitted to the group's overseas headquarters and was approved in mid 1983. The equipment, with an expected physical life of 10 years, was ordered straight away and commissioned a year later. Despite delays in bringing the equipment into use, the early results seemed reasonable, although the group finance director was reserving judgement until after the 12 month post investment review, one of three routine reviews of project performance.

The financial evaluation was based on the increase in pre tax profit (after interest and central administration costs) expressed as a percentage of the amount invested. This was compared to a target which had been laid down some years ago by the parent group's chairman. The target was unusually high, and clearly bore little resemblance to the group's cost of capital; few of the projects evaluated actually achieved this target but many were accepted which fell short of it. This project was thought 'clearly profitable' although the return was below the target.

The additional profit was prudently calculated on the basis of improved productivity, but did not include a quantified estimate of the possible costs of serious breakdowns and disruption resulting from the state of the old machine. Taxation was not taken into the calculation of profit and leasing was not considered as a means of financing. As the capital expenditure would not have affected the parent's reported tax liability in the slightest, it appears that there was no direct consideration of taxation incentives when the investment decision was being taken.

The possibility of the pre 1984 tax system indirectly influencing the investment, vis-a-vis the system proposed in the 1984 Finance Act, also appears remote. The recent trading losses would have given rise to similar tax liabilities under either system, so the company's liquidity and ability to invest were not enhanced under the old system. The 'target' for projects would not have been influenced by the UK taxation system, particularly in view of the group's lack of UK tax capacity. The acceptance of the investment would not therefore have been dependent on the tax system artificially holding down a hurdle rate. Similarly, the lack of taxable capacity in the UK makes it unlikely that the group's perception of the attractiveness of investment in this sector depended to any significant degree on the pre 1984 tax incentives. It was the interviewee's clear view that taxation had played no part in the decision. The finance director was also of the opinion that the 1984 Finance Act would not change the group's policy towards leasing as they still hoped for a return to taxable profitability in the near future.

The group had not tried to take advantage of the first year of the transitional arrangements and, having few short life assets, would not be very interested in the depooling concession offered in the 1985 Budget. The group had benefited from regional development grants in the past, but the location of investment was largely determined by the availability of mineral reserves, project returns being increased where the grants were available, but rarely by a critical margin.

Case 28

This is the wholly owned subsidiary of a large public group which has extensive interests in the extractive sector. The parent has substantial overseas earnings and a record of high dividend payments resulting in large amounts of unutilised ACT, some of which has been written off in the accounts. This has been influential in reducing the marginal rate of corporation tax on UK profits, while trading losses in some activities, as well as various tax allowances, have also had an effect on the average tax charge.

The subsidiary, which produces aggregates and related products, has grown both internally and through acquisition. It is an extremely important profit and cash generator within the group and has a history of very substantial investment. Since 1980, it has leased new assets whenever possible, usually financing about one-quarter of its total capital expenditure in this way, with the remainder generally being funded internally.

The company has well defined corporate planning procedures and a very sophisticated approach to the appraisal of capital investments. The criteria used vary in different tiers of the organisation's structure and according to the nature of the investment, with a distinction in the case of aggregates being drawn between three main types of project expenditure. For mineral reserves, which usually account for about 10 per cent of total capital expenditure, the aim is to replace the approximate value of minerals extracted each year. Replacement investment is based on a target percentage of the depreciation charge on a current cost basis and varies according to the profit and cash flow position of the group and the state of the assets which are, on average, at half life. The criteria used to evaluate the third type of investment, which is broadly categorised as expansionary, is illustrated by the project studied.

This project, which cost nearly £5 million, was designed to expand capacity and reduce operating costs at one of the company's major quarries. It was chosen for study because it was a large and fairly recent investment. The trigger for the investment was the success of a planning application which provided a significant increase in extractable reserves but limited the hours of the day in which the machinery could be operated. Although the quarry contained good quality stone, the lack of adequate reserves with planning permission had previously limited investment at this site. Part of the existing crushing machinery was obsolete, expensive to operate and did not have the capacity to cope efficiently with the new reserves in the hours allowed for operation. In addition, a 40 year old coating plant, which was closed some years ago for environmental and safety reasons, had not been replaced, and facilities at another site had been used for this process.

The proposed expenditure on installing a new crushing plant and adding a stone coating plant was included in the 1983-84 budget and, in view of its size, had to be approved through the various tiers of the company and ultimately by the main board of the parent. Final approval was given in September 1983 and the first orders were placed immediately. The installation was completed in March 1985, a delay of two months on the anticipated date, due to bad weather. Post installation audits are an important aspect of the group's procedures but they are carried out on the first and second anniversaries of completion, so it is too soon for the performance of this investment to have been assessed.

The investment proposal was produced at regional level and contained a very thorough financial evaluation, with all the assumptions clearly specified. It was based on the incremental cash flow advantages of the project assessed over an 18 year period. The comparison was between making the proposed investment or continuing the existing operation as before at currently achievable levels of sales, excluding the estimated £1 million of replacement capital this would require. The calculation was carried out, as usual, on the basis of purchasing the equipment and a 52 per cent tax rate was used. As capital allowances were carried forward rather than 'sold' to the group, no tax bill was shown until year five.

The internal rate of return on the after tax net cash flow was about 10 per cent above the relevant target rate for expansionary projects of this type and even further above the minimum hurdle rate. A sensitivity analysis was used to examine the effect of changing the underlying assumptions and five key results were shown in the proposal - a restriction in the life of the scheme by one-third, a 10 per cent increase in either the capital cost in the first year or in the total costs of production, and a 10 per cent decrease in either throughput or the sales price of the incremental tonnage. The increase in the total costs of the scheme reduced the internal rate of return most sharply but, even here, it was still marginally above the target rate and well above the relevant minimum hurdle rate. Other indicators of return included the payback, which was well within the required period and the rate of return on capital employed (before interest and tax) which was very high.

This financial evaluation formed only part of what appears to be a very thorough proposal which also assessed the strategic, commercial and operational aspects of the investment. It will have been reconsidered in the light of the effect on the parent company as a whole, including any corporate expenditures which would be incurred as a result, and the choice of funding made as a separate aspect of the decision before ultimate approval by the parent board.

The financial calculations presented in the proposal were reworked applying the post 1986 system of tax, both including and excluding the transitional arrangements. The effect of the new system is to increase the after tax return on this investment by approximately 2 per cent, if the transitional arrangements are excluded, and marginally less if they are taken into account. Thus, if anything, the direct effect of the pre 1984 system of investment incentives would have been to reduce the attractiveness of this investment. Most of the equipment was not separately identifiable and therefore not suitable for leasing but about £1 million of the expenditure was eventually leased. The leasing component will have allowed some advantage to be taken of the tax benefit but, in view of the relatively small proportion of the investment financed in this way and the group's ACT problem, the tax savings on the expenditure are unlikely to have been crucial.

The interviewee stated that the total sum allotted for capital expenditure in any year depended on the cash flow position of the group but that projects which are expansionary, in accordance with strategy and meet the various evaluation criteria, are at most delayed by cash constraints. The expected returns on this project were so high and its strategic importance so clear that the necessary finance would almost certainly have been forthcoming in the absence of any accumulated additional liquidity from the system of investment incentives prevailing up until that time. The tax advantages of past investment had been greatly reduced by the overall ACT position and, although some benefits had accrued since 1980 through leasing, the character of most assets generally acquired made them unsuitable for this form of finance.

No adjustment has yet been made to the hurdle rates as a result of the 1984 Finance Act since the change would be within the margin of error on such calculations and would slightly decrease the company's cost of capital. The effect of tax changes on the attractiveness of investment in this industry was seen as very marginal and the only effect mentioned by the interviewee was in relation to ACT, which probably made the parent more interested in investing in the UK than it would have been otherwise.

It seems clear that the decision to carry out the project and its timing would not have been sensitive to the post 1986 reduction in allowances and corporation tax rates. In fact, the interviewee thought the Budget changes to investment incentives would be beneficial to this company in the long term and this seems likely given the steady stream of investments and the long life of the assets involved. No additional deferred tax provision had been raised as a result of the Budget changes and it was expected to be at least eight years before the parent company would be paying tax at the full rate, so leasing was expected to continue whenever possible.

Some investment had been accelerated because of the transitional arrangements but only a small proportion, due to long lead times. The company has benefited from regional development grants but these were not regarded as crucial to the investments concerned, particularly in view of the need to locate near to the primary reserves and the market. However, the availability of Section Eight aid to subsidize rail transport costs was mentioned as important. At a recently replanted quarry, this had reduced the costs of the project by an important percentage and such assistance was thought to govern the efficiency and scale of the investments concerned.

Case 29

This public group has its base in the aggregates sector, with nearly half of its profits coming from this activity. A similar proportion of the group's total activity is overseas and altogether turnover is between £500 million and £1 billion. The group has steadily improved profits and gearing during this decade through acquisitions and internal growth. Overseas earnings and a record of high dividends have given rise to surplus ACT, some of which had been written off in the accounts. The group financial director took part in the case study and the group's project evaluation procedures, which he described, were among the most impressive encountered in this fieldwork.

The project involved capital expenditure of £1-5 million on static plant and machinery, which added value to the mineral extracted at one of the group's UK aggregates sites. The investment was designed to reduce costs by replacing older, less sophisticated machinery and was identified during the annual strategic 'look forward' in 1981. Approval was given to go ahead in March 1983 and the installation occurred during the next 12 months. Although post investment audits are considered an important part of the group's procedures, it was regarded as too early for the performance of this investment to be assessed accurately.

The financial evaluation compared the cash flows over 15 years associated with making the investment, by direct purchase, and with continuing as before, the assumed throughput being identical with existing projections in both cases. Inflation of 5 per cent was built into the costs and revenues and the discounted internal rate of return calculated on the net post tax difference between the two sets of flows. This return was adjusted for inflation and compared to the target real rate of return used by the group, which in turn derived from a text book calculation of real cost of capital. The return shown by the project was considerably in excess of the target rate.

In common with most of the group's capital expenditure, the plant was bought outright and was evaluated as a purchase. The group had 'endlessly' calculated the effect of leasing, which was always marginal and dependent on when it was assumed the group would exhaust its ACT. Any advantage was never clear enough to justify a policy of leasing. The financial director regarded sensitivity analysis as a very important aspect of project appraisal and, in this case, the effect of both not obtaining certain savings and a lower throughput had showed results still above the target return. This careful and detailed financial analysis formed only a part of the very thorough project appraisal.

The group financial director was of the firm opinion that none of the group's major direct investment had been affected by tax considerations. The return on this project would actually have been marginally higher if calculated under the proposed post 1986 system of writing down allowances and rates, due to the marginal rate of 22 per cent being applicable to the early years of the project under the pre 1984 system. Leasing was not considered as part of the decision, so no tax benefit was recognised in that way. The possibility of any influence through concern about the effect on the reported tax charge appears negligible because of firstly, the group's ACT position; secondly, the fact that the investment was not to be made in the immediate financial year and thirdly, the financial sophistication of the executive directors. There is little doubt that the existing system of investment incentives had no direct effect on this investment decision and it certainly did not represent a decisive influence.

The possibility of the pre 1984 tax system conferring an indirect push to this or other investment also appears unlikely. Although the group did not go ahead with all projects which met its cost of capital requirement in the 1979-83 period, the reason was one of strategic quality rather than insufficient funds. The group actually wrote off some millions of pounds of ACT as irrecoverable during the late 1970's and early 1980's, slightly in excess of the benefits reported as being due to accelerated capital allowances. The post 1986 tax system would not have increased tax payments significantly in this context. In addition, the group's gearing was low enough for the marginal tax cash flows not to be necessary to fund strategically desirable projects, so investment was not dependent on any liquidity generated by the old capital allowances system. The effect of the ACT position on the group's cost of capital means that, with the post 1986 tax system and a return to a full marginal tax rate, the group's weighted cost of capital will actually fall slightly. This effect would be to increase rather than decrease the chance of marginal projects taking place, though such projects were said to be extremely rare.

The group financial director did not regard the pre 1984 tax system as conferring any significant advantages to investment in the aggregates sector which would not exist under the post 1986 tax system. However, although stressing that the group's recent expansion overseas had been purely for commercial purposes, he believed that the proposed system would remove most companies' ACT surplus and with this , one disincentive to investment abroad. He also said that a recent major UK acquisition by the group did have a tax element, as it allowed the expansion of UK taxable capacity and the relief of some of the group's unutilised ACT. The interviewee stressed the overriding importance of business strategy in investment decisions and expressed scepticism over how long the proposed low corporate taxation regime would be maintained. The group had accelerated about 20 per cent of its annual capital expenditure into the period before 31 March 1985 in response to the transitional arrangements, but only by two or three months.

It appears that the project chosen for detailed study was strategically sensible, relatively low risk and had a high return, so that it would have gone ahead under either the pre 1984 or post 1986 tax systems. With negligible effects on liquidity or sector competitiveness, the only way in which the tax system could be said to impinge indirectly on the decision is through the influence of unrelieved ACT, under the pre 1984 system, on the relative attractiveness of UK and foreign investment. However, even this minor influence must be viewed against the financial director's clear opinion that it is 'very dangerous to take long term decisions based on today's tax regimes, whether in the UK or overseas'.

Case 30

This UK publicly quoted group has a strong presence in the non energy extraction sector in the UK and in related fields. Worldwide turnover is in excess of £100 million and the group's ratio of borrowings to shareholders' funds is modest. The group finance director explained that the most important element of capital investment in its extraction activities is in the acquisition of mineral reserves. The acquisition of such reserves is 'a matter of knowing when they are on the market and taking the opportunity to buy them' and would 'not be affected in any way' by tax considerations. As the markets for the group's extracted minerals have been fairly static for some years, capital expenditure in the UK on extractive and processing machinery was mainly for replacement. Fixed processing plant, with the exception of crushers, tends to have a very long life at a permanent site while crushing machinery usually lasts four to six years.

The group has recently paid substantial mainstream corporation tax in the UK, easily utilising its ACT and benefiting only marginally from stock relief and accelerated capital allowances. The finance director was of the opinion that the 1984 Finance Act would benefit the group, restoring the balance in relation to its more capital intensive competitors. Decision making in this group is very decentralised and group involvement in approving capital expenditure is largely a formality.

The interviewee stressed the relative importance of expenditure on mineral reserves, with the group often acquiring companies in the UK in order to secure reserves in a good geographical position. The pre 1984 tax system had not impinged on these decisions, according to the finance director.

110

The group's direct expenditure on replacing crushing machinery throughout the UK was less than £0.5 million in 1982, very small compared with the scale of investment in mineral reserves. All the replacement decisions were taken at operating company levels on 'purely commercial' grounds. No financial evaluations had been made, the decision being simply based on the deteriorating technical condition of the old crushers. The interviewee clearly regarded the group's approval of such expenditure as a formality and he would not have interfered with a 'commercial' decision on the basis of tax considerations. As demand tends to be strongly localised and technical considerations require on-site knowledge, local operating managers in this sector are better placed to take decisions than would be the case in a sector where wider strategic considerations play more part.

The group finance director appears correct in his view that the replacement of crushing machinery in 1982 was not significantly influenced by any differential effect of the pre 1984 tax system. The absence of post tax evaluation, the fact that leasing of such assets by this group is extremely rare and the lack of any consideration, at group level, of the impact of such capital expenditure on the reported tax charge, rule out first year allowances having any direct effect.

Indirectly, the group's tax bills, post tax profit and hence liquidity would have been improved over the last four years under the tax system proposed by the 1984 Finance Act. Any effect on the post tax cost of capital would not have influenced these decisions, which were patently not made in respect of any such criteria, and the group's perception of the attractiveness of investment in this sector has not been altered by the 1984 Finance Act. The tax incentives on plant and machinery expenditure are greatly diluted by the much less attractive allowances on mineral reserves, which have recently formed a large proportion of investment in the sector. The importance of the extraction sector to the group's other activities also makes it extremely unlikely that the group's willingness to invest in this sector would have been any different had the tax system proposed by the 1984 Finance Act been in force earlier.

Some operating companies had taken 'very marginal' advantage of the transitional arrangements by accelerating some expenditures. However, no expenditure had been brought forward by more than one or two months and the tax advantage was always weighed against commercial considerations. For non replacement investment decisions in the extractive sector, the group normally uses pre tax payback and return on investment criteria and the interviewee doubted whether any such investments had

111

ever been sensitive to the taxation system, apart from possible marginal timing considerations.

Case 31

This large UK owned public group has more than 10,000 employees and a turnover in excess of £500 million, of which about half is overseas. The group has diversified in recent years but its base is still firmly in the extractive sector and specialist interests in mining and quarrying account for the majority of its profit. The group as a whole has been consistently profitable, with a record of high dividend payments in recent years, and it has a strong balance sheet. Overseas operations have resulted in some surplus ACT over the period 1979-84, but this has been relatively insignificant, giving rise at most to six or nine month delays in usage. The group has paid substantial mainstream corporation tax each year but, until recently, these tax payments have formed a fairly low proportion of its UK pre tax profit due to the capital allowances on its considerable investment programme and to stock relief. As far as leasing is concerned, the group tax manager, one of the two interviewees present at the discussions, explained that it was company policy not to lease anything, even cars, in view of the group's position as a prime borrower and its ability to benefit from capital allowances directly.

The project chosen for detailed study was a £1.1 million investment in a plant to produce high quality concrete blocks. The proposed plant was to be sited at a recently acquired subsidiary, replacing the existing works, which were in poor repair with ageing equipment and insufficient capacity. The purpose of this investment was seen as strategic - to safeguard and increase the firm's share of the market for concrete blocks in the region by allowing an increased output of higher quality blocks to be produced, while ensuring a larger internal source of demand for the output of the group's nearby quarries. It was also estimated that the improved method of block manufacture would cut the cost of production and reduce manpower requirements, with at least eight fewer employees required than using previous methods.

The project was appraised by calculating the pre tax, pre interest return on capital for the works as a whole, taking into account the existing capital for the five years beginning in 1981-82. The calculations (which incorporated the expected sales increase and cost reductions) showed a return averaging about 23 per cent over the first five years. There were no rigid guidelines against which projects were assessed when this

112

proposal was being considered, although investments would certainly have been expected to have yielded a return of more than 10 per cent at that time. This project, which showed initial returns of about 16 per cent and rising, would therefore have been comfortably above the relevant informal guideline. The project was approved by the main board in March 1981 and the plant was fully commissioned by June 1982. While the group does not carry out routine post investment audits, this plant, with an expected life of over 15 years, has performed well, despite somewhat lower throughput than anticipated due to the recession.

The interviewees firmly stated that this project, like the group's pre 1984 investment in capital equipment generally, would not have been affected if the post 1986 system of taxation had been in operation at the time, and all the available evidence supports their view. Investments within the group are always appraised on what was described as a 'commercial pre tax profit judgement' and then, after the decision to go ahead has been taken, they are financed at least possible cost.

The evaluation of this concrete block works was typical in that it was conducted on a pre tax basis, so the calculated returns would not have been affected if they had been carried out under the post 1986 tax regime. The financing decision was taken after it had been decided to go ahead with the investment and leasing was never considered, so tax effects could not have influenced the decision in this way. When the subsidiary at which the investment took place was acquired, it was known that it was only a matter of time before major improvements would become necessary, so this decision had a certain inevitability after the takeover. Approval of the project was clearly based on a commercial and technical judgement about the type of investment required and its timing, rather than any sophisticated financial appraisal.

Turning to possible indirect effects, an analysis of the accounts suggests that total tax payments over the 1979-83 period would have been little changed if the post 1986 system of allowances and corporation tax rates had applied at the time, so the ability to finance investment is unlikely to have been dependent on the funding implications of the pre 1984 tax regime. A provision for deferred tax has been made as a result of the 1984 Budget but this has not significantly affected the group's ability to borrow. The group had no formal hurdle rate when the project was appraised and the interviewees felt that these tax changes, unlike the proposed changes in mineral depletion allowances, would have no effect on sector attractiveness.

No grant aid was received on this investment, although the group have benefited from regional development grants and other selective assistance. All investments are normally evaluated on a pre grant basis and the availability of regional development grants was described as generally having no direct effect on investment decisions, with the main consideration in the location of investment being the siting of the resources and, in the case of aggregates, proximity to markets. The company has accelerated investment when possible to take advantage of the transitional arrangements but only a small amount of planned expenditure could be brought forward in this way. The regional development grant deadlines were described as more important and instructions had been sent to operating managers to ensure that target dates were met within their current projects. As far as the proposed depooling arrangements are concerned, it was thought likely that the company would either disregard the provisions or apply them to a very limited class of assets, in view of the administrative problem of tracking individual items of equipment.

Case 32

The representative of this small family owned company withheld permission for the publication of the case study, although he agreed with the finding that the investment discussed had been tax driven. Replacement equipment had been purchased at least nine months before it was needed due to an aversion to tax payment on the part of the company's owners. When brought into operation, the machinery proved technically troublesome and the haste to make this investment before the year end was considered partly responsible for the poor choice of equipment. A policy of taking tax driven investment decisions without any formal appraisal of the effects on actual returns had eliminated significant taxable profits in the recent past and probably resulted in the scale of past investment being increased, as well as the acceleration of the specific project studied.

Cases 33 and 34

This private company was purchased from its family owners in the mid 1970's by two individuals, one of whom, a chartered accountant and managing director of the company, took part in the case. The company extracts a very specialised mineral which it sells throughout the world, supplying around 20 per cent of the world market. Turnover is approximately £1 million per annum and rising and, since 1980, the company has had a very good profit record.

The company's recent investment history has reflected two essential factors. Firstly, the existing reserves of the high quality mineral are expected to be exhausted after only two more years at present rates of extraction so the company has little incentive to invest in anything except essential plant. Secondly, as the main extraction process is contracted out, the company only invests in plant and machinery to support and process the work done by its subcontractors. The original decision to contract the extraction out was an important operational decision, rather than a tax driven decision, and has been very successful. Tax losses from earlier years ran out in 1983 but the company's low capital expenditure and close company status offer little scope for significant tax planning and the interviewee regarded tax planning as unimportant to the firm's activity.

During 1983, the company bought two excavating machines to replace two existing excavators. Both were secondhand and cost £5,500 and £4,550 respectively. The first was bought virtually immediately after a similar excavator was stolen from the site. It was needed desperately and purchased before agreement with the insurers had been reached, though this was eventually forthcoming. The machine formed a vital part of the quarry working and, against a background of very profitable supply contracts, simply had to be replaced. No calculations were thought necessary to show that the investment was worthwhile. Similarly, an old wheel loader used for trenching became physically impossible to repair later that year and another was purchased to replace it. This machine again played an important part in the processing operations and failure to replace it would have impeded output.

The managing director made both decisions himself without reference to the board. He did not think the tax environment at all important to the decisions and did not take it into consideration, neither directly nor by looking at a leasing option. Indirectly, the low level of capital expenditure since the takeover of the company and the tax losses, which only ran out in 1983, meant that investment under the pre 1984 tax system added nothing to liquidity either by tax savings or via lease finance (which the company has never used). According to the managing director, the attractiveness of their highly specialised activity is so dependent on markets, control of extraction costs and the availability of mineral reserves that taxation is virtually irrelevant. The investments in the two excavators were for replacement and therefore of low risk, apart from possible technical problems. The equipment was vital to the highly profitable operation. The speed and decisiveness with which the replacement occurred is indicative of the essential nature of such investment, whereby profitable operation can be impaired by a relatively minor gap in the system of plant and machinery.

The company has only invested in essential items for some time. The frugality in office provision and in the careful maintenance of secondhand machines is immediately evident on visiting the firm. Capital investment has been designed to ensure profitability within the limited time horizon of the mineral reserves, rather than the reduction of tax liabilities. The most recent capital expenditures (on a crusher and screener to improve the quality of output) happened to fall before March 1985; the timing was not due to a conscious decision but simply dictated by the operational need. The company appears to make investment decisions totally in accordance with physical needs within its carefully thought out method of extraction, whereby subcontractors carry out most of the heavy work and own the main machinery.

7 Pharmaceuticals

The pharmaceuticals industry manufactures a range of products, including prescription or ethical drugs, over the counter drugs, veterinary preparations, certain food additives and bulk active ingredients. It is a high technology industry, with substantial sums being spent on R and D. Its research intensity, together with the heavy expenditures required to promote new products and the typically short product life cycles, mean that the industry has become international in scope, often through the establishment of local subsidiaries in overseas markets. The companies selected for study were either the subsidiaries of foreign multinationals (cases 35-39) or UK based companies with substantial overseas markets and interests (cases 40-42), reflecting the important role of foreign subsidiaries in Britain and the industry's significant export activity, which in 1984 accounted for 40 per cent of its total UK output.

The British pharmaceutical industry has grown rapidly and been highly profitable in recent years, despite the recession; output rose by 16 per cent between 1979 and 1984, compared with a decline of 8.6 per cent in manufacturing as a whole. It is a relatively capital intensive industry and, according to industry sources, has been investing between £215 million and £240 million in capital projects over the last four years; in 1984, it accounted for 4.4 per cent of total capital expenditure and 2.2 per cent of total net output in manufacturing as a whole. Much of the investment has been in increasing manufacturing capacity (as in cases 35, 40, 41 and 42) or improving productivity (cases 36, 38 and 39). The industry has a strong record of growth in R and D expenditure and it is estimated that, while Britain accounts for 4 per cent of the world pharmaceutical industry's sales, it accounts for 11 per cent of all research. The maintenance of 100 per cent allowances for capital expenditures on scientific research in the 1984 Finance Act is therefore examined in the context of an investment in new R and D facilities (case 37).

This industry is subject to a wide range of national and international controls and the British government recently introduced stiffer regulations in an effort to curb NHS expenditure on drugs. As well as substantially reducing the returns allowed to drug companies on NHS sales contracts, the range of branded products which doctors can prescribe was restricted, prescription costs raised and promotional expenditure on drugs further limited. These changes were being introduced just as the fieldwork began, so their possible effect on profitability, capital investment and research expenditure in the UK was a major issue in the industry at the time.

CASES

Case 35

This UK subsidiary of a major European based pharmaceutical and fine chemical company accounted for less than 10 per cent of the group's $1 billion turnover and under 5 per cent of its worldwide employment of nearly 50,000 in 1984. The group has historically enjoyed healthy profits and cash generation on the basis of mature but exceptional ethical products. The UK operations consist mainly of research and capital intensive fine chemical manufacture, together with the uncomplicated 'bulking up' of active ingredients for the UK market, and these have accumulated extensive tax losses which should last well into the 1990's. The group's investment in the UK has been substantial and forms an important part of the group's worldwide research and production strategy, although not particularly profitable yet. The group has had a sound balance sheet throughout the last decade with gearing of approximately 20 per cent. The interviewee was the company's UK treasurer, who was closely involved in evaluating and arranging the financing of the investment examined in detail.

The project was the construction of a very sophisticated

plant, costing over £100 million, on an existing greenfield
site in a UK development region. This now forms the group's
biggest single production facility for a particular fine
chemical which is also a common pharmaceutical product. The
availability of grants was vital to the decision to locate the
plant in the UK but the influence of tax incentives in the
form of first year and initial allowances was not even
considered until after the project had irrevocably started,
mainly because of the background of heavy UK tax losses.

The group's central decision makers realised, during their
1976 strategic planning exercise, that the need for a
particular fine chemical could not be met in the long term by
its existing plants. The following year, it was decided to
construct a plant somewhere in the world for completion in the
early 1980's to 'secure for the 1990's the group's requirement
for this fine chemical'. From then until the end of 1978, the
question was not 'is this economically justifiable?' but
'where can we get the best deal?'. The choice quickly lay
between four democratic and industrially mature countries. The
case for siting in the UK was based on three main advantages:

1.   the UK company already owned a suitable greenfield site,
     with labour and other inputs readily available,
2.   regional development grants would be available on capital
     expenditure, and
3.   selective financial assistance could also be obtained from
     a UK government anxious to encourage additional productive
     employment in the country.

The UK's case won; there were press announcements, site
preparations, grant claims on expenditure and the international
design team commenced work - all by January 1979. Shortly
afterwards, the UK financial management realised that if the
plant and machinery for this project in a development area were
leased, total leasing payments could actually be below its
capital cost, net of grants, over a five year period. The
reason for this 'negative interest' was checked and rechecked
and the bulk of qualifying expenditure was eventually leased.
However, it took over a year to convince a conservative foreign
parent board that there was no hidden trap, during which time
all major contracts were placed. Thus, although there has been
a substantial saving in finance costs due to leasing, this was
purely a windfall for the group and was never considered as
part of the decision to invest.

The plant was completed in 1983 and employed 260 additional
people directly, as well as creating additional ancillary
employment. Due to the world recession, demand for the product
was not initially as high as anticipated. With 90 per cent of

output exported and most of its value added in the UK, the project would seem to represent a very useful investment from the UK's view, turning the country into a substantial net exporter of this fine chemical instead of an importer.

There was no direct incentive from the pre 1984 accelerated capital allowances system for the project. No post tax evaluation was carried out, the effect of leasing was not considered and capital allowances would have had no impact on reported group taxation. Similarly, the indirect effect of the pre 1984 system was negligible in that trading losses, and the absence of significant leasing in the past, meant that no tax savings had accrued to the company from capital allowances. The original decision was to expand worldwide productive capacity in a familiar sector and the UK tax system would have had no effect on the attractiveness of this global market. If the original decision to build the plant had been assessed on a post tax discounted cash flow basis, the UK tax system would not have had the slightest effect on the discount or target rate used by a European company considering a global decision. The interviewee's contention that UK taxation was totally irrelevant to the decision first, to build the plant and then to build it in the UK, is fully supported by the facts and circumstances of this case.

The group has continued to invest in the UK and built a new R and D building here in 1983. For the future, the government's policy towards pharmaceutical companies is viewed by the group as infinitely more significant than the 1984 Finance Act and, as a result of the effects on its sales, the company has already announced a large number of redundancies. Surprisingly, the group has not been leasing everything since its 'discovery' of tax based leasing in 1979. The sheer administrative headache of monitoring each single piece of equipment to the completion of the contract is seen as offsetting the financial advantages, unless the equipment is easily defined and simple to track. The company did not accelerate any significant capital expenditure to take advantage of the transitional arrangements introduced by the 1984 Finance Act.

Case 36

This company is the main UK subsidiary of a foreign owned group with interests in several sectors and worldwide turnover in excess of £300 million. The company manufactures and sells consumer products, ethical drugs and 'over the counter' medicines, including some important lines used by the NHS. It has invested steadily in the UK in recent years, although no major expansions in capacity have been made. Instead, investment has tended to fall into one of four categories, namely cost saving (a constant thrust to reduce the labour content on high volume lines), new product related (often as simple as new packaging equipment), legally necessary (in line with safety or health regulations) and replacement of worn out assets.

Both the company and the group have strong balance sheets and profits have risen consistently in the last three years, after a rather static period following the worldwide economic downturn at the beginning of the decade. The UK company has been paying mainstream corporation tax for 'as long as the records go back' and has fully provided for deferred taxation for many years. The finance director who helped with the study shares, with the managing director, the responsibility for screening projects before they go for group approval, as well as for the final evaluation and approval of items included in the capital budget prior to ordering. The group operates a system of post investment audits which had regularly vindicated the quality of the UK company's investment proposals.

The specific project was the purchase for just under £100,000 of granulation equipment for the grinding and mixing of active and bulk substances before testing and packaging in various forms. The investment was part of a defensive strategy to increase productivity and reduce unit manufacturing costs and was the first stage of a three stage project. The initial proposal and screening occurred early in 1983, when the roughly calculated payback was found to satisfy the group's guideline for screening. A detailed proposal then went to the group's overseas headquarters and, as a result, was included in the 1983-84 capital budget and later in the very detailed list of budgeted investments. Final calculations of the payback and internal rate of return were made just prior to ordering in early March 1984. These were still attractive in relation to the group's guidelines, so the project received final approval and orders were placed.

The investment proposal was extremely thorough, containing analyses of the technical, operating, commercial, safety and financial aspects of the investment. In the discounted cash flow calculation, 100 per cent first year allowances were treated as giving rise to an inflow with a one year timing delay. This specific investment was not reexamined following the 1984 Budget but other similar projects were, and the results showed 'virtually unchanged returns'. The investment project had no effect on employment but did increase the capital labour ratio, reduce unit costs and improve competitiveness. The products affected are mainly sold in the

UK and, as no significant additional sales were being sought, there was no major market related risk. The expected life of the equipment is 10 years, although the evaluations looked only at the first 5 years.

The pre 1984 tax system did not have a direct incentive effect on this decision. The projected return would have been similar under the post 1986 rules, leasing was not considered and there could have been no attractive effect on the reported tax charge of a company providing in full for deferred taxation. Indirectly, the pre 1984 system resulted in higher tax bills in the past compared to what would have occurred under a post 1986 system. The new system would have added over 3 per cent to capital employed had it been in force since the mid 1970's, with some form of stock relief, so the old tax system added nothing to the ability to fund this project. The returns on typical projects appear unchanged by the new tax system, and this, together with the swamping effect of the new DHSS regulations on the industry, makes tax considerations less relevant to the company's view of the attractiveness of investment in this sector.

As the group's guidelines for acceptable project returns are not sensitive to changes in the UK tax system and the interviewee's perception of the local cost of capital is 'linked solely to base rates', it appears that there is little basis for suggesting that the pre 1984 tax system has indirectly encouraged this company's investment vis-a-vis the post 1986 system. Similarly, in view of the company's strong financial position, it is unlikely the reduced tax payments, which would have applied if the new system had operated prior to 1984, would have resulted in any additional investment.

The finance director was of the opinion that the 1984 Finance Act had a largely neutral effect on the company's potential projects. The deferred tax provision had been reduced by nearly one-third of its 1983 level following the proposed reduction in tax rates and amounted to less than 5 per cent of shareholders' funds. The company had accelerated 'minimal' capital expenditure as a result of the transitional arrangements and the finance director did not think tax considerations had previously affected timing, even the timing of replacement investment. The company's policy was described as to 'make decisions for business rather than tax reasons'. Government grants have had little influence on investment programmes, particularly as there has been no major expansion of capacity in recent years. The company leases very little apart from car fleets and the financial director thought it unlikely that the use of lease finance would increase in the future.

Case 37

The UK operations of this US multinational pharmaceutical group employed more than 3000 people (over half in manufacturing) and accounted for approximately 15 per cent of the group's worldwide turnover of nearly $2 billion in 1983. The group invested almost £50 million in the UK in the 1977-82 period. This was financed largely from the parent's retained profit and, to a lesser extent, back to back US loans. The large investment programme resulted in an average corporate tax rate close to 35 per cent, although the marginal rate was always 52 per cent. This increased the management's awareness of the direct significance of capital allowances and it was group policy only to lease motor vehicles and computers. The interviewee was the UK director of corporate finance, who was with the group during the period of heavy investment. The UK operation was, in his words, 'subject to a high degree of control from the USA', from where UK investment was normally seen in terms of a worldwide research and production strategy and its proximity to the EEC market.

The specific investment was the building of an R and D centre on a wholly dedicated greenfield site, close to an older manufacturing unit, which was upgraded at the same time as part of an independent project. Although regional development boundaries changed during the project's life, government assistance was received initially. The capital cost of the project was over £10 million and the site ultimately employs 275 people and has been very well received in the local area. The requirement for a research centre grew, in the late 1970's, out of the group's policy of enhancing its R and D effort worldwide. The UK research director 'went out and fought for the project to come here'. He was successful; in mid 1980, the decision was made to go ahead in Britain and the installation was finished in September 1982.

R and D tends to be regarded by head office as an overhead with an unquantifiable payback. Although not attempting to challenge this premise, the group's UK management provided a simple evaluation which set the cost of the investment so neatly against the UK's regulatory, fiscal and market situation that it appeared a very attractive proposition, with a 1.7 year payback and a net cost of only 36 per cent of the total outlay required before tax allowances and grants.

The proposal also pointed out that by widening the group's UK asset base and increasing capital employed, the investment would enable the group's UK prices, calculated under the government price regulation scheme, to be slightly higher, resulting in additional profit in the first full year of 22 per

cent of the capital cost.   While this effect was not evaluated
in the proposal by showing the price increases as an annual
return, the effect on revenue would have been expected to
continue into the future, reducing payback further.

The final decision was taken in the USA, where the fiscal
authorities were in the process of introducing attractive
allowances for R and D. Despite this, and an exchange rate of
$2.4 = £1, the UK option was accepted. The group treasurer is
in no doubt that 'at that time, without the 100 per cent first
year allowances, the project would certainly have gone to the
States'.   This appears reasonable in view of the significance
of the capital allowances in the calculations, which dwarfed
the other attractive 'benefits'. The unquantifiable advantages
of the UK location (e.g the tradition of pharmaceutical
research) tend to be shared by the US and therefore are
unlikely to have been significant in a UK versus US decision.

Indirectly, any liquidity effect of the pre 1984 tax system
did not specifically affect this project, which was financed
from the USA by means of a back to back loan via a UK
investment fund. The high profits of the UK operations enabled
the group to absorb the capital allowances generated by its
investment programme and the effective tax rate was close to 35
per cent. Looking at the years 1982 and 1983, the difference
between a 35 per cent charge on taxable profits before
accelerated capital allowances and 52 per cent on taxable
profits after accelerated capital allowances is less than £1
million in each year, so the group's tax bills would not have
been reduced, vis-a-vis the post 1986 tax system, by enough to
affect the UK group's liquidity during its intensive investment
phase. The need for parental support does not seem to have had
an inhibiting effect. The position appears to have been that
strategic reasons and both fiscal and regional incentives led
the group to wish to invest in the UK and the necessary funds
were available. It seems unlikely that any significant part of
the group's investment, and particularly the R and D centre,
was dependent on the relatively marginal liquidity advantages
of the pre 1984 tax system.

As regards the effect of taxation incentives on industry
attractiveness and on the UK as a potential location, the
interviewee was firmly of the opinion that the change in the
government's attitude to the pharmaceutical industry 'swamped'
any tax consideration, and regional development grants had
normally been more important than taxation when presenting
investments to the US decision makers. The lower proposed tax
rate still had 'some way to go' to compete with certain other
jurisdictions in an environment where there is 'increasing
competition for investment from other countries'.

This project was atypical of the group's UK investment in that it was an 'overhead', but typical in that the incidence of regional development grants was important. The group's investments between 1977 and 1982, if judged by the return on capital employed, appear to have been reasonably successful. Exports account for about 20 per cent of the UK group's sales, assisted by both the specific project and the general manufacturing investment.

The relatively limited use of the UK as an export base, and the consequently greater importance of the UK prescription market, has intensified the effects of the government's restricted list and recent price cuts on the group. Budgeted UK employment for next year is 250 below the 1983-84 level (including 150 in manufacturing) and a reduction in sales is forecast. Such considerations, rather than taxation, are expected to dominate future manufacturing investment, although the group did attempt to accelerate around £2.5 million of capital expenditure into the period to 31 March 1985. This emphasises that the taxation implications of investment will rarely be ignored by a financially aware business.

The effects of tax were important in bringing this specific investment to the UK. However, the 100 per cent scientific research allowances will still be available under the tax system proposed by the 1984 Finance Act. Although the reduction in the tax rate under the new system would have lengthened the payback on this project from 1.7 years to 2.4 years by reducing the tax shelter from the allowances, it is unlikely that this would have been critical to the decision.

Case 38

The firm is the UK holding company of a large US multinational engaged in the production and supply of pharmaceuticals and other related activities. The US parent is highly profitable and, after a period of very rapid and sustained growth over the last 10 - 15 years, reached a turnover of over $2 billion in 1984 (80 per cent in pharmaceuticals). With its turnover of less than £200 million, the UK subsidiary represents a relatively small part of operations worldwide but it has also experienced rapid growth and has a strong cash flow and profit record. The group has been paying mainstream corporation tax in the UK over the last decade, although the effective rate of payment has been much reduced by stock relief, accelerated capital allowances and losses surrendered by group companies.

The interview was carried out with the UK company secretary and the UK financial director; the latter had worked at the corporate headquarters until recently, so he was in a particularly good position to discuss the influences on the parent's investment decisions as well as the determinants of capital expenditure from the UK perspective.

At the outset, a sharp distinction was drawn between the factors affecting the major strategic investments of more than £1 million, which are initiated from the USA, and relatively minor programmes which tend to be initiated locally. As the company already has a well established capital base in the UK, most of the recent investment has been of the latter type, involving smaller sums, typically of £0.5 million, needed to maintain the efficiency of the established plant. In view of this, a locally initiated investment project costing just over a £250,000 was chosen for detailed study.

This investment package was part of an ongoing programme to improve efficiency by upgrading the instrumentation at the distillation facilities of an existing factory in the UK. The proposal, a largely technical submission, was prepared at local level for approval first by the UK head office and then, given the size of the expenditure, by the parent company. The cost of this part of the programme was £280,000, to be phased over one year, beginning in the last quarter of 1983, with the bulk of the expenditure occurring in the first part of 1984.

The financial evaluation consisted of a comparison of the cost of purchasing and installing the equipment necessary to improve the recovery of the solvents with the likely annual savings, and it was estimated that annual expenditure on solvents would be reduced by approximately £186,000. The expected economic life of the equipment was estimated to be about 10 years. The investment, which was eligible for a 22 per cent regional development grant, was approved and the non grant element funded internally by the UK company from retained profits.The equipment is now operational but its performance has not yet been assessed using the company's post completion audit procedures.

The interviewees stated that although the regional development grant may have influenced the decision, it was very unlikely to have been crucial, and they were firmly of the opinion that tax was not important either directly or indirectly to this investment. In view of the fact that the expenditures had been included in the 1983 capital plan and the obvious cost savings and low risk involved, a sophisticated financial evaluation was not thought necessary and the annual savings were estimated on a pre tax basis.

In theory, the ability to fund this investment internally

could have been influenced indirectly by the effect of the accumulated tax benefits of past investments on the UK group's liquidity position, the group having benefited through lower tax bills by an amount equal to approximately 7 per cent of capital employed vis-a-vis the post 1986 system. However, this indirect effect is unlikely to have been of critical significance. This is both because the UK company was in such a strong cash position at the time anyway, and because the parent's attitude to a locally initiated cost saving programme of this size and return would hardly have been different if funding was being sought, as well as approval for the expenditure.

The main constraint on locally initiated investments in the past was said to be the limited opportunity for obtaining suitably high yields rather than finance, particularly in view of the parent company's extremely high credit rating. Although the UK company had raised a large deferred tax provision in response to the Budget tax changes, this was definitely not expected to affect the company's ability to borrow. However, it was recognised that despite the multinational's favourable access to finance, the 'purse strings' were held quite tightly by the parent company, so smaller investments in the UK probably had been facilitated in the past by the availability of internal funds, which had 'made it unnecessary to compete so much for the corporate pot of money'. These internal funds will have been partly due to first year allowances, although stock relief also played an important role in reducing the group's effective rate of UK mainstream corporation tax payment.

Although tax incentives under the pre 1984 system seem to have been unimportant in the case of the relatively small investment studied, they were thought a very important element in the large, long term strategic decisions initiated and funded by the US parent, which are always based on an after tax assessment. This was illustrated by reference to a location decision taken some years ago concerning the production of a new antibiotic. Three possible countries were considered by the head office before it was decided to site the factory, which cost over £5 million, in Britain. At that time, the tax regime in the UK, including the available investment allowances, the benefits of dual nationality status and regional grants, played an important part in increasing the attractiveness of the British site, with regional development grants perhaps the most important of these. However, the UK investment incentives were only one of a number of considerations, which also included the availability of EEC grants, the tariff position and comparative labour and distribution costs.

Another location decision is currently being taken, this time concerning a major agricultural chemical, with the USA and UK as likely candidates. The interviewees thought that the effect of the removal of first year allowances would be approximately cancelled out by the reduced rate of corporation tax, as far as the relative attractiveness of Britain as a site for this non pharmaceutical investment was concerned. As regards future investment in pharmaceuticals, the tax changes announced in the 1984 Finance Act were described as being 'lost in the shuffle of everything else', with recent government restrictions on rates of return making the UK unattractive to new investment in this sector.

The group had tried to accelerate their investment programme to take advantage of the transitional arrangements but this was felt to be easier to say than to do, particularly in multidisciplinary projects. The tax position was being reviewed as part of normal planning procedures and the company was expected to move progressively towards tax payment at the full rate over the five year planning period. After the rapid growth of recent years, the company was entering a period of more stable growth in both the UK and worldwide and it was against this background that it had been decided to consider even minor investment decisions more carefully in future. A new set of corporate guidelines had been introduced, with standardised procedures for project evaluation and a more sharply defined hurdle than previously. The company's changed growth prospects also meant they were becoming more sensitive to tax considerations and the financial director commented that 'ironically for this company, investment incentives were not needed so much when they were here, because of our exponential growth, but now they would be more useful, they are going away.'

Case 39

This company, with a turnover in excess of £50 million, is the UK subsidiary of a major, profitable, foreign owned pharmaceutical group with a worldwide turnover of over $3 billion. The UK company only manufactures a small proportion of the ethical products it sells, but has substantial manufacturing capacity for household products and some non ethical pharmaceutical products. Its manufacturing capacity, which is in a regional development area, was extensively restructured in 1983 and investment continues in upgrading manufacturing equipment.

Following its considerable investment and reorganisation in 1983, the UK company generated tax losses, leading to tax

repayments and the anticipation of a low average tax charge for
the next two or three years. The UK company has no difficulty
in financing capital investment and is restrained only by the
group's worldwide manufacturing strategy and the clear
awarenesss that the UK management is judged by the pre tax
return on capital employed. This latter factor dominates the
evaluation of investments and the choice of finance.

The parent requires, in the absence of a predetermined global
dividend policy, that any post tax financial evaluations use
the tax rules of the home rather than the host country. This
requirement has resulted in virtually every lease or buy
decision showing a post tax leasing cost of approximately four
per cent. Despite this, the UK company tends only to lease
short life office equipment. The interviewee, an accounting
services manager, attributed this to the adverse impact on the
key pre tax profit criteria of leasing plant and machinery on
a lease period which is less than the economic life of the
asset.

The investment decision examined in detail was the
installation of a new computer system in late 1981. The
capital cost of the equipment was £231,000 but it was leased
via a specialist computer leasing company. The object of the
investment was to increase the company's data processing
capability by stepping up to a new system rather than
continuing the regular additions to the old one which would
otherwise be required, given forecasted utilisation. The
company planned to use the facility extensively for production
planning, inventory control, management information and
accounting. The investment was considered for some time and
the manufacturer's delay in launching the new system, meant the
need was even more apparent by the time it was available.

The alternative financing options were examined before the
new system was evaluated against the old. A lease from a
specialist computer leasing company was chosen because of the
opportunity to exchange the machine in the future without
penalties. This was judged to be significant enough to justify
a slightly higher interest cost than a simple finance lease
from a traditional lessor, and was calculated to be more
attractive than buying a machine outright or renting from the
manufacturers. The lease rentals and other costs of the new
system were then compared with those of keeping the existing
leased facility, leasing additions to it as required. This
showed the new system would have a downward effect on pre tax
profit in the first year, followed by rapidly rising positive
effects. It was clear, virtually at a glance, that the new
system was financially very attractive. The pre tax internal
rate of return would have been 72 per cent (payback 2 years)

and post tax, using the parent's tax system, 71 per cent (payback 1.3 years). The company's management and the parent group approved the investment.

The most obvious effect of the pre 1984 tax system on the decision would have been through the leasing cost used to compare the proposed and the existing systems. However, given the extremely high project returns and the choice of a specialist lessor, it appears most unlikely that the effect of the pre 1984 system of first year allowances in reducing lease payments was critical to the decision, particularly since the alternative (the original equipment) was also benefiting from leasing. In common with other companies studied, the advantages of investment in data processing facilities were not quantified but rather the costs of alternative facilities were compared. It is not likely that lease finance would have been critical to the original decision to move to electronic data processing, as such decisions tend to be very difficult to quantify and dependent on the company's culture and the competitive environment. The use of a pre tax evaluation and the unimportance of short term reductions in UK tax charged, in the eyes of the parent, tend to rule out any other direct tax based motive in favour of undertaking this investment.

It is unlikely that this profitable company benefited significantly from the pre 1984 tax system before 1981; indeed, it is probable that, under the tax system proposed in the 1984 Finance Act, the company would have benefited more from the reduced rate of tax than it would have lost in terms of less attractive capital allowances. In any case, the group is highly profitable, so it appears very unlikely that any tax savings due to the pre 1984 tax system would have been essential to the company's ability to make this investment. Similarly, the bias in favour of debt financed investment in plant and machinery under the old system would not have artificially reduced the company's hurdle for accepting projects, enabling this project to slip through. The group's target pre tax return of 25 per cent is set abroad by reference to the parent's tax system and the return on the project greatly exceeded this criterion.

The pre 1984 tax system does not appear to have made the UK a more attractive manufacturing or research base for this group. Unlike some other foreign multinationals, the tax incentives attaching to capital investment have not tempted the group to establish either a major pharmaceutical manufacturing centre or a large research establishment in the UK. The group's capital investment in the UK is mainly orientated to the domestic market in non ethical products; this type of manufacturing investment in relatively bulky, highly packaged goods which cannot as easily be sourced from far flung dedicated manufacturing centres, is attracted by the proximity to the market rather than tax incentives. In this group's case, in the absence of a pre determined dividend strategy, the pre tax profits arising in the UK would be regarded as ultimately taxable in the parent's fiscal environment and the treatment of those profits by the UK tax system, and therefore the attractiveness of the investment producing such profits, is largely irrelevant.

The UK company has accelerated some investment in 1985 to take advantage of the phased reduction in first year capital allowances and, more importantly, the change in regional development grant rules. The interviewee did not regard the 1984 Finance Act as significantly affecting the group's future investment. Although he recognised that the measures would affect the cost of leasing, he was aware that intense competition between lessors was keeping rates very competitive and could not forecast the pattern of the group's leasing after April 1986.

Case 40

This UK owned public group has a large turnover, including pharmaceuticals, and no shortage of funds with which to finance investment projects. It has paid considerable mainstream corporation tax in recent years at the full marginal rate. Some benefit has arisen from UK stock relief and accelerated capital allowances but over the last six years, the group would have benefited more from a 35 per cent tax rate, as proposed by the 1984 Finance Act, than it gained by way of accelerated capital allowances and stock relief under the pre 1984 tax system. The interviewee was a senior financial manager in the group's headquarters responsible, among other things, for strategic planning and evaluation of large projects.

The specific project was the setting up, on an existing UK site, of a dedicated manufacturing facility for a drug which was about to go into large scale production. Some building work was involved but the bulk of the capital expenditure was on plant and machinery and the total cost will be over £5 million by the time the project is complete. The interviewee explained that the product had been under development for about 10 years and a production facility had been included in strategic plans since 1980.

The development of a drug is constantly monitored before further R and D is approved and the cost of such activity means considerable sunk costs have built up long before the decision to launch large scale manufacturing. By this stage, returns on manufacturing have to be very high, in relation to any conventional cost of capital, in order to provide a surplus to cover the R and D expenditure. The interviewee pointed out that the expected returns from such manufacturing projects could be much lower than the high target set by the group but still be worthwhile if they exceeded the group's cost of capital. Manufacture would proceed in such cases but research in that area would be searchingly re-examined.

The post tax internal rate of return on manufacturing and selling this product was well within the higher target range, indicating that not only was manufacture worthwhile but that the product would contribute substantially towards ongoing R and D costs. While the decision to go ahead with manufacture was an easy one, the questions the group faced, as the successful product trials brought national launch dates nearer, were where to manufacture and what size of plant to build. The interviewee explained that the group had the option to manufacture in relatively low wage, low tax countries and location decisions often hinged on the anticipated takeoff of the new product. For a quickly accepted drug, launched in fairly rapid succession in a number of markets, the early profits would quickly absorb the setup costs and then benefit from a low tax rate, so a low tax country would tend to be favoured. Alternatively, a product might have a slower, steadier takeoff period; in a low tax regime, where a greenfield site had been utilised, this would mean the gradual absorption of heavy setup costs postponed any taxable profits and made the low tax rate relatively less important.

For projects such as this, the siting of a plant in the UK provided an immediate tax advantage by relieving taxable profits on other activities, without waiting for profit on the project to come through. This product was judged to be a relatively slow, steady developer. The option to build the plant in the UK was compared, using post tax internal rates of return, with a potential overseas site. The UK option provided the higher return, 'significantly' assisted by the availability of first year allowances. Prior to the 1984 Budget, the decision to go ahead in· the UK was taken and implemented almost immediately. The project is not yet completed but it is expected to increase employment and contribute additional exports to the UK's balance of payments.

The pre 1984 tax system, particularly accelerated capital allowances, significantly improved the attractions of a UK site for this project in a fairly narrow decision. However, the interviewee had looked again at the figures following the 1984

132

Budget (not with a view to reversing the decision) and was of the clear opinion that although the old tax system had made the decision to site in the UK 'much more comfortable', the decision would almost certainly still have gone the same way under the UK tax system proposed in the 1984 Finance Act, but by a much finer margin. Neither the possible effect of leasing on project profitability nor the potential impact of accelerated capital allowances on the reported tax charge were considered in the decision. It appears that although 'significant', the first year allowances were not directly critical in bringing this investment to the UK.

There is little ground for arguing that this decision might have been affected indirectly by the pre 1984 tax system vis-a-vis that proposed by the 1984 Finance Act. The group's liquidity would have benefited from a lower tax rate regardless of the reduced allowances, no conceivable impact on the post tax cost of capital could have affected the viability of this project, while the attractiveness of investment in manufacturing drugs is a function of R and D success rather than tax considerations.

The interviewee explained that the investment might be accelerated for tax purposes, where possible within the strategic plans, and this had happened in respect of the reduction in first year allowances on 1 April 1985, although he could not quantify the extent of this timing change. It was thought that the tax changes had not and would not make a material impact on the group due to the nature of its businesses; tax relief on capital expenditure formed only a small proportion of total costs of the research based pharmaceutical operations. The tax changes would not alter the group's policy of buying virtually all its UK assets outright. The group has in the past located some plants in assisted areas but this possibility was not considered in the case of the manufacturing plant studied.

Case 41

This UK based publicly quoted group has a turnover in excess of £1 billion. Turnover and profits have grown steadily for the last 10 years, with pharmaceuticals contributing around half of profit before taxation and accounting for one-third of the group's worldwide employment of over 30,000. Roughly 40 per cent of its employees work in the UK and these generate around 30 per cent of trading profit. The group has had a strong investment record in the UK, in both pharmaceutical and non pharmaceutical manufacturing and research, including investment in regional development areas. Despite suffering from recent government action on pharmaceuticals supplied to the NHS, the group has maintained its commitment to the UK, announcing several major projects recently and 'went to great lengths to buy from British engineers, despite major hassles and major risks'. The group has had a strong balance sheet for many years with substantial cash balances, while high dividends and the level of UK taxable capacity have led to £60 million of ACT being written off since 1979.

The project discussed with the finance director of the UK pharmaceutical division concerned the expansion of the productive capacity used to manufacture a basic pharmaceutical material for use worldwide throughout the group. The cost of the additional facilities was £5.5 million, £4.8 million being in plant and machinery, the remainder in industrial buildings.

The project was triggered in 1982, when the normal forward planning procedures indicated that the group's need for this basic pharmaceutical product was likely to exceed current productive capability within a few years. In late 1982, a suitable sum was included in the group's long term financial plan but the project was described only in vague terms. The technical options were discussed during early 1983 and a particular technology chosen, only part of which would be susceptible to technological change. Formal project approval was then sought in a detailed paper completed in October 1983. The main board approved the project in November 1983 and commissioning began shortly afterwards. The facility is due for completion by the end of 1985 and current projections of the group's need for the material and its world price indicate that the outcome will be at least as good as forecast. The facility is in a regional development area, and has an expected life of at least 15 years.

The group uses discounted cash flow techniques and has a model which generates its cost of capital (although the interviewee would like to see this improved). However, for most projects, a simple payback is seen as the clearest and most effective measure, with discounting being used for comparisons and for more complex flow patterns. The division normally evaluates projects without grant or taxation incentives because, although the former are often attractive, the group had suffered in the past from sudden withdrawal of government incentives and now likes projects to stand by themselves. If tax is brought into the analysis, it is included at the effective marginal rate. This particular project was comfortably within the group's payback criteria without the grant or tax incentives. The choice of project finance is regarded as a separate decision and the evaluation included the capital costs as an initial outlay.

Tax therefore had no direct effect on the project, neither through inclusion of capital allowances in the evaluation nor from tax based leasing. The need to buy equipment outright to qualify as capital employed under the government's price regulation scheme reduces the attractiveness of leasing in the pharmaceutical division. The division had not been concerned with the potential impact of capital allowances from the project on the group's reported tax change, but the interviewee could not speak for the main board and its various committees. However, in view of the group's philosophy towards such incentives and its 22 per cent marginal taxation rate, it is very unlikely that such considerations would have had any weight. The system of first year allowances almost certainly did not directly affect the attractiveness of this project.

Indirectly, there can be no doubt that the group benefited to some extent from accelerated capital allowances and had accumulated £170 million (gross) net acceleration by 31 March 1984, with the bulk of this being reflected in a lower tax charge rather than deferred taxation. However, in view of the group's level of unutilised ACT and double taxation relief, it appears that the marginal rate of tax on UK profits was 22 per cent during the last 6 years and would have been 5 per cent under the post 1986 system of allowances and rates. The group would probably have paid slightly less in tax under the latter system, assuming no change in the dividend policy or the pattern of remittances from abroad. The group's already strong liquidity position cannot therefore be attributed in any way to the pre 1984 taxation system vis-a-vis the post 1986 model. Had the new system been in force in the past, the improvement in group liquidity would have been only one per cent or less of shareholders' funds.

A change in the group's calculated cost of capital as a result of the change in the tax system appears likely if the group's model is updated. Whether this would present a lower or higher hurdle for project acceptance will depend partly on the group's perception of its marginal tax rate. This will potentially affect only those few projects where discounting is used which, given their long term nature, tend to be strategic in purpose and less dependent on marginal financial considerations.

The interviewee was convinced that any effect of the tax changes announced in the 1984 Finance Act on the attractiveness of the UK pharmaceutical sector would be lost in the very strong reaction of the industry to the government's stricter policy towards pharmaceutical pricing and profits. He said that, while the group's continued investment in the UK seemed at variance with its public stance on the potential damage of the government's policy, the recent investment had been in the group's home base for overriding strategic reasons. He regarded the withdrawal of regional development assistance as 'much more far reaching' than the tax changes, and said 'this incentive is being withdrawn just when we most need it'.

It therefore seems unlikely that the project, or any significant part of the group's recent UK investment, has been indirectly influenced by the pre 1984 tax system through liquidity, cost of capital, or sector attractiveness. The group's investment was described as being generally market led, but depending considerably on the results of its R and D. Where possible, some of the group's UK investment was accelerated to fall before 31 March 1985 but attention was focusing more on the November 1985 regional grant deadline. The division has never leased on any scale and there 'was nothing in the 1984 Budget to change our minds so far'.

Case 42

This chemicals company is a subsidiary of a large UK based multinational. Company turnover in 1984 was £42 million, generating a 20 per cent pre tax return on shareholders' funds and loans, a recovery to the level earned in 1980. The group has had surplus ACT since the mid 1970's, as a result of a high proportion of overseas earnings and mixed UK profitability. In 1981, all UK subsidiaries were formally asked to use a 22 per cent rate of corporation tax in their financial evaluations to reflect this. Some years ago, the group circulated its estimated long term cost of capital, and later a higher target rate of return for use in project appraisal by its subsidiaries. The rates have now remained unchanged for many years. The group usually looks at operating profit on capital employed and cash generation when assessing current operations of subsidiaries.

The chemicals subsidiary was set up in the early 1970's and has built up considerable expertise in a particular chemical and its potential compounds. These compounds are difficult to handle and require sophisticated and significant capital investment. Few other chemical companies use the technology involved. The company has had three major investment projects since 1972. Two new chemical installations in 1974 and 1981-82, together costing over £10 million, were both largely leased in view of the group's low marginal taxation rate. The third major project, in 1978-79, was a plant to produce certain pharmaceutical intermediaries on a large scale and was financed by a short term bank loan. Apart from major market related, strategic projects which have accounted for approximately one quarter of recent investment, the bulk of capital expenditure has historically been aimed at reducing costs, with only a small proportion of simple replacement investment.

The project discussed with the company secretary and a senior financial analyst was the building of the major plant in 1978-79. This was dedicated to the production of a variety of pharmaceutical and agrochemical intermediaries, based on a compound in which the company had considerable specialist experience. A pilot plant was already producing small quantities of these intermediaries and in 1977, two major pharmaceutical companies expressed interest in taking large quantities for new drugs they were preparing to launch, one now a very well established product. The company was faced with the question of whether to invest in the large plant necessary to fulfil possible contracts with the pharmaceutical manufacturers. The technical risk was low as the technology was known to the company, but the ultimate success of the investment was dependent on the performance of the final drugs, which at that stage appeared to be promising.

The total investment was £2.85 million, of which all but £0.4 million was on plant and machinery. The plant could be built with or without a small second phase extension after 2 years and both possibilities were evaluated using discounted cash flow techniques over a 5 and 10 year life. The results looked as follows:

	Years evaluated	IRR vis-a-vis target	NPV at group cost of capital
Without second phase	5	Well below	Negative
	10	Same	Significant
With second phase	5	Below	Small
	10	Well below	High

The proposals were prepared by the chemists in the business development section of R and D and the evaluations checked in the finance department. The tax rate used was 52 per cent but capital allowances were carried forward, rather than 'sold' to the group, with the result that the original projections showed no tax flows until a modest tax bill in year five. The proposals had to go through various divisions to the central executive, which approved the project in January 1978. The plant came on stream in October 1979 and the second phase was added in due course. There were some problems initially with one of the contract customers and in 1982, a post investment audit concluded that, although the return on the project was above the cost of capital, it was below the group's target. Since then, the market conditions have improved greatly and the capacity of the plant has been extended.

The prevailing system appears to have had no direct effect in improving the attractiveness of this project vis-a-vis a system of 25 per cent writing down allowances and a 35 per cent corporation tax rate. In fact, on reworking the evaluations under the latter system, the projected return with the second stage is 4 per cent greater over both 5 and 10 years and the net present value significantly higher. Leasing was not considered as part of the appraisal and the reduction in short term UK taxable profits would have been of little interest to a group struggling with surplus ACT.

Indirectly, the liquidity of the group was almost certainly not helped by the pre 1984 tax system vis-a-vis the post 1986 regime. The level of timing differences arising from accelerated capital allowances was low relative to total taxable profit. Under the post 1986 tax system, this would probably have suffered tax at a 5 per cent marginal rate until at least the early 1980's. This 'saving' would have been less than the effect of a drop from a 22 per cent marginal rate to a 5 per cent marginal rate on UK taxable profits. Mainstream corporation tax under a post 1986 tax system, given an unchanged dividend policy, would therefore have been less than actually paid, but the effect would not have been significant in relation to group capital employed.

The 1984 Finance Act has not persuaded the group to alter either its cost of capital calculation or its target internal rate of return. The pre 1984 tax system is therefore unlikely to have increased the attractiveness of capital investment through its effect on hurdle rates. As regards industry attractiveness, this company would appear firmly insulated from sectoral preferences based on relative tax merits. Although the pharmaceuticals sector is fairly capital intensive and therefore attractive to investors with taxable capacity, this company's involvement in pharmaceuticals arose from its expertise in a particular field within its chemicals business. Pharmaceuticals accounted for just over 2 per cent of the company sales in 1984, although the proportion is likely to rise to 3 per cent in 1985.

Overall, the company appears to be part of a group which correctly treats tax as a flow within a time horizon. No more emphasis than is financially appropriate seems to be given to taxation in an investment decision. The group's ACT surplus,

reducing its pre 1984 marginal tax rate to 22 per cent and the
practice of carrying forward capital allowances within a
project (rather than immediately offsetting them against other
income) have reduced this potential impact to practically zero,
making it unlikely that the differential effects of the pre
1984 taxation system contributed critically to the investment
of this group in recent years.

The 1984 Finance Act has thrown the group's projected
marginal tax rates into the melting pot again. This issue, as
well as how to account for previously unprovided timing
differences, exercised the tax planners throughout most of
1984. A central instruction to try to take advantage of the
higher capital allowances available up to 31 March 1985 was
accepted by the company but tempered by the need to get
important structural equipment right ('we don't want to rush
and make a hash of it'). In future the group's leasing policy
will depend solely on its taxation position; the company and
the division have banks 'queueing up' to lend money at very
favourable rates and will therefore only lease if there is a
post tax financial advantage. The measures in the 1985 Budget
affecting short lived assets will be of limited significance to
the company and group policy as regards depooling has yet to be
decided.

8 Printing

BACKGROUND

The eight cases presented in this chapter focus on the general printing industry, particularly firms engaged in book, periodical and security printing. As most of the major printing companies in the UK are British owned, only one foreign multinational is studied (case 43). Some of the largest printing companies are involved in security printing (e.g. case 44) and this has been one of the main growth areas in recent years, showing relatively high profits in an industry which has been badly hit by recession. A large proportion of activity in the industry is accounted for by numerous small concerns, many of which are privately owned, and it is estimated that the leading ten firms together are responsible for only about 30 per cent of total output.

The printing industry has been subject to fierce competition in recent years and recession in the home market, together with increased competition from foreign printers for both domestic and overseas sales, has meant many firms have operated well below capacity. The resulting pressure on prices at a time of rising input costs, notably due to the high wage settlements in the industry and rapid increases in the cost of paper, have squeezed margins and cash flow problems have been widespread amongst the smaller firms. Much reorganisation has taken place and closures, particularly of undercapitalised family businesses catering beyond the local market, have been common.

The relatively poor performance of the printing industry generally is reflected in the cases, with only one of the firms studied paying substantial mainstream corporation tax. Low taxable profits have lead to considerable use of leasing, and three of the projects were leased (cases 45, 46 and 49).

Much of the recent investment has been primarily to replace obsolete equipment rather than to expand capacity due to the low levels of demand and uncertain prospects, as well as rapid advances in printing technology. The need to modernise in order to survive in an increasingly competitive environment has been a major concern in many firms, and printing is in the process of transformation from its former reliance on relatively traditional methods to become a high technology industry, with increased capital and reduced manpower requirements.

CASES

Case 43

This company is a subsidiary of a very large foreign group. The company's printing activities are highly specialised and relate to the group's major activity in the UK. Total UK turnover of group companies has been in excess of £25 million for some years, but recent trading results were poor and the group is unlikely to return to taxable profit for a few years. The group has invested heavily in the UK, despite its disappointing profits and this, together with re-equipping, rationalisation and selective disinvestment, led to a halving of numbers employed since the mid 1970s, although the real value of turnover has risen. The group secretary, a chartered accountant, helped with the case study and provided copies of the project proposal.

The project concerned the purchase of two large, specialised printing machines costing over £1 million. Following considerable discussion in the operating company, an investment proposal was made to the group's overseas headquarters in mid 1981 and approved in time for implementation, in 1982, by outright purchase. The purpose of the investment was to replace very outdated machinery, improving reliability, cost effectiveness and quality as well as increasing capacity. The limitations of the old machines were threatening to jeopardise the loyalty of the company's existing customers, as well as restricting its market share in a profitable sector. The proposal included a detailed financial evaluation and explained that failure to agree to the proposed investment would virtually signal the end of the group's interest in its specialised printing activity. The project has been successful, 'making a profit from the very beginning'. Despite being expansionary, it did not involve any additional employment.

The financial evaluation of the project was thorough and completely pre tax, which is understandable in view of the group's UK tax position. A pre tax payback and a pre tax internal rate of return were calculated for 'realistic', 'optimistic' and 'pessimistic' outcomes. The parent group tends to favour investments with paybacks of under three years and the forecasts satisfied this criterion, as shown below.

	Payback (years)	IROR (%)
Realistic	2.49	28
Pessimistic	2.95	21
Optimistic	2.21	31

The evaluation was based on the outright purchase of the machines and included additional working capital. No reference was made to the potential benefits which might have accrued if lease finance had been chosen. The purchase of the machinery would have had no effect on the group's reported tax charge in the year. It therefore appears that the pre 1984 tax system had no direct effect on this decision vis-a-vis the system proposed in the 1984 Finance Act.

It is also unlikely that the pre 1984 tax system had any indirect effect on the investment decision. The group's tax losses did not arise principally from capital allowances and therefore little tax would have been paid under either system. The group did finance some of its investment through leasing but the indirect tax benefits from this would not have been significant as early as 1982, and certainly would not have been enough to be vital to the financing of such a major project. The UK tax changes will have little effect on the group's perception of the attractiveness of investing in printing because the group's main activities tend to be more capital intensive than printing so, if anything, the attraction of investing in printing from a tax viewpoint, when the company returns to tax payment, may increase. As the parent group's cost of capital would be unchanged by the UK tax reform, it is not likely that the guideline applied to this project would have been altered under the new tax system. The only possible way in which the tax system proposed in the 1984 Finance Act could have influenced this decision, compared to the pre 1984 system, is by changing the group's perception of the attractiveness of investment in the UK. However, as it had set up a large operation in the UK prior to 1973, and the printing operation was one of the most profitable UK activities, it seems unlikely that the decision would have been any different under the post 1986 tax system.

The company did not consider the possibility of obtaining regional development assistance for this project but regional grants had been an important factor in determining the location of some other investments. The printing investment studied is probably not wholly representative of the group's recent UK investment as it was expansionary and in a profitable business, whereas investment in other sectors has tended to be very heavily concerned with rationalisation and job shedding. It is doubtful whether returns from such projects would have been any more tax sensitive than the case studied, although the availability of low cost leasing might have enabled some investment to proceed when the group were unwilling to sanction outright purchase. The group had examined the possibility of timing a recent computer lease to fall prior to 31 March 1985 but, for business reasons, it was decided not to accelerate this investment and the deadline was allowed to pass.

Case 44

This is a large UK owned multinational group with over 4000 employees worldwide and a turnover exceeding £100 million. It is primarily engaged in specialised printing, publishing and packaging and has spent sizeable sums recently on upgrading its manufacturing plant and machinery as well as on acquisitions and group restructuring. Although pre tax profit has been rising over the last six years, the group has not paid mainstream corporation tax recently at the full marginal rate. This is due both to capital allowances and the tax losses available from the restructuring programme, which have resulted in unutilised ACT at the group level.

The specific project discussed with the group's finance director was the design and installation of a new generation of electronic security printing machinery, which will ultimately cost just under £6 million. The purpose of this major investment was described as 'strategic'; it was seen as necessary to ensure the future of one of the group's specialist businesses, due to increasing pressure on prices and margins from a powerful group of major customers. The existing printing machinery was very sophisticated and the only apparent scope for reducing costs of production significantly was in the verification process. This operation was extremely labour intensive and was performed by teams, mainly of female employees, who were responsible for checking every item of output individually. The quantum leap made in this investment was through the introduction of LED technology to carry out the necessary verification electronically. At the same time, the software controlling the system has been changed to increase flexibility and accommodate customers' changing requirements.

Over 250 redundancies are planned as a result of the eventual replacement of all manual checking by LED verification, a 25 per cent reduction in the work force of the subsidiary where the machinery is being installed. The machines are being introduced in phases over two years and by September 1984, six months after the announcement of the investment programme, 100 redundancies had taken place under voluntary schemes negotiated with the unions. As the investment will not be complete until 1986, it is too early for it to be assessed on the basis of the post investment audit procedures recently introduced in the group. However, the possibility of using the technology for cost effective short run publishing within other group companies has now been recognised and the group also hopes to sell the technology, both at home and abroad.

Evaluation of this project was first initiated by the relevant operating subsidiary in 1981 as part of its strategic five year plan. Formal presentations to the main board were made in mid 1982 and the group was irrevocably committed to the decision in December 1982, when the necessary technology was purchased from the USA for further in-house development. The investment was evaluated within the group's established corporate planning procedures, which allow considerable scope for decentralised decision making.

Briefly, each operating company submits a strategic five year plan at least every two years, including a rough estimate of projected capital expenditure to indicate the cost of following strategy proposed. Once this strategic plan is approved at group board level, the detailed numerical projections, as well as a list of the individual items of capital expenditure required, are given in the annually produced two year budget. The finance committee of the group board, of which the group finance director interviewed was a member, then reviews the budgets for consistency with the most recently approved strategic plan and sees, after consolidation, whether all the proposed investments can be financed.

If the proposed capital expenditure is approved in principle, a formal case has then to be made to the appropriate divisional board. The returns from the project are appraised in terms of the payback period and the discounted or undiscounted cash flow (depending on how the operating subsidiary chooses to present the case), but divisional management are encouraged to focus on

the strategic logic rather than the numerical justification to
see the project has been 'examined, debated and interrogated'
before approval is given to place the order. Certain minimum
pre tax returns are required, however, depending on the nature
of the business and the risks involved in the investment. In
essence, projects are decided first on the basis of their
commercial and industrial logic, subject to the availability of
finance and their ability to meet a minimum pre tax return.
The finance director stated that it was group policy never to
turn down strategic investments for lack of finance and
emphasised that finance and tax planning came afterwards, as a
consequence of the investment decision, rather than playing any
part in reaching it.

In this case, the strategic need to reduce costs in the
verification process in order to survive profitably in the
business in the long term was clear and accepted by the group
board. The initial proposal was to buy in the latest equipment
but an evaluation showed that this would not have allowed the
cost reductions necessary to ensure the future health of the
business. Instead, the basic technology was purchased and
developed in-house; the availability of a technology grant to
cover a quarter of the development cost was described as quite
a factor in this decision. The project was appraised both in
terms of its payback and the pre tax return for the subsidiary
as a whole over a five year period and showed the short payback
period and high return thought necessary to go ahead with this
risky investment.

The project was not specifically financed (apart from the
grant element) but the group had recently raised substantial
funds through a rights issue, in accordance with a policy of
maintaining relatively low gearing. The R and D element of
the cost has not yet been written off, as it will be amortised
over the period in which the benefit is expected to accrue, and
the group's tax position meant the first year allowances on the
equipment were of no immediate significance.

The finance director firmly stated that tax considerations
were immaterial in this 'strategic and commercial decision' and
the available evidence supports his view. The strategic case
for the investment was extremely strong; it was necessary to
survive in a business which has typically made a large
contribution to the group's profit and which was seen as an
attractive growth area if costs could be reduced sufficiently
to offer customers the lower prices they were beginning to
demand. The required rate of return was a pre tax one and the
hurdle rate was not altered frequently; in addition, any tax
planning was described as occurring after the decision to go
ahead. So many aspects of the quantum leap in technology

involved in this investment were new and difficult to predict that potential tax effects, much reduced by the group's tax position, would have been swamped anyway by the larger uncertainties. Any indirect effects of first year allowances appear negligible; in particular, the finance director said that capital rationing is not applied to strategic investments so the accumulated benefit of allowances could have had no influence here, unless it affected the ability to be sure of raising the necessary finance, which seems very unlikely.

This project, like most of the group's investments, can be described as strategic but it was unusual in that it involved extensive high risk development work. The irrelevance of tax considerations to the decision typifies the group's approach to investment, which is decided on a commercial pre tax profit judgement and 'no commercially justifiable investment decision is ever influenced by tax'. The group's policy of maintaining a flexible gearing has recently resulted in all capital expenditure programmes being re-evaluated and non strategic 'nice to have' expenditures (accounting in 1984 for about one quarter of the total investment originally proposed) are only accepted either on an emergency basis when a breakdown threatens or after a further three monthly review. However, the finance director firmly rejected the possibility that any reduction in tax payments under the pre 1984 system, compared with the model proposed in the 1984 Budget, would have affected the firm's ability to fund such investment.

A government grant was a material factor in this case and the interviewee also said that regional grants might have an influence in choosing a new factory location, although the actual investment would have to be viable without this incentive. The group did not alter any decisions before 31 March 1985, but the installation of two or three major pieces of equipment was accelerated slightly in order to obtain more attractive leasing rates.

Case 45

This specialist printer was acquired in the late 1970s by a large UK owned multinational, as part of a policy of diversifying from its traditional base in packaging into new growth areas. It has about 350 employees and grew rapidly in recent years to reach a turnover of over £30 million in 1984. This still represents a very small proportion of the parent's total operations but the subsidiary is regarded as having excellent future prospects and has already made a significant contribution to overall profit and cash flow. Its performance record is in marked contrast to that of the organisation as a whole, which has been somewhat static in recent years. The parent's effective rate of corporation tax payment has been much reduced by overseas earnings, incentives gained on capital projects abroad (particularly in 1983) and ACT, with some ACT actually being written off in the accounts. For the past three years, all the taxable profits of the printing subsidiary have been covered by group relief and this is reflected in the use of leasing to finance its substantial investments.

The investment programme chosen for detailed study cost approximately £650,000 (excluding the associated working capital requirement of £250,000) and accounted for the bulk of capital expenditure in the subsidiary in 1983-84. Both the financial director of the subsidiary and the divisional financial director participated in the enquiry, so the general determinants of capital expenditure in this part of the organisation could be discussed as well as the specific investment, for which copies of the relevant proposals were provided.

The main purpose of the investment was to allow expansion in a fast growing part of the printing market, in which the subsidiary is a market leader. The investment was the logical outcome of a decision in 1982 to establish a new department to serve those areas of the market which could not effectively be supplied as part of its well established operations. This department had achieved a turnover of about £600,000 by 1983 and re-equipping was considered essential for further progress. Thus, given the wish to expand, the main trigger for this investment was the inadequacy of the existing machinery to meet anticipated demand. The investment also had a strong defensive element, with the machinery being specified to allow a gap in services to existing customers to be filled.

The investment was screened as part of the annual five year planning procedure and was included in the 1983 and 1984 budgets. The first detailed proposal was put forward in mid 1983 and the programme was then separated into two parts for detailed evaluation. The first proposal, for a large press costing £260,000, was approved in October 1983, with installation due to start the following month; the second £391,000 proposal was mainly to acquire three smaller presses and the final written approval was given on 20 March 1984. Both were installed by the end of 1984. Indications in early 1985 suggested that some expectations about their performance had been mistaken; for example, the value of average orders had been about twice that expected but the flow of work had not been as smooth as anticipated. By mid 1985, however, the large press was reported as working on three shifts.

A financial evaluation of both projects was carried out separately on a post tax basis, assuming that they would be purchased and that tax was payable at the full rate, despite the group's overall tax position. The basis of the two tax calculations differed as the proposals were written at different times. The evaluation for the large press was carried out under the pre 1984 tax system, with the 100 per cent allowances shown as carried forward and a 52 per cent tax charge; the second proposal used the 1984 Budget information to calculate future tax payments so only a 75 per cent allowance was shown on the original investment and the lower corporation tax rates were introduced. The results appear below.

Project Returns

	Project 1	Project 2
IROR	40.0	58.4
Payback	2.5	2.5
ROCE (first year)	30.3	31.7

The interviewees were of the opinion that this investment programme was not tax sensitive and that both projects would have been carried out under the post 1986 tax regime, a view which accords with the available evidence. While no precise targets are set, projects in this area of operation would generally be expected to show an internal rate of return of at least 25 to 30 per cent, hurdles which have not been revised to take account of the tax changes. Recalculations of the project returns show that with the post 1986 reduction in tax allowances and corporation tax rates, the hurdle would still have been achieved in both cases. Had the internal rate of return on the first project been calculated using the post 1986 system, the return would have been reduced to approximately 33 per cent and the payback period increased to 3.3 years. The effect on the second project (which had already taken the transitional arrangement into account) of a post 1986 start would have been less noticeable, with returns falling to 52.5 per cent and the payback increasing only marginally. Given the company's real tax position, the effect on the internal rate of return of the new tax system would actually have been negligible.

While full financial evaluations are normally carried out, the company places more emphasis on the strategic justification for expansionary investments of this type than on marginal financial calculations. In planning terms, the company is considered a 'star' and new developments are regarded favourably. The investment did have a strong strategic motivation as it expanded an activity in which the subsidiary

is a market leader and provided an important defensive
capability, an advantage which was emphasised in the original
proposal but was not included in the financial evaluation. It
is worth noting that it was the first project, with the lower
quantified return, that was expected to play a major part in
this defensive move.

Although the investments were evaluated as purchases, the
equipment was in fact leased, so the company will have
benefited indirectly from the tax based reduction in leasing
rentals. The effect of the tax advantages of previous leasing
and accelerated capital allowances on liquidity has been
slight, especially in view of the group's heavy surpluses of
ACT, which meant the estimated gain from the old system had
been less than two per cent of capital employed. The effect of
tax changes on this specialised area of printing is hard to
predict but the high returns and growth make it likely that the
subsidiary will benefit from the changes. It was thought
improbable that anyone would either mount a strong competitive
attack on or leave this segment of the market as a result of
the new tax regime, so anticipated sales from the investment
were not thought to be sensitive to the tax environment.

The interviewees firmly believed that the availability of tax
incentives had no effect on the investment programme studied
and little, if any, effect on investment in this subsidiary
generally. It was suggested, however, that this might not be
the case for the group as a whole. The slow growth and high
gearing of the parent mean that it has been subject to tight
cash constraints and even slightly reduced tax payments and the
indirect tax benefits of leasing would possibly have resulted
in more investment than otherwise. Instructions to accelerate
investment in the transitional period had been sent through the
divisions to all group companies but the management of this
subsidiary had not been able to bring any investment forward,
due to long lead times. The division is still leasing all new
equipment costing over £10,000, but this policy is likely to be
reviewed because the group is rapidly moving towards tax
payment at the full rate.

Case 46

The group is a medium sized public company with under 1,000
employees and a turnover of a little less than £25 million. It
has interests in a small number of very diverse activities
including a printing division, which accounted for about one-
third of the group's turnover in 1984. The group made losses in
1981 and 1982 but recovered significantly in the last two
years, largely due to the increased profitability of its

printing operations.   Despite this upturn, net trading losses over the 1980-84 period as a whole meant the group had little taxable capacity, with tax losses in several subsidiaries (including the printing firm considered here), as well as at group level.   Gearing is high, and there has been extensive reliance on leasing to finance the group's relatively modest investment programmes.

The project chosen for detailed study was an investment in a new £1.8 million web offset press.   This investment, which with the necessary support machinery cost about £2.0 million, was the only significant investment in the printing division in recent years and was wholly financed by leasing.   The firm had leased its existing web offset machine in 1976 and, in view of the age of the machine and recent technological advances, needed to install a more modern press to ensure the future health of the business and even its survival in web offset printing. Although the existing machine was fairly profitable in the 1983-84 period, this partly reflected the peppercorn rental being paid on entering the secondary term of the lease and an upturn in demand.   The lack of any in-house backup to this ageing machine was seen as reducing the firm's potential market and leaving it only a breakdown away from a serious loss of customer confidence.   The operation was considered particularly vulnerable as magazines, with their tight delivery schedules, accounted for over half the throughput of the machine.

The first proposal for a new machine was rejected by the main board in 1983 but approval was given to a second submission the following year.   The machine was installed early in 1984 alongside the existing web press, which is still in use, and this expansion in capacity resulted in about 25 additional people being taken on at the printing plant.   The group does not carry out any formal post installation review of investments but the new machine had serious teething troubles with a stacker, did not prove as quick and profitable as had been anticipated and the management had initially been forced to take large, low margin jobs to maintain capacity utilisation.   A few months after the interview, the efficiency and profitability of the machine was reported to have improved.

The interviewee, an accountant in the printing company, provided a copy of the investment proposal, which runs to nearly 40 pages.   The group was described as using recent results to guide its investment decisions, with approval much more likely if the division or subsidiary had performed well in the immediate past.   In his view, the proposal was turned down in 1983 as the subsidiary's profit in the previous year had been very modest but was allowed subsequently because of an

upturn in profits, rather than any improvement in the potential
return from the project.

The interviewee admitted that the projections included in the
proposal were somewhat optimistic and a detailed examination
suggests it was written as an attempt to justify rather than to
appraise the project. It begins with lengthy market survey and
concludes that the company could probably double its share of
web offset printing with the new machine. However, details of
likely sales in terms of customer numbers, frequency of orders
and average run sizes (rather than the market share forecast
provided) would have given the decision makers a much clearer
view of how likely expansion of the required magnitude was.

The proposal does not include a DCF analysis of the
investment; it neither provides complete long term projections
of the establishment's output, employment and financial results
with and without the new machine nor evaluates all the relevant
assumptions, including the likely development or contraction of
sales without the new machine. Instead, the main calculations
concern the basic total and hourly costs of the machines,
assuming three shift working, and a pre tax profit and loss
forecast for three possible sales levels over only one year.
Increased productivity was central to the case but no
information was presented to support the very significant
increase predicted. Altogether the financial analysis has a
number of shortcomings, some fairly obviously designed to throw
a favourable light on the investment.

The interviewee believed the sales outlook was always much
more important than marginal financial effects to the company
and he was of the firm opinion that the tax changes announced
in the 1984 Budget would not have affected the web offset
decision. The available evidence supports this view.   The
accumulated tax losses, which were largely due to earlier poor
trading results, meant that there were no direct tax incentives
for this investment, although the advantages were obtained to
some extent through leasing. The appraisal, if carried out in
a post 1986 tax environment, would have included higher lease
rentals on the new machine. A reworking of the original
analysis on the basis of higher leasing charges shows it to be
very improbable that the likely magnitude of future increases
in leasing costs would have been sufficient to have affected
the decision; the leasing costs accounted for less than one-
third of the estimated annual costs of the new machine, so the
increase in total costs associated with the project would have
been relatively small.

The group board appears to apply standards other than strict
financial appraisal to their investment decisions, particularly

as the inadequacies of the financial analysis could have been
exposed by a board member intent on a clear financial
justification. In its summary, the project report makes no
specific mention of the financial appraisal but instead is
couched in the rather hazy and optimistic generalisations which
seem to have guided this decision. The importance of the
investment to the subsidiary and its acceptance on the basis of
a financially imprecise evaluation by the board make it
extremely unlikely that the project would not have gone ahead
under the post 1986 tax regime.

Indeed, it is unlikely that the pre 1984 tax system
stimulated recent investment expenditure by this group in any
way. The group's main interests lie outside manufacturing and,
unlike the printing division, are not capital intensive. The
modest investments required, together with the net trading
losses in many subsidiaries and overall over the 1980-84
period, mean that first year allowances have had little effect
on capital expenditure and the rate of corporation tax would
have been largely irrelevant. If anything, the post 1986 tax
regime may be expected to stimulate this group's investment
programme, if the current revival in its fortunes continues.

Case 47

This quoted UK publishing group has a printing division which
carries out work for the publishing division of the group and
for third parties. Group turnover is over £100 million, of
which printing for third parties constitutes a substantial
proportion. The group had not paid mainstream corporation tax
for some years up to 1984, mainly due to trading losses and
stock relief. It also had surplus ACT which, until recently,
had been written off annually. As a result, much of its
investment in plant and machinery had been financed through
leasing, although a mixed financing strategy had been adopted
so some non leased assets would appear on the group's balance
sheet.

The group projects its anticipated tax profile annually,
giving operating divisions the effective rates of taxation to
use in the post tax discounted cash flows calculated in all
major investment proposals. For printing investment, such
evaluations are compared to a relatively high target rate,
which is not related directly to the group's cost of capital
and largely reflects the degree of risk attached to such
decisions.

The specific investment discussed with the group treasurer
was in a four colour litho press, proposed in late 1982 and

delivered in late 1983. The machine cost approximately £0.5 million and was financed by leasing. The decision to lease was taken well after the press was ordered, by looking at the group's financial position and tax profile just before delivery. The investment aimed to increase output and lower unit costs and the group are very happy with the machine, which has a minimum life of at least 8 years and is on a 7 year primary lease.

The investment was evaluated as an outright purchase on the basis of the group's tax profile as projected in 1982. The post tax internal rate of return was comfortably above the high target for such investments. This evaluation formed part of a complete capital expenditure proposal which was presented to the group's board and approved early in 1983. In 1982, the group would have envisaged a 2 year tax holiday, then a 22 per cent rate for 4 years and, subsequently, a full marginal 52 percent. Under the post 1986 system, assuming some relief for inflation, the tax horizon would probably have been 2 years at 5 per cent, followed by a return to a full marginal rate of 35 per cent.

This lack of immediate taxable capacity means that the impact of taxation on the calculated return would have been small under either tax system and the estimated return similar to that which would have arisen if the post 1986 system had applied at the time. The expenditure qualified for regional assistance, as does most of the group's capital investment. Regional development grants are important to the group as a whole, but were not thought significant to this individual decision.

The pre 1984 tax system would not have had a significant effect on this project, compared to the system proposed in the 1984 Finance Act. The calculated post tax returns would still have been comfortably higher than the target criterion, there was no consideration of the tax advantages of leasing prior to the decision and the investment would have had no impact on the short term reported tax charge due to the group's tax profile under either system. The attractiveness of this particular investment was therefore not enhanced significantly by the pre 1984 tax system vis-a-vis that proposed in the 1984 Finance Act, due mainly to the lack of taxable capacity, which arose from factors other than past capital allowances.

Indirectly, the profits of this group up to 1983 would have given rise to small payments of mainstream corporation tax under the system proposed by the 1984 Finance Act, assuming some measure of stock relief. This, together with the accumulated effect of the tax based interest savings through leasing, would not have been significant in relation to a strong balance sheet, to the group's ability to fund the investment. The post tax target used for assessing projects was not a cost of capital measure and would probably not have been higher in 1982-83 had the tax system proposed in the 1984 Finance Act been in force. The group's perception of the attractiveness of investment in its important printing division would not have been significantly influenced by its relative tax treatment at that time, given the presence of other factors, such as technological and market changes, and the group's tax position. It therefore appears unlikely that the pre 1984 tax system indirectly affected the ability or the willingness of the group to undertake this specific investment.

The group treasurer recognised that when the group emerges from the tax shelter provided by some exceptional losses in the late 1970's and by stock relief, the change in the rules for capital allowances would reduce the marginal post tax returns on some capital investment projects. He was not able to forecast whether investment in plant and machinery would fall as a result and thought that this would depend on shareholders' expectations and the attractiveness of alternative investment possibilities. This fall in anticipated returns would be even more serious due to the changes in regional development grants.

The group is looking at the 1985 depooling proposals but does not expect these to help significantly, due to the likely administrative burden. A small amount of investment was accelerated to fall before 31 March 1985 but there was little emphasis on this, as a large reorganisation programme assisted by grant aid had been agreed prior to 13 March 1984 and will qualify for full first year allowances up to 31 March 1987.

Case 48

This case study focuses on the investment in a new six colour press by a subsidiary of a medium sized unquoted group. The group's core activity is high quality specialised printing and the subsidiary accounts for approximately 20 per cent of the group's printing turnover and an even greater proportion of operating profit. The group has been growing for a number of years and has made substantial direct investment in advanced equipment and techniques, as well as selective acquisitions both inside and outside the field of specialised printing. As a consequence of these investments, the group's gearing has risen sharply while group profits have been reduced by the related startup and reorganisation costs, as well as trading losses in an existing subsidiary.

The group has not paid significant mainstream corporation tax for some years. Although the tax efficient timing of capital additions has previously helped reduce or eliminate taxable profits, the group's lower profitability plus the build up of some ACT made this a less important factor when a decision on the specific investment studied was being taken. At the same time, following the appointment of a new finance director, the group was beginning to make financial evaluations of proposed investment projects. The group's investment profile previously depended almost entirely upon the judgement of its highly respected chairman and tax considerations played a part within 'the fundamental desire for a strong group'. The interviewee was the group's finance director, a chartered accountant, who had been closely involved with the specific investment decision.

The purchase of a six colour press for nearly £0.5 million in 1983 was by far the largest capital investment by the group in that year, the cost price exceeding total pre tax profit. The new machine was requested the previous year when the subsidiary company found itself under increasing pressure from competitors with much newer machines. The group board turned down the request in October 1982 but, as competitive pressure continued, the request was repeated and was considered at a special board meeting in June 1983. Between October 1982 and June 1983, the group's chairman had drawn up a list of the probable capital investments within the group during the next financial year (to March 1984) which included the six colour press. The finance director helped the subsidiary company to evaluate the proposed investment, the first time in the group such an exercise had taken place.

The investment was approved on the basis of the subsidiary's case, the chairman's judgement and the financial evaluation. The order was placed in July 1983 and the press, which was financed by hire purchase, was delivered in December 1983. The finance director was still uncertain how far expectations of the new machine had been met by the time of the interview. It had been very busy but he thought that this was partly due to accepting lower margins, as well as shifting work which could have been done on an existing machine. The subsidiary's management accounts were not showing as high a profit as anticipated. The effect on the number employed was negligible and the revised manning levels and rates had been previously negotiated with union officials.

The financial evaluation consisted of a complete reworking of the subsidiary's budget for the year on the basis of full utilisation of the new machine, including new manning levels and rates, additional selling costs, increasd turnover and additional working capital. This projection showed a significant extra profit after depreciation and hire purchase interest. The most vital assumption was that of a 20 per cent increase in sales and this was the most closely examined aspect of the decision. Although the evaluation was not framed in terms of payback, it is interesting to note that the payback, before interest and depreciation, would have been approximately 2.5 years compared to the 4 year guideline which the group now use. Taxation was not included in the evaluation and the availability of first year allowances was not mentioned as a point in favour of making the purchase.

The direct incentive of capital allowances was not, therefore, considered by the decision makers. The financial evaluation was pre tax, leasing was not considered as a means of financing the investment, while the remoteness of the group's next year end (nine months) and the recent reduction in taxable capacity evidently made even an unquantified tax benefit too small to be mentioned. Indirectly, the group had in the past seen capital allowances reduce or eliminate mainstream corporation tax liabilities, resulting in tax payments significantly below those which would have taken place under the post 1986 model. This gain was equivalent to approximately 20 per cent of shareholders' funds.

The group has made substantial acquisitions and increased gearing considerably since the decision to purchase the six colour press, yet the finance director still has no difficulty in arranging hire purchase finance. The financing of this press or any other strategically important asset, is therefore unlikely to have been adversely affected if the group had not had the accumulated benefit from the pre 1984 system. Instead, it seems that the decision would have gone ahead with hire purchase finance, regardless of the advantages of the pre 1984 tax system for this capital intensive company.

The group has not altered any strategic or investment plans as a result of the 1984 Budget, and the finance director has not changed his opinion that the borrowing rate, considered pre tax, is the effective cost of capital to the group. He believed the changes in the tax system have not affected the outlook of any of the group's managers but pointed out that, if profits were 'not up to expectations', this, together with possible taxation payments and provisions, might mean shareholders' funds would be insufficient to support planned group investment. If profits are as expected, no such problem will arise.

Case 49

This private printing company was bought from its parent group in 1983. Although the company's turnover has slowly risen to over £5 million, numbers employed have fallen by more than 150 in the last five years. Its finances were significantly reorganised on the change of ownership but gearing remains high. The new owners anticipated a heavy capital expenditure programme during the initial three years, to be financed largely by leasing. The company had tax losses well in excess of accelerated capital allowances and the takeover agreement stipulated that sufficient tax losses would be left in the company to prevent significant tax liabilities arising in the near future. The finance director assisted with the study; he had been in this position for some years, was closely involved in the takeover and is now deputy managing director of the new company as well.

The company provided the project evaluation which formed the basis of an investment decision taken in 1983, just after the change of ownership. This concerned the acquisition of a £97,000 printing press to increase existing capacity in an established, high quality sector of the market. The resulting increase in turnover was expected to require additional working capital of £66,000 when the machine was fully operational on two shifts. Only after the decision to go ahead had been taken, was it decided to lease the press. The machine was fully operational in February 1984. No post installation appraisal has been carried out, although a larger piece of equipment, installed at about the same time, has been formally appraised.

The proposal to acquire the press was subject to a full financial evaluation, in line with company policy for all investments over £50,000. The anticipated margin on the additional output constituted the pay off, which was expressed in real terms, and this was compared over seven years with the fixed and working capital costs, on the assumption of outright purchase and full taxable capacity. The evaluation focused on the return on the investment and payback, with payback shown after tax as well as pre tax. The original calculations were reworked using the original assumptions but incorporating the tax rules proposed by the 1984 Finance Act and, in addition, the real post tax internal rate of return was calculated under both systems. This showed the results would have been virtually identical whichever tax regime had applied at the time the investment was being appraised. The pre tax payback was 4.2 years and the post tax payback increased from 4.75 years to 4.77 years under the post 1986 tax system. The internal rate of return was 18.0 per cent on a pre tax basis and approximately 17.7 per cent post tax under either system.

Soon after the evaluation, the investment was approved without reference to any formal guidelines. The company has only subsequently defined its target criteria for investment returns and although these targets, 3 year paybacks and 25 per cent internal rate of return, are actually higher than the levels calculated on the project, estimated returns are still comfortably above any conceivable real cost of capital. Bearing in mind that the pre and post tax returns would have been almost identical under either tax system, the fact that the leasing option was chosen after the decision was taken and that, as a private company, the marginal effect of the investment on the published tax charge would not have been a significant inducement to make capital expenditure, it would appear that the pre 1984 tax system did not directly make the project more attractive than the system proposed by the 1984 Finance Act.

The possible indirect effect of the pre 1984 tax system on the company's investment plans and on this investment needs careful consideration. Although individual investments have been assessed on the basis of outright purchase and finance decided afterwards, the company's new owners at the outset had a 'rough feel' for the capital expenditure budget for some years ahead and had assumed considerable reliance on leasing in the short term, with a lull in capital expenditure in 1986-87 to reduce gearing. The anticipated ability of the company to carry out this investment programme would have owed something to the availability of low cost leasing, which the finance director estimated cost 6-7 per cent less, pre tax, than conventional bank finance, as well as having less stringent collateral requirements. Had this differential not existed, would the takeover of the company, with the same inherent capital expenditure plans, have proceeded?

The finance director thought that the 1984 Finance Act would not affect the company's broad capital expenditure plans, and the transitional arrangements and intense competition between lessors was expected to mean relatively low cost lease finance would continue to be available until March 1986, by which time much of the planned capital expenditure would have been made. If the post 1986 tax rules had applied since the takeover, the additional finance costs associated with the projected new leasing commitments before the 1986-87 'breathing space', would have been approximately £60,000, with no corresponding benefit from lower tax rates. To provide for this at the outset, and maintain the existing gearing ratio, would have meant equity participants investing around 4 per cent more than they had actually provided. This would have slightly reduced the prospective return to the new owners but it seems unlikely, in view of the uncertainty affecting more significant variables

158

and the strong personal motivation of the investors, that the takeover, and hence this investment, would not have gone ahead under the post 1986 tax system.

In early 1985, the company was considering the acceleration of some major capital expenditures to take advantage of lower leasing rates in the first quarter. The investment examined above did not qualify for grant aid and the finance director did not envisage that capital grants would play a significant part in future investment decisions, although the company had invested in assisted areas in the past.

Case 50

This investment programme concerns the phased introduction of two advanced typesetting machines to modernise part of an existing plant. It was the largest recent investment undertaken by a small printer, with less than 100 employees and a turnover of about £1.5 million. The firm is an unlisted close company, and although another printer has a large equity stake,the decision making still largely rests with the original family owners. The firm specialises in photosetting and lithographic printing for the book trade and has been relatively profitable, despite the recession, largely because of its established reputation for high quality work.

The purpose of the investment, which cost just over £200,000, was to improve the speed and quality of the firm's typesetting process by replacing two outdated machines with a new advanced electronic system. This was installed in two phases; the first phase was carried out in 1982-83 and the programme was completed the following year. The managing director explained that the rapid advances in typesetting technology virtually forced the company into the investment in order to maintain its position at the quality end of the market. The management carefully monitor and evaluate all technological developments which might improve the quality of their services and reduce costs, as failure to introduce the right machine at the right time would undermine the firm's competitive strength in its chosen market niche.

The firm has missed only one generation of pre press technology and that because the quality produced by the newly available scanning system was considered too low for the investment to be worthwhile. In the case of the project under investigation, three years elapsed after the technological breakthrough before the available machinery was considered to produce quality high enough to warrant its introduction and, by then, the managers had amassed enough information to be able to assess the alternative systems fairly rapidly and select the one which was actually installed.

The new system, which is expected to have a 5-6 year life, is about ten times as fast as the old machines and much more flexible, especially where corrections are concerned. The old typesetting process cccasionally led to bottlenecks in the flow of work through the factory, even when two shifts were being worked, and these have now been eliminated, with one shift working and substantial capacity to spare. 2-3 jobs have been shed and this reduction has been accommodated through natural wastage.

While the technical and commercial appraisal appears to have been very thorough and the decision justified by actual performance,the financial implications of the project were not evaluated fully; such calculations as were made were not formal enough for records to be preserved. The cost implications, particularly recovery of initial costs, were worked out informally and the investment was assessed with particular regard to its effect on the total return on capital employed by the firm as a whole. This 'back of the envelope' approach appears surprising in view of the relatively large sums involved, but may reflect both the necessity of the machine and the lack of in-house financial expertise.

The investment was financed internally from retained profits and the firm's tax liabilities were considerably reduced by the first year allowances, both because taxable profits were reduced and because the firm was brought fully within the small companies' tax threshold, reducing the effective marginal rate of tax. However, the managing director specifically stated that, had the post 1986 tax system existed at the time, it would not have made any difference to this decision. Given the lack of any formal evaluation of the financial and tax implications, as well as the necessity to make this investment in order to remain competitive in high quality typesetting, a vital part of the business, it does appear that this view is correct and the decision would not have been sensitive to the post 1986 tax changes. Indeed, given recent developments, especially the increased strength of overseas competition, the managing director believed that 'if we hadn't made the move, we wouldn't have a typesetting department now.'

The company would definitely have paid less tax under the system proposed by the 1984 Finance Act over the last five years and almost certainly in the 1990's if it had applied then as well. As the company was cash rich even under the old system and as no major additional investments in upgrading other facilities had ever been restricted by lack of funds, the tax advantages of the new system would have been unlikely to have stimulated capital expenditure.

However, whereas this decision to modernise an existing line of activity appears to have been dominated by technological requirements, it is interesting to note that a possible future move by the firm into a new area of colour printing may be sensitive to changes in the tax system. Such diversification would require capital expenditure of approximately £400,000 on a four colour press. It was said that this potential investment is likely to be appraised more closely than the typesetting machinery, by looking both at cash flow effects and whether expected sales to existing customers would exceed marginal costs plus depreciation over an 8-10 year period; however it does not appear that the tax flow effects will be evaluated precisely, but instead will be treated as an unquantified advantage. Although the investment would be evaluated 'in its own right', the managing director was of the opinion that it was unlikely to go ahead unless the expenditure could be brought forward into the March 1985 year end to take advantage of the transitional arrangements and eliminate the company's budgeted tax bill. It has subsequently been reported that the new printing machine was ordered at the end of March 1985 on the basis of a detailed financial appraisal, undertaken with the aid of an outside accountant.

9 Road haulage

BACKGROUND

The transport of goods by road is usually split into two sectors, namely road haulage and 'own account' operations. This chapter focuses on road haulage, defined as the carriage of goods for hire and reward, rather than the haulage carried out on their own account by integrated concerns.

Until recently, the road haulage industry was heavily dependent on general haulage for its revenue. This casual hiring of vehicles to carry goods when required is a risky business, with the utilisation of fleets fluctuating substantially according to demand, which varies both seasonally and cyclically. While the many small operators in the industry are still primarily engaged in general haulage and operate under very competitive conditions, the larger hauliers have tended to diversify from their traditional transport operations into areas with higher potential growth and returns.

There is an increasing tendency for manufacturers and retailers to contract out many of their distribution activities to specialists and the number of dedicated contracts, or exclusive arrangements between customers and large hauliers providing a range of services, are growing. The cases include three firms from among the market leaders in such activities, which require investment in buildings, racking and automated equipment, as well as vehicles (cases 51, 52 and 53). The main

162

investment outlays of the small operators, many of which are unincorporated (see cases 59 and 60), are on vehicles, which are relatively short life assets, with little resale value, requiring regular replacement.

The road transport industry has suffered a great deal in the recent recession because it has been faced not only by falling demand, but also by a steep rise in operating costs, particularly fuel costs. Intense competition in the general haulage section of the market has led many firms to keep vehicles for longer periods than otherwise, as the depressed profits made it difficult to finance the high cost of vehicle replacement. Some of the smaller operators have reduced costs by relying on secondhand rather than new vehicle replacements. Others have disposed of or 'mothballed' vehicles until conditions improve, and closures have not been uncommon. Although there has been some use of leasing to finance investment by firms with little taxable capacity, many of the smaller firms have preferred to rely on retained earnings and bank borrowing.

The Road Haulage Association, which has about 12,000 members, most operating less than five vehicles, expressed considerable concern that the tax changes introduced in the 1984 Budget would have a serious effect on their members' investment prospects, at a time when not only were conditions already very competitive, but they were also being required to invest heavily to meet increased environmental and safety standards. One of the main concerns was that the future writing down allowances would not be sufficient to meet the accounting depreciation of the average haulier. Results from a postal survey of members were used to demonstrate this, but the study was based on a very limited sample and the results do not appear to be very representative. The association called for straight line writing down allowances for short life assets, rather than the depooling provisions which were announced in the 1985 Budget.

CASES

Case 51

This company, which runs 300 vehicles, is part of a large UK quoted group. The group has diverse interests and a turnover of over £1 billion, while the company's turnover of over £20 million derives from providing transport services on a 'hire and reward' basis. The group's debt to equity ratio has been comfortably below 40 per cent since 1981; dividends have been high relative to UK taxable earnings, resulting in a continuing

surplus of unutilised ACT.   This led the group to direct, in
1982, that the company's new vehicles should, where possible,
be leased under the group's bulk leasing facility, instead of
continuing to buy them outright.

The specific decision, discussed with the company's chief
accountant, was taken in the 1982-83 financial year.   It
involved the replacement of over £1 million of vehicles, as
part of its normal replacement policy.   The policy, which had
been in operation for a number of years, envisaged the
replacement of vehicles when they were 7-8 years old.   The new
vehicles not only replaced the old vehicles but also tended to
incorporate changes in specifications, to reflect developments
in the company's business and of its client's needs.   The basis
of the policy was the need to maintain the technical
reliability and the 'image' of the company's fleet.   In the
opinion of the interviewee, the company had not taken taxation
incentives into account, neither when setting the policy nor
when deciding the exact replacement requirements in 1982-83.
The company did not financially evaluate its replacements as
'projects', prefering to put its energy into obtaining the most
competitive quotation.   The group had never tried to influence
the company's replacement policy for taxation reasons, except
by specifying the change to leasing finance.

The pre 1984 tax system does not appear to have had any
direct effect on this company's 1982-83 vehicle replacement
decisions.   The absence of a formal financial evaluation and
the company's autonomy from the influence of group tax planning
policies as far as the level of gross capital investment was
concerned, rule out any consideration of the possible tax
benefits on investment through accelerated capital allowances.
In addition, the interviewee clearly stated that the change to
lease finance had not in any way altered the company's attitude
to replacement of vehicles.

Indirectly, the group would almost certainly not have had
surplus ACT if the tax system proposed in the 1984 Finance Act
had been in force since 1973.   Under such a system, tax
payments would probably have been slightly less up to 1984, so
the group's ability to invest was not enhanced by the pre 1984
system.   The group's cost of capital was not artificially low
due to the pre 1984 system; in fact, due to the move from
persistent surplus ACT to full tax paying status, the group
would have been more, rather than less, likely to make marginal
investments if it had applied strict capital budgeting
principles.   Similarly, the group's surplus ACT position would
have muted any considerations of the relative attractiveness of
investment in the sector based purely on taxation
considerations, particularly since the group's other UK

activities tend to be of similar capital intensity to road haulage. It would therefore appear unlikely that the group's ability and willingness to make the 1982-83 investment in vehicle replacement in this company were significantly improved by the pre 1984 tax system.

The above decision is representative of the company's investment in vehicles. Most of its other investment tends to be in dedicated depots which tend to arise on the initiative of customers. The company did not significantly alter its investment plans to take advantage of the stepped reduction in first year allowances and corporation tax rates, up to 31 March 1985, and no instructions were issued by the group to consider such action. The latest annual report of the group described the changes in the tax system as being 'relatively neutral in their effect on the group once the transitional period is over' and the deferred taxation provision created in response to the changes was fairly small.

Case 52

The provision of road haulage services is one of the core businesses of this UK public group. The group has a worldwide turnover well in excess of £400 million and operates over 2500 vehicles in the UK through a number of specialist and general distribution companies. The group's specialist operations have been growing steadily in recent years, although the total number of vehicles and employees in the UK has been falling slowly since the late 1970's. Annual investment has been substantial and real growth in fixed assets has been most noticeable in buildings, equipment and specialised vehicles connected with specialised distribution and storage, reflecting the growing emphasis on providing such services.

The group's net borrowings have typically been less than 50 per cent of shareholders' funds during the 1980's. The group has been profitable and has been paying mainstream corporation tax in the UK at the full marginal rate, although the average UK tax charge has been somewhat reduced by accelerated capital allowances. The group does not lease on any scale, except for short term operating leases, mainly due to this tax profile. However, the group has provided leasing facilities to those operating companies which feel strongly that leasing is best for them.

The interviewee was a senior finance manager at the group's headquarters with responsibility for reviewing and evaluating capital expenditure proposals. He emphasised that the key criterion used by the group to judge existing and potential operations is return on capital employed, expressed before finance charges and before taxation.

The specific investment was the building of a new distribution store as part of a five year distribution contract with a 'blue chip' customer. The proposal arose and was evaluated in 1983 and the contract was entered into before the 1984 Budget. The total capital costs exceeded £5 million and comprised, in addition to the building which was leased, extensive racking and automated handling equipment, which was purchased outright. This contract represented the type of specialised distribution service which the group believes it can provide more effectively than can clients' 'own account' operations. The acquisition of a major and prestigious contract provided another incentive to make the investment, in addition to the estimated financial return on the capital expenditure.

The financial evaluation looked at the charges under the distribution contract which would relate directly to the provision of the equipped building. This income was evaluated as a return on capital employed, after depreciation but before interest and taxation, in accordance with group practice for investments of this kind. The difference between the estimated project returns and the group's average return on capital over the last two years were as follows:

Period	Return compared to average (%)
First full year	+ 2.5
First five years	+ 4.7
Ten years (if extended)	+ 9.6

These returns were more than adequate for the contract and the associated capital expenditure to appear financially attractive and board approval was given. The contract has started and appears to be going well, although it is too early for a full post investment evaluation.

This investment does not therefore seem to have been directly sensitive to the pre 1984 tax system vis-a-vis that proposed by the 1984 Finance Act. The evaluation was totally pre tax and did not include leasing but looked at the project capital cost as an outlay. The board were not influenced by the possible effect of capital programmes on the average tax charge, as the group's main tax policy is to attempt to take at least enough taxable profit in the UK to cover the ACT on its dividends.

The existing tax system did not significantly reduce mainstream corporation tax payments by the group up to 1983.

166

The accumulated taxation on accelerated capital allowances, up to 1983 at 35 per cent, would have been approximately £13 million but a similar figure would have been saved had UK taxable income between 1977 and 1983 been taxed at 35 per cent, rather than 52 per cent. Given this tax neutrality, which the group clearly perceives, and the absence of a post tax cost of capital hurdle for such projects, it appears unlikely that the pre 1984 tax system had any indirect effect on the group's ability or motivation to undertake this investment.

The interviewee believed that the tax changes would be to the group's benefit from 1989 onwards. From 1984 to 1986, however, effective tax rates will be well in excess of the statutory rates because vehicles, which had been the subject of 100 per cent allowances, are being replaced by ones where capital allowances are given at lower rates. £7 million has been provided in the company's accounts as an estimate of the additional tax payable in the transitional period. The need to generate funds to meet this tax liability must be considered when any new decision is being taken on capital investment. Once the system proposed by the 1984 Finance Act becomes fully established, probably by about 1989 in this group, most of the vehicles last purchased under the pre 1984 system of capital allowances will have been replaced and the effective tax rate will again be 35 per cent. Some effort had been made to bring capital investment into the period prior to 31 March 1985 but the acceleration affected only a few projects and was limited to a couple of months.

Case 53

This group has extensive haulage interests throughout the United Kingdom, as well as interests in related sectors and overseas. A decision taken in 1983, to build a large distribution depot, provides the focus of the case. The depot was built as part of a regional distribution contract with a well known high street retailer and was the largest single investment which the group had undertaken recently. Building work began in January 1984 and the depot was fully operational within eight months. The interview was with a senior finance manager of the group who had participated in the appraisal of this investment. He was adamant that tax considerations were not a factor in either seeking or winning the contract and firmly believed that the investment would have gone ahead if the post 1986 tax regime had applied at the time.

The scale of the capital expenditure programme was dictated by the customer's distribution requirements and the contract was first screened by looking at the costs and benefits of the contract over its five year term. The internal rate of return was calculated with a sensitivity analysis based on projected throughput at the depot. As the results met the group's pre tax, pre interest hurdle rate, the wider strategic financial and tax implications were then considered, as usual on a project of this size, before deciding to go ahead. The investment was looked at in the context of the group's planning strategy and clearly fitted in with corporate policy by extending its interests in high quality specialised contracting markets. Indeed, this was regarded as a prestigious contract which could help in generating future business with both new and existing customers, an important but unquantified advantage.

Building costs formed the major item of expenditure and these were financed by borrowing, whereas the vehicles, plant and machinery, together accounting for about one-third of the capital cost of the project, were leased. The decision to lease the equipment reflects the tax position of the group. Tax losses existed to varying degrees in some group companies, no mainstream corporation tax had been paid by the group for many years and no mainstream corporation tax became due in respect of the year in which the investment was made; moreover at the time of the decision it seemed unlikely that the group, with its accumulated losses and large capital expenditure programme, would be tax paying for some years. While the group was eligible for accelerated allowances on the building work, the group's tax position clearly would have reduced their potential impact substantially and, according to the interviewee, the availability of the initial allowances in no way affected the investment decision.

The use of leasing to finance the necessary equipment undoubtedly allowed some benefit from first year allowances. Although the lease rentals were built into the costings, the interviewee was firmly of the opinion that the reduced rentals available from leasing would not have made the contract more competitive from the client's standpoint or significantly increased the contractor's profit margin. This was mainly because of the relatively small magnitude of the savings compared with the other costs involved (e.g. wages and fuel) and the competitive nature of the business. The interviewee explained that contract hauliers are essentially concerned with developing contracts of a back to back nature on a cost-plus pricing basis; 'the primary decision to invest lies with our customer and he will decide whether it is a worthwhile project, taking into account the net returns that such an investment would give him in developing his business'.

In this case, our calculations indicate that the client

concerned was paying substantial mainstream corporation tax at the full marginal rate during the period 1981-84. The tax incentive to carry out distribution activities on an 'own account' basis would therefore have been greater than under the system proposed by the 1984 Finance Act, making it more, rather than less likely that the choice to contract out would have been taken if the post 1986 tax system had prevailed at the time of the decision.

This evidence accords with the manager's firm assertion that tax considerations were not a material factor in this investment, either directly or indirectly. All the detailed evidence concerning the evaluation procedure, the strategic importance of the decision to the firm, the haulier's tax position, the tax position of the client, as well as the competitive behaviour in the industry, lends support to this conclusion.

The manager stated that the total amount of capital expenditure carried out by the group has not been affected by taxation but the timing of its investment has occasionally been altered on tax grounds, although the seasonality of the business was by far the most important influence. In particular, the group has tried to accelerate the acquisition of new vehicles to take advantage of the transitional tax arrangements, with the assistance of its customers. However, as contracts are usually finalised very quickly anyway, the scope for accelerating such investment was felt to be limited.

On a broader front, the activities of the group were thought to be far more affected by changes in interest costs and the level of activity in the economy than the corporate tax environment. One possible effect of the Budget tax changes, and the consequent higher post tax cost of funding vehicles, would be for 'own account' operators to reassess their activities and possibly further increase the amount of distribution work put to outside specialist contractors.

Case 54

This quoted group has grown, mainly through acquisitions, to reach a turnover in excess of £50 million. Despite having a core business in a very competitive part of the road haulage industry, the group has enjoyed healthy profitability. With non acquisitional capital investment growing modestly and relatively low stock levels, the group has been paying substantial mainstream corporation tax for some time. Since the late 1970's, this taxable capacity has been partially reduced by the group's role as a lessor. Group liquidity has tended to vary considerably with the level of leasing activity and the funding of acquisitions, although the group's gearing has been kept within sound limits.

The decision discussed with the group financial director was the order of 100 trailer chassis, in February 1984, for delivery over the next 2.5 years. These were ordered, at a cost of approximately £10,000 each, as part of the group's long established policy of regularly replacing its vehicles when they reach a predetermined age. This policy is put into practice by a director with special responsibility for the vehicle fleet and followed strictly, unless there are exceptional engineering circumstances. The finance director had never tried to persuade the engineering director to alter his technical decisions for taxation purposes, and he pointed out that the in-house leasing company, rather than the company's own capital investment, had recently provided any accelerated tax allowances the group wished to obtain.

To assess whether the extent or timing of the February 1984 chassis replacement order was in any way tax orientated, it is necessary to look at the original decision to lay down definite replacement ages and adopt a policy of steady replacement expenditure. The steady net investment in new vehicles over the last four years indicates that this original policy was closely followed by the group.

The finance director believed that in the early 1970's, at the time of this policy decision, the group had been aware of the tax advantages of a steady level of capital investment and of faster rather than slower replacement. However, he surmised that the policy had been 75 per cent a sound business decision, reflecting the technical and cash flow advantages of regularly replacing ageing vehicles, and '25 per cent for tax efficiency'. He would not comment explicitly on whether the replacement age of trailers in particular would have been higher under a tax system of 25 per cent writing down allowances, but believed that the first year allowance rules had 'a significant bearing', although no formal post tax evaluation had been carried out when the policy was first adopted.

It appears likely that, over the three categories of vehicle for which replacement ages were defined, the tax incentive of first year allowances would have contributed, in at least one category, to slightly earlier replacement than a purely technical judgement might have indicated. Since the 1984 Budget, 'the tax aspect hàs virtually disappeared' and the group have decided to review the target replacement ages, although the finance director thought that tightening market conditions would, by now, have led the company to consider extending the lives of some assets for purely commercial reasons anyway. It therefore seems likely that the pre 1984 tax system led to shorter replacement periods, effectively accelerating and increasing the firm's total investment in vehicles in the years prior to March 1984.

The group has not altered any 'hurdle' rate by which it judges capital projects as a result of the 1984 Finance Act. An active policy of diversifying out of its core haulage sector has been due to market rather than tax reasons and the main areas of diversification continue to be relatively capital intensive. The liquidity of the company would almost certainly have been better under the post 1986 system. From 1981 - 84 the level of taxable profits, in relation to net accelerated capital allowances, was high and the savings of tax through a lower tax rate would have been roughly similar to taxation on the additional chargeable profit. However, the firm's activities as a lessor, while reducing the tax charge and mainstream payments, made a major demand on cash resources. This lost liquidity due to the tax orientated leasing operations did not, in the finance director's opinion, curtail any direct investment plans of the group. It would therefore appear that,despite its direct influence on the vehicle replacement policy, the pre 1984 tax system did not affect the company's investment indirectly, vis-a-vis the likely position under the post 1986 system.

The group's entry into and experience in the leasing business was examined to see whether devoting finance and management time to this activity adversely affected other areas. The group had surplus cash and heavy tax payments in the late 1970's and became a lessor principally to reduce the group's tax charge and thus improve earnings per share. There was a clear understanding at the outset that the company would 'never borrow to lease'. However, continuous growth in the value of assets leased is required to benefit fully from the tax sheltering capacity of leasing and prevent tax payments on rentals received. As assets for leasing grew, the group's cash reserves turned into net borrowing during 1981, and the directors, 'in a cleft stick', were faced with a jump in the tax charge per share if leasing was not expanded. The 'overriding tax considerations' prevailed and assets held for leasing and net borrowings grew side by side until a rights issue to finance potential acquisitions decisively eliminated borrowings.

The finance director is convinced that the leasing business, which was conducted mainly through brokers, was not a drain on the group's non cash resources. The leasing subsidiary was sold

within a year of the 1984 Budget, together with its future
taxation liabilities, although the group continues to have a
small in-house leasing operation to give it flexibility in
financing.

Looking at the group's main non vehicle investment, the
finance director explained that the acquisition and fitting out
of depots tended to follow a carefully thought out strategy,
with a group 'blue print' of physical layout. The opening of
new depots could be accelerated to take start up losses into an
earlier financial year but the seasonal pattern of trade was
normally a much more important determinant of timing. Grant
incentives were not considered a significant influence on the
group's investment decisions, particularly following the
refusal, in the past, of a grant application which the group
believed would be readily approved. The group did not plan to
advance capital expenditure significantly in response to the
transitional arrangements but anticipated negotiations with the
Inland Revenue when trying to claim allowances on orders placed
just prior to 13 March 1984.

Case 55

This warehousing company is part of a private group whose main
activity is wholesaling in a consumer goods industry. The
company, employing around 80 people and with a turnover of £2-3
million, operates a small haulage fleet as part of its services
to customers. The fleet has consisted of 6 or 7 vans and
approximately 10 trailers for a number of years. Horse units
to draw the trailers are hired as and when they are needed.
Investment in vehicles has tended to vary according to the
condition of the fleet and is normally less than expenditure on
plant and equipment for the warehousing operation. For many
years, the group was able to take considerable advantage of the
stock relief rules, resulting in virtually no mainstream tax
being paid in most group companies.

The warehousing company has generated modest taxable profits
in some years, although first year allowances on capital
expenditure have sometimes reduced or eliminated these. The
group's expansion of fixed and working capital has been
financed by retained earnings and normal overdraft limits for
many years and this was, in the opinion of the finance
director, due largely to the way stock relief had removed
virtually all tax liabilities. The group finance director, who
helped with this study, is responsible, among other things, for
monitoring the financial performance of all companies in the
group and reporting this to the chairman, who is in overall
control.

The investment examined in detail was the purchase of six trailers early in 1984. In late 1983, the advanced age of some of the existing trailers and the possibility of increased business led the management of the company to propose the acquisition of the new ones, mainly as a replacement but partly to expand capacity. The chairman visited the company in December 1983 and, after discussing plans and prospects with the management team, agreed to the inclusion of the trailers in the 1984 budget. Such a decision was 'normally conclusive'. The order was placed in February 1984 and the trailers, with an expected life of five years, were delivered a couple of months later at a cost of £61,000. The investment has proved a 'good operating decision' to date, although there have been one or two idle periods.

The finance director was of the opinion that tax had no influence in this decision. The purchase took place nearer the beginning than the end of the financial year, reflecting the operating need rather than any tax avoidance motive. There was no formal evaluation which could have taken tax into account. The group does not lease and possible tax benefits from this source were not considered when taking the decision; any effect on the reported taxation charge would not have been relevant to a private group with limited ownership. There does not, therefore, appear to have been any direct effect on this decision from the pre 1984 tax system vis-a-vis that proposed the 1984 Finance Act.

Indirectly, the pre 1984 tax system greatly enhanced the liquidity of the group and member companies. This was mainly due to stock relief, rather than accelerated capital allowances, which had enabled the expansion of working capital and, to a lesser degree, fixed assets within the cash flow afforded by retained earnings and a trading overdraft. The finance director was of the opinion that the decision would still have gone ahead under a less advantageous tax system but that the trailers might have been financed separately rather than from the normal trading cash flow.

The 1984 Finance Act has not made the group rethink its investment criteria or its commitment to the warehousing company and its haulage operations. The group still plans to expand its haulage activities in the future, despite the less attractive capital allowances. It therefore appears that the pre 1984 tax system had no significant impact on this investment decision, apart from a liquidity effect on the method of financing, which derived principally from stock relief.

The interviewee explained that when the warehousing company

was expected to make taxable profits, they had sometimes looked to see if any capital expenditure could be accelerated into that financial year. He gave an example of investment in warehouse mechanisation which had been brought forward for tax reasons some years ago. The group had taken no steps to benefit from the transitional arrangements.

Case 56

This private company is owned and managed by two brothers and has an annual turnover of about £130,000. Having once run a haulage fleet of 22 vehicles, the company currently only employs 7 people, runs 4 vehicles and concentrates on skip hire, salvage and the haulage of scrap. On the advice of its accountants, the company has normally distributed its taxable profits to its owners by way of salaries, thereby incurring personal rather than corporate taxation. 'Cut-throat' competition was regarded as making it difficult to operate profitably and this, together with the very heavy wear suffered in skip and scrap haulage, has meant that the company purchases secondhand and occasionally, damaged vehicles. In each of the years to 31 March 1983 and 1984, two secondhand vehicles had been bought to replace existing vehicles which had reached the end of their working lives.

Detailed discussions with the senior of the two owners focused on the two vehicles purchased outright at a total cost of £7,000 in the year to 31 March 1984, both before the March 1984 Budget. The interviewee explained that ageing vehicles had needed replacing and that the two vehicles purchased both appeared to be 'at the right price at the right time'. He did not consider the tax implications or consult his accountant before making the purchases. The evaluation of each investment was a commercial and technical one, concerning whether the condition and price of the used vehicle made it a good buy, given that a replacement was needed. On each occasion the need for a replacement was based solely on the condition of the oldest vehicle in the fleet. There was therefore no element of direct tax incentive affecting either purchase decisions.

The 1984 Finance Act has not changed the interviewee's commitment to the business nor the return he hopes to make from capital investments, although he described the changes as 'another kick in the teeth'. The only way in which the level of investment in this company could possibly be affected by the post 1986 tax system vis-a-vis the pre 1984 rules is if the new system would have affected the availability of funds for capital expenditure.

As all taxation has been through personal income tax and national insurance contributions, it would at first sight appear that the company would have lost the benefit of earlier capital allowances but not enjoyed a compensating reduction in the rate of taxation. The pre 1984 system probably had given the company £6-7,000 in additional capital allowances by 1983, reducing income tax and national insurance contributions by 45.5 per cent of this, that is £2,700-3,150. Under the post 1986 tax system, the small companies rate will be 30 per cent of taxable profits whether left in the company or paid by way of dividend. This may be more attractive, subject to the best use of personal tax allowances and national insurance thresholds, than declaring all taxable profit as salaries and suffering 44.7 per cent income tax and national insurance thereon. If the business had been facing the post 1986 tax system in the past, it seems unlikely that any change in total tax and national insurance paid would actually have been significant enough to affect capital expenditure decisions.

Although taxation was not considered in the decision to purchase the vehicles or the timing of this investment, the interviewee did say that his accountant had for many years written before the company's year end pointing out the tax advantages of timing prospective investment to fall prior to that accounting date. On occasions in the past, this had prompted the company to 'look around' and to bring forward a purchase if the replacement price was suitable. In the year to 31 March 1984, the necessary purchases for the year had been made before tax efficiency was considered and the scarcity of finance meant only essential vehicle replacement were possible.

Although very averse to tax payments, the owners of this company have been prevented, by the recurring physical need for replacement of quickly depreciating vehicles and the financial necessity to take advantage of suitable opportunities for acquiring secondhand vehicles, from engaging in significant tax avoidance through the timing of vehicle purchases. The company had no plans to accelerate any future expenditure into the period prior to 31 March 1985.

Cases 57 and 58

This owner-managed private company specialises in heavy industrial removals and haulage involving the use of mounted cranes. The company, which was only incorporated recently, has run seven vehicles for the last few years and has a turnover of over £250,000. The business has been successful for 20 years and grew to its present size on the basis of retentions and bank borrowing, without any reliance on instalment credit or leasing.

Until the 1984 Finance Act, the proprietor assessed the likely taxable profits each year with his accountant and then planned what capital expenditure should be made before the company's year end in June. This policy was based on the view that it was better to use cash to expand or update the fleet, rather than 'give it away' in tax.

In the year ended 30 June 1983, the company made two major investments: a new mountable crane costing £25,000 (case 57) and a £8,000 secondhand truck (case 58). These were bought following the normal assessment of likely taxable profits, which revealed that considerable tax would become payable if no first year allowances were available. The vehicles were both bought outright in the May - June period, duly qualifying for first year allowances. The owner explained that the choice of vehicles was based on his business experience, an assessment of the state of the fleet and likely future needs. He described the truck as replacing a vehicle which would have needed replacing quite soon anyway; the tax incentives had 'speeded up the decision'. He could have waited 6-9 months before demand was expected to make the additional crane commercially necessary.

It is clear that the initial driving force to make these two investments at that time came from overall tax considerations, and the commercial possibilities were then examined to see what possible qualifying expenditure could be made. The additional crane was purchased before demand justified the decision, but the risk that demand might ultimately prove inadequate for the expanded capacity was considered worth taking in view of the clear tax advantages. The owner has no regrets about the decision, particularly as demand did later come up to expectations and as the additional crane gave the company more flexibility. The earlier replacement of the truck involved only a couple of months acceleration and the results of the investment were as expected.

The direct consideration of the tax incentives by the company's owner would have been reinforced by the indirect effect of his policy of making tax efficient capital expenditure. The policy undoubtedly saved tax and, as the fleet was fully occupied, the earning capacity of the business was increased using tax savings; this in turn strengthened the company's financial position which enabled additional investment to take place.

The risk of such a policy is that assets are purchased which are not commercially viable, in which case the outlay could exceed the tax savings and the associated revenues, putting the business in a worse position than if it had simply paid the tax. In the cases studied, the early replacement of a truck was not particularly risky and the level of demand in the firm's market niche has sustained the tax driven, expansionary investment in the crane, enabling the company to take real advantage of the first year allowances.

The owner recognises that there will be no such tax advantage to investment under the system proposed by the 1984 Finance Act. Instead of buying new vehicles in the future, he believed that the company would make more investment in tax efficient pension schemes and pay more tax. Over the transitional period, the company may replace vehicles where necessary and, if possible, the replacements would be timed to fall before March 1986. The owner was aware that fellow hauliers had been taking considerable advantage of 75 per cent first year allowances available up to 31 March 1985. He was concerned that this 'hiccup' might lead to some excess capacity in an already difficult market place.

Case 59

This unincorporated haulier entered the sector in 1974 and by 1979 had built up a fleet of seven lorries, following profitable work between the Mendip quarries and motorway construction nearby. The fleet size has stayed constant since 1979 and consists of both dump trucks for quarry work and articulated vehicles for longer haulage.

Although using the services of a professional accountant, the proprietor usually relies on him only for basic tax advice and preparation of accounts. The business replaced one or two vehicles each year until 1984, except in the financial year ended 31 May 1982, when the absence of any additions resulted in a jump in taxable profits and, despite considerable use of pension schemes, the owner had to pay the top personal tax rate of 60 per cent on some of this profit. His reaction was to change from his previous accountant, who had not given sufficient warning of the likelihood of this problem. The owner has since regarded regular assessment of likely taxable profit as an important part of his task in running the business.

Detailed discussion focused on the last vehicle purchased prior to the 1984 Budget, a dump truck for use in quarry work. This was purchased outright early in 1984 for £40,000, to replace a similar three year old vehicle in time for the beginning of the main quarry working months. The prime reason for the purchase was to obtain first year allowances and thereby avoid higher rate personal taxation. The proprietor was clear that this had been the major motive for the purchase, which followed his regular assessment of likely profits. Although the vehicle would have needed replacement eventually, it was only three years old and would have been run for another year had it not been for the 100 per cent first year allowances. No financial evaluation was done to assess or justify either the decision or the outright purchase of the vehicle. The proprietor has never leased and was adamant that 'I like to own my vehicles'.

By early 1984, the existence of 100 per cent capital allowances had given this business an estimated £75,000 more in tax allowances than under a system of 25 per cent writing down allowances, a tax saving of £20-45,000. This extra liquidity would have facilitated higher capital expenditure, but this indirect effect would simply have reinforced the strong direct incentive to buy new vehicles.

Following the 1984 Budget, the proprietor did not wish to see any fall in his capital allowances over the near future. To prevent such a fall, he decided to invest heavily prior to 31 March 1985 but to claim only the 25 per cent writing down allowances. By doing this, purchasing 3 new tractors and 2 new trailers, he hopes to ensure that a stable level of capital allowances prevents taxable profit reaching higher rates over the next few years. The proprietor emphasised that the chance of extra work had come up and enabled him to buy these vehicles. He had not wanted to expand and would not have done so but his perception of the 1984 Budget was 'expand even if you don't want to or pay tax and reduce in size'.

The proprietor's view, that these decisions were primarily tax based, seems correct and understandable in view of his position as an unincorporated trader and the specific experience in 1981-82 of paying tax at 60 per cent. The pre 1984 tax system therefore resulted in the business maintaining a newer fleet than technically necessary, while the transition to 25 per cent writing down allowances persuaded the proprietor to expand the fleet when he would not have otherwise, although the availability of work for the extra vehicles was essential to the decision.

Case 60

This unincorporated road haulier now runs seven vehicles generating a turnover in excess of £200,000. The owner of the business has invested steadily in recent years, increasing his fleet by one vehicle in 1983 and replacing ageing lorries with new vehicles soon after they are five years old. The business does not lease and finances this capital expenditure from retained earnings and borrowings.

The owner participated in the study and clearly believes that each new vehicle must stand on its own as a viable investment. However, with help from his accountant, investments have in the past been timed to reduce taxable profit to a level chargeable to income tax at the basic rate after personal allowances. The business accounts have provided in full for deferred taxation but borrowings, and therefore gearing, have been reduced under the pre 1984 tax system providing greater scope to increase the fleet when demand allowed.

The decision to acquire the new vehicle in 1983 was discussed in detail. Early in that year, the possibility of additional work appeared reasonable enough to consider the purchase of a new vehicle. The owner consulted his accountant and together they evaluated the effects of a new vehicle on cost, revenue interest and taxation. On looking at the new vehicle's ability, on a post tax basis, to support the additional capital and interest costs, the owner and his advisor believed that it would just be viable as an outright purchase prior to the end of the financial year in August 1983. This provided a substantial projected saving (40 per cent plus of the qualifying cost) in the owner's income tax liability which greatly reduced the outstanding investment.

The lorry was purchased for £23,000 and to date has been a 'good vehicle'. The first year allowances were granted and reduced the taxable income after personal allowances into the 40 per cent (£15,401-£18,200) band for the 1984-85 tax year. The actual tax saving from the investment would therefore have been around 50 per cent of qualifying cost in the next year's tax payment. The owner of this business was convinced that with 25 per cent writing down allowances, instead of a 100 per cent first year allowance, the vehicle's potential revenue would not have supported the additional operating and borrowing costs and he would have bought a much cheaper, secondhand vehicle.

Following the 1984 Finance Act, this business is intending to extend the life of existing vehicles, rather than replacing them with new ones every five years or so, and to consider buying secondhand vehicles instead of new ones. The owner said that this was also partly a response to the highly competitive market conditions, which made it difficult to cover the cost of a responsibly maintained and managed fleet.

In this case, the decision maker took the tax incentive represented by 100 per cent capital allowances into the evaluation. The effect of the 1984 Finance Act on the returns from the investment would have been purely negative because the business was unincorporated, so would not gain from the lower corporate tax rate. This growing business had accumulated considerable tax savings through first year allowances, which would have reduced borrowings. Under the tax system proposed in the 1984 Finance Act, this relief would have been largely lost and the ability of the business to make this and other investments would have been reduced.

The owner's opinion that the pre 1984 tax system led to more investment appears correct, in the light of the uncompensated effect of the removal of first year allowances directly on the attractiveness and indirectly on the ability to fund marginal projects. The other direct mechanisms, namely reduced leasing charges and the effect on reported earnings, did not enter this decision and the change in tax system did not affect the investment through the indirect mechanisms of perceived cost of capital or sector attractiveness.

The business took care to bring a vehicle purchase intended for the year to 31 August 1985 forward to fall before 31 March 1985 in order to qualify for 75 per cent first year allowances. Future investment plans depend very much on the availability of haulage work at reasonable rates.

PART 3
THE FINDINGS

10 Overall results

INTRODUCTION

The tax implications were considered in a large number of cases before the project was carried out, but the approval, scale and timing of the investments would generally not have been affected if the post 1986 system of allowances and tax rates had been in operation at the time. In nine of the sixty cases, the decision would have been different under the post 1986 tax regime (see Table 10.1). In six of these (cases 8, 23, 32, 57, 58 and 59), the timing of the investment rather than the decision to undertake it would have been affected, with the investment being accelerated in the pre 1984 environment for tax reasons. Two investments would have been scaled down under the post 1986 tax rules (cases 54, where the timing would also have been affected, and case 60), but only one project would have been abandoned completely (case 26).

The detailed evidence on which the findings were based was presented in Chapters 3-9. The next two sections provide an overview of the analysis of the effects of the tax changes, looking first at possible direct effects and then at the indirect effects of tax. The importance of grant aid in the investment decisions is then discussed, followed by a summary of the rather limited evidence on the relative quality of the sixty investments. The final section of the chapter broadens the focus to consider the tax sensitivity of other investment undertaken by the sample firms, apart from the projects chosen

Table 10.1

Main features of tax regime sensitive cases

Case	Sector	Ownership	Employment	Profit/tax position	Project cost	Nature	Effect of tax
8	Data processing	PLC	100 - 499	First major tax charge about to be incurred at the time of investment.	£359,000	Expansion	Timing
23	Mechanical handling	Private company	500 - 4999	Profitable up to 1979 but with little tax. Since 1982, rental profits sheltered by IBA.	£400,000	Replacement	Timing
26	Mechanical handling	Private company	1 - 99	Corporation tax liabilities removed by FYA's from reinvestment of profits.	£375,000	Expansion	IBA essential to decision
32	Non energy extraction	Following the writing up of this case study the interviewee, while not disputing the basic findings, decided that he did not wish the details to be published					
54	Road haulage	PLC	500 - 4999	Healthy profits; mainstream tax paying for many years	£1,000,000	Replacement	Timing and extent
57	Road haulage	Private company	1 - 99	Profitable with taxable profit taken as directors remuneration.	£25,000	Expansion	Timing
58	Road haulage	as 57	as 57	as 57	£8,000	Replacement	Timing
59	Road haulage	Sole trader	1 - 99	Profitable with taxable profit subject to personal tax rates.	£50,000	Replacement	Timing
60	Road haulage	Sole trader	1 - 99	Profitable with taxable profit subject to personal tax rates.	£23,000	Expansion	Extent of expenditure

for detailed study, and collects together the evidence on firms' reactions both to the transitional arrangements and the proposed depooling procedures.

DIRECT EFFECTS

1) Project returns

Table 10.2 summarises the direct effect of the pre 1984 tax system on the project decisions, and a more detailed breakdown by sector and firm size appears in Appendix 1.1. Just over one-third of the investments were not formally evaluated and this approach was typical of the smaller firms. In seven such cases, it was the effect of 100 per cent allowances on total tax paid or reported which led to a tax based acceleration of the investment (cases 8, 23, 32, 54, 57, 58 and 59) as well as affecting the scale of one of these. In the latter case, the recognised, but unquantified effect of a regular and early vehicle replacement policy, established after the introduction of 100 per cent first year allowances in the early 1970s to reduce the level and increase the stability of tax payments, had both accelerated individual investments and increased their scale over a number of years. The other six provided examples of deliberate acceleration of the particular project in order to reduce or eliminate potential short term tax bills. They included the investments by the two unincorporated hauliers, as well as by a medium sized data processing firm, where the main concern was to reduce the reported tax charge in the first year after flotation.

   In the remaining fifteen cases where no formal evaluation was carried out, the motive for making the investment and the tax position of the firms involved appeared to support the interviewees' contention that tax considerations had played no part in the decisions. Eight of these projects were carried out by firms which were tax exhausted and did not envisage the use of financial leasing, so it was clear that tax could not have played any direct part in the decisions (cases 9, 11, 17, 18, 33, 34, 55 and 56). Of the investments by tax payers or lessees, the only leased investment was a programme of vehicle replacement which was necessary to maintain the technical reliability and image of the road haulier's fleet (case 51), and the replacement of a very worn crusher by a firm in the non energy extraction sector was similarly regarded as non discretionary (case 30). Three of the other five investments where returns were not quantified, all by firms in a tax paying position, were in response to strong demand pressures on existing capacity (case 6, 24 and 25). The investment in advanced typesetting equipment by a small printing company was necessary for competitive survival (case 50) and the installation of a paint booth by a mechanical handling firm made important improvements to employee safety and the finished quality of its products (case 20).

Table 10.2
Direct effect of the tax system

Nature of project appraisal	Effect of tax system	Number of cases
Not quantified	Pre 1984 tax system critical	7
	Taxation and leasing ignored or insignificant	15
Pre tax	Taxation and leasing ignored or insignificant	18
Post tax	Pre 1984 tax system critical	2
	Returns well above the target criteria	7
	Returns similar under both systems	7
	Returns lower under post 1986 system but not critically	4
Total		60

Eighteen projects were evaluated on a pre tax basis with no consideration of leasing in reaching the decision to invest (even though five of these were eventually funded, in whole or part, by leasing). In seven cases where a pre tax appraisal was used, the company's tax exhaustion at the time of the investment and lack of a tax horizon in the immediate future would have made any consideration of tax cash flows irrelevant (cases 3, 4, 16, 19, 27, 35 and 43). In four, tax would have had little significance because tax capacity was negligible (cases 5, 12, 13 and 48). The main tax policy of the UK based international group described in case 52 was to attempt to take at least enough taxable profit in the UK to cover its dividend payments, while a multinational pharmaceutical company with strong cash flows and surplus ACT was not concerned with the tax implications of a relatively small, cost saving investment (case 38).

In five firms making substantial mainstream corporation tax payments, the pre tax nature of the appraisals reflected the view that any consideration of tax issues, including possible tax efficient methods of financing, should always follow the decision to go ahead with the investment and project approval should be based on 'purely commercial criteria' (cases 21, 22, 31, 41 and 44). The latter case provides an excellent example of methods reflecting this attitude, whereby potential investments are identified on the basis of well developed strategic planning procedures, yet evaluated solely on a pre tax basis.

Although five of the investments which were evaluated pre tax and without including lease rentals in the cash flows were eventually leased, the possible tax based advantages of leasing in the pre 1984 tax environment did not appear to have affected either the decision to go ahead with these investments or their timing (cases 3, 5, 12, 13 and 35). This was usually because the investment and financing decisions were deliberately separated and the evaluation of the project was based on purchasing the plant and machinery outright. However, there was one particularly interesting example of the delayed recognition of significant savings possible through lease finance in the late 1970s by a major foreign based phrmaceuticals company, with tax losses in the UK (case 35).

Tax effects did enter the appraisal of twenty investments, either because capital allowances and corporation tax payments were shown as tax cash flows or because lease rentals, with their implicit tax subsidy, were included in the calculations. The effect the post 1986 tax system would have had on the returns expected from these projects was estimated, as described in Chapter 2. Two expansionary investments, which were based on the ability of post tax returns to repay borrowings, would have been sensitive to the post 1986 tax regime. One of these, an industrial buildings project, would have been abandoned completely without the benefit of 100 per cent allowances gained on small workshops under the pre 1984 system (case 26), and the other, an investment in a vehicle, would have been scaled down (case 60). The remaining eighteen appraised on a post tax basis would not have been affected under the new tax system.

In seven cases where tax entered the appraisal, either directly or through leasing, the calculated returns were regarded as well above any target rates and clearly would not have been sufficiently affected by the new tax regime for the investment decision to have been altered (cases 1, 7, 14, 28, 37, 39 and 45). Four of the investments with very high projected returns were actually financed through leasing. In three of the leased cases (cases 7, 28 and 45), the firms involved would not have been able to benefit fully from capital allowances because of thir overall tax position. Nevertheless, the equipment was evaluated as an outright purchase, assuming tax would be paid at the full marginal rate. The other leased investment was carried out by a foreign multinational pharmaceutical company which did incorporate the expected lease rentals in the project appraisal. This investment showed a pre tax internal rate of return of 72 per cent, while the post tax calculation reflected the home country's tax system and again showed a very high return on the investment (case 39).

The only investment in R and D facilities within the sample falls in this category and is worth highlighting in view of the provision within the 1984 Finance Act for first year allowances to be maintained on R and D expenditure (case 37). This decision by a US multinational to place a pharmceutical research and development unit costing over £5 milion in the UK was critically dependent on the first year allowances gained on all the capital expenditure. However, since allowances on expenditure on scientific research are to continue at 100 per cent, this project would still have qualified for 'free' depreciation under the post 1986 tax rules. Although the UK tax shelter afforded by the project would have been reduced from 52 per cent to 35 per cent of the capital outlays under the new regime, this was unlikely to have had a critical effect on the decision.

In the remaining eleven cases where it seems that using the new tax system in the evaluation would have been unlikely to have altered the original decision, the returns anticipated were less exceptional. The seven which would have shown either similar or higher returns under the post 1986 tax rules will be discussed first. Two of the three leased projects falling in this category were evaluated as purchases, assuming full tax payment at the marginal rate of 52 per cent. The effect of the loss of 100 per cent first year allowances on these projects, both in the printing industry, would have been almost exactly balanced by the lower corporation tax rates (cases 47 and 49). The third leasing case concerned the decision by a major road haulier, with substantial tax losses, to build a large distribution depot (case 53). Here, it was thought that any burden of the 1984 tax changes could have been shifted forwards onto the customer, leaving the profit margin on the investment virtually unchanged.

Two of the four non leased investments where the unexceptional returns anticipated would have been either similar or higher in the post 1986 environment, were undertaken by firms with substantial surplus ACT. In one of these (case 29), the project was evaluated using the 22 per cent rate of corporation tax which would have been applicable in the early years of the project under the pre 1984 system; returns would have been marginally higher if the post 1986 tax rules were applied and the firm does not anticipate altering its hurdle rate, although a slight decrease in the cost of capital in the new tax environment is expected. The other concerns a company with a long history of surplus ACT stretching back to the mid 1970s (case 42). It was not until 1981 that the subsidiary making this investment was formally asked to include a 22 per cent tax rate in its appraisals, and the evaluation of the project studied was based on a 52 per cent marginal tax rate. However, the effect of tax on project returns was minimal, as capital allowances were carried forward within the project, rather than being immediately offset against other group income, and would have been higher if the post 1986 tax rules were applied using the same assumptions.

Referring again to Table 10.2, there were four investments which offered unexceptional returns when appraised on the basis of the pre 1984 tax rules and would actually have shown lower quantified returns if they had been assessed under the post 1986 tax rules. Two of these were by UK firms and financed by leasing and, in both cases, the cost of lease finance was included in the project appraisal. Even if higher leasing costs had been included to reflect the reduced tax shelter available to lessors under the post 1986 system of writing down allowances, these projects would still have gone ahead, according to the interviewees, primarily because of their unquantified strategic advantages (cases 15 and 46).

The two other investments which would probably have shown lower returns under the post 1986 tax rules and been very near to the relevant criteria for acceptance, were both carried out by the subsidiaries of foreign multinationals. The first concerns a relatively small investment by a large multinational in the internal provision of an advanced network of workstations (case 2). The aim was to demonstrate the successful use of such a network within the organisation as an example to potential customers, a strong unquantified benefit. The investment appeared marginal when assessed in strict financial terms under the pre 1984 tax system. The interviewee was certain, however, that if even lower returns had been shown, the company would not have abandoned the project but rather asked the operating managers to 'commit' additional productivity benefits, essentially shifting the burden of tax to the employees.

The second case relates to the establishment of a dedicated manufacturing facility in the UK for a drug about to go into large scale production (case 40). The returns on manufacturing and selling the drug were very high, so it had definitely been decided that the manufacturing facility would be built. The critical issue was where it would be located. The advantages of building the plant on an existing UK site in a non assisted area were compared with a potential site in the Far East and, in a fairly narrow decision, the UK option was found to provide the higher return. The pre 1984 tax provisions, particularly the accelerated allowances, were seen as assisting significantly in the decision to favour the UK site, although, in the interviewee's opinion, the same decision would almost certainly have been taken under the post 1986 tax regime, but by a much finer margin. This investment, with its heavy start up costs and slow take-off period, provides an example of the type of investment for which the pre 1984 tax provisions were particularly favourable.

2) Overall tax charge

As discussed earlier, there were six examples of deliberate acceleration of investment in order to reduce or eliminate potential short term tax bills, including investments by the two unincorporated traders in the sample (cases 8, 23, 32, 57, 58 and 59); in one of these (case 8), the main concern was to reduce the reported tax charge in the first year after flotation. In case 54, the known, but unquantified, effect of regular and early vehicle purchases on reducing the level, and increasing the stability of tax bills, was said to contribute to the setting of a policy which was otherwise '75 per cent a commercial decision'. In the other fifty-three cases studied, the interviewees did not regard the possible effect of the investment on total tax paid or reported, as having an impact beyond that included in any post tax evaluation of returns. The available evidence, particularly regarding the nature of the investment, the firm's overall policies towards capital expenditure, their tax positions and the deferred tax provisions of US subsidiaries, all supports this view.

As Table 2.2 showed, a large number of the projects were by firms which were either tax exhausted or would have expected to pay a negligible amount of corporation tax, both when the main orders for the investment were placed and in the immediate future. Against this tax background, such firms would have been able to derive little benefit from 100 per cent first year allowances directly and the investment would have had no significant influence on tax paid or reported. Seven investments were carried out in groups with substantial surplus ACT and the effect on reported after tax earnings in this context, if considered at all, would also have been seen to be insignificant. In several of the firms which were tax exhausted, paid relatively little mainstream corporation tax or had substantial surplus ACT, the investment was leased, so the lessor will have derived the immediate benefit of tax shelter anyway.

Of more interest in this context are the seven businesses where the payment of mainstream corporation tax had been significantly reduced by capital allowances over a number of years. In one such case, the specific investment studied was deliberately timed to reduce the tax charge (case 32), but the reduction of taxable profits did not appear an important factor in the other six decisions by firms in this tax category. The investment in security printing machinery detailed in case 44 was a large and strategic investment involving research and development which would have made the timing of expenditure difficult to control for tax purposes, even if this had been the intention, an idea which the group financial director firmly rejected; case 10 refers to an investment by the subsidiary of a US multinational required to provide in full for deferred tax, thereby nullifying any reporting benefit; cases 17 and 25 involved very strong demand pressure; case 38 showed a very fast safe payback and the investments in cases 26 and 48 were crucial to competitive survival.

Of the fifteen firms where substantial mainstream corporation tax was being paid under the pre 1984 system, only in case 54, discussed above, was any unquantified value attached to the fact that the capital investment could reduce reported tax charges and short term tax payments. In five of the remaining fourteen cases, the firms provided in full for deferred taxation and were clearly cash rich, nullifying any reporting advantage of accelerated capital allowances and any perceived need to reduce short term tax bills (cases 1, 2, 36, 37 and 40). Six firms had explicit pre tax evaluation procedures reflecting a deliberate policy of not letting quantifiable tax advantages, much less unquantified ones, influence decisions (cases 20, 21, 22, 30, 31 and 52). The remaining three firms paying substantial mainstream tax were case 5, where a quick pre tax payback and strong behavioural factors dominated the decision, case 6 which involved acute, unquantified capacity pressure in a highly profitable market, and case 50, the only investment which reduced the firm's tax liability by bringing the firm fully into the small company's tax threshold. The importance of this was examined carefully at the interview, but the managing director of the company specifically stated that the decisive influence on the investment was the need to

modernise in order to stay competitive and the availability of
a new generation of proven typesetting equipment, rather than
potential reductions in their tax bill.

INDIRECT EFFECTS

1) Cost of capital

Although in theory changes in the tax system will alter the
firm's cost of capital and so, at the margin, influence its
investment decisions, the fieldwork provided few examples of
firms, even among the largest and most dynamic organisations in
each sector, which actually used such finely tuned calculations
in the context of the sample projects. Similarly, there was no
evidence that such criteria as were applied in the evaluation
of investments would generally have been stiffer under the new
tax regime. Although some firms had altered their methods of
appraisal since the decision studied, these changes were not
due to the 1984 Finance Act.

Table 10.3
Use of hurdles and targets in project appraisal

Type of evaluation	Number of cases
No quantified evaluation	22
No definite yardstick	
pre tax appraisal	4
post tax appraisal	5
Definite yardstick	
pre tax appraisal	14
post tax appraisal	15
Total	60

*classified according to main criterion,
where more than one used

About half of the projects were approved without reference to
a target rate of return or other precise yardstick. These
included seven of the tax regime sensitive cases which had not
been formally assessed, except insofar as the effect on the

firm's tax bill or reported earnings were concerned, fifteen cases where the project had been assessed with no consideration of tax or leasing and nine where evaluations had been carried out, but not in a framework which allowed assessment against precise financial targets. It is still, of course, possible that changes in the tax system would have given rise to the feeling that the returns on projects would 'have to be better' for the investment to be justified, but there was no evidence that such a change in attitudes was likely.

A pre tax target was used in fourteen cases, normally the undiscounted payback or rate of return on capital employed. In fifteen of the twenty where tax was taken into account in assessing the project, the returns were evaluated against established post tax criteria. Two tax regime sensitive decisions by small firms involved judging the post tax income formally against the ability to repay borrowings (cases 26 and 60), two cases saw post tax evaluation but no target or norm (cases 7 and 49) and in one case, lease rentals were incorporated into an evaluation which was not measured against any formal criteria (case 46). Five of those evaluated post tax were carrred out by foreign multinationals. Two of these were judged in relation to undisclosed internationally set criteria (cases 1 and 37), while three were assessed against specified criteria used internally for UK investments (cases 2, 10 and 36).

The post tax criteria were usually defined in terms of round figure internal rates of return on cash flows. There were only four instances where precise calculations of the firm's cost of capital (based on its financial structure, rather than the borrowing costs associated with the particular project) featured in the decision. In one, the calculated cost of capital happened to be a round figure and the safety margin added was 8 per cent; the group had not changed either for over a decade and there was no indication that they would be changed following the 1984 Finance Act. Of the other three which had a cost of capital hurdle rate, two had recalculated their cost of capital soon after the 1984 Budget. Both expected rapid utilisation of surplus ACT as a result of the tax changes and their calculated cost of capital fell slightly, but by too small a margin to justify altering the target (cases 28 and 29). The third had not attempted to change its notional cost of capital in view of very large tax losses carried forward (case 42).

2) Liquidity

Table 10.4
Indirect effect of the tax system on liquidity

Effect on liquidity*	Impact on specific cases	Number of cases
Significantly improved by pre 1984 system	Significantly aided	6
	Not significant	8
Similar had post 1986 system operated	Nil	38
Significantly improved had post 1986 system operated	Not significant	8
Total		60

*Ignoring the abolition of stock relief in periods of high inflation

Table 10.4 summarises the effect of differential past mainstream corporation tax payments and lease costs under the pre 1984 and post 1986 tax systems on the ability to fund the projects studied. A more detailed analysis by sector and firm size is presented in Appendix 1.2. The liquidity effect appeared to have an important impact in six cases, all of which were directly sensitive to the tax regime. Amongst them were the investments by the two unincorporated road hauliers (cases 59 and 60) who had accumulated considerable tax savings through 100 per cent first year allowances, thereby reducing their borrowing requirements. Under the system proposed in the 1984 Finance Act, the relief would have been largely lost, with no compensation through reduced tax rates, and their ability to fund this and other investment would have been significantly impaired.

One of these sole traders had replaced his vehicle about a year earlier than otherwise (case 59) and, in the three other cases where the timing of the project had been accelerated to reduce or eliminate a tax bill, past tax savings had undoubtedly provided additional funds enabling the momentum of tax avoidance to be maintained (cases 32, 57 and 58). The new tax system would have also adversely affected the industrial buildings project considered in case 26, by making the borrowings necessary to fund the investment more difficult, so reinforcing the critical direct effect of the old tax system (case 26).

The liquidity effect did not appear significant in the remaining fifty-four cases. A further eight firms did benefit from the pre 1984 tax system, seven of them through lower tax payments than would otherwise have been enjoyed, and one with heavy trading losses through its reliance on lease finance. However, for a variety of reasons these relative gains under the old system did not have a critical influence in funding the projects studied. Three firms would have been in a relatively strong position to fund their investment anyway (cases 10, 38 and 48) and the nature of the other five projects meant that they would not have been subject to capital rationing even though, under the post 1986 tax system, funding might have been more difficult. Two were very strategic (cases 15 and 44), two were demand led and additional borrowings could have been made on the strength of this (cases 17 and 25) and one tax accelerated replacement was also regarded as a priority (case 23).

Total tax payments in the years just prior to the investment would have been little affected in the majority of cases if the post 1986 tax provisions had been in operation in the years preceding the investment. In twenty-three of these, relatively unprofitable trading would have given rise to very low tax payments under either tax system and no significant advantage had accrued from reduced lease rentals. In a further seven cases, there was sufficient unutilised ACT to make the post 1986 system at least as beneficial in terms of tax paid, while in the remaining eight firms, the high level of profits compared with fixed capital expenditure would have given rise to tax payments below or similar to those actually experienced under the pre 1984 tax system.

A small minority of highly profitable, usually large, firms with relatively small capital expenditure programmes would have benefited substantially through lower tax bills under the post 1986 system (cases 2, 20, 30, 36, 40, 50 and 54). Without exception, their financial strength makes it extremely unlikely that the tax cash savings would have removed any formal capital rationing. Six had cash and short term investments in excess of borrowings in their latest balance sheets. Of the remaining two groups, one had gearing of net debt to equity of around 20 per cent while the other group had gearing in the UK of 8 per

cent, and its foreign parent had worldwide gearing of 3 per
cent.   These interviewees emphasised that funding ability had
never constrained investment;   instead, capital expenditure
tended to be limited by either the lack of suitable investment
opportunities or the non financial resources necessary to carry
them out.

3) Sector attractiveness

The indirect effect of the tax changes on the strategic choice
of investment areas proved difficult to evaluate.   Particular
types of investment which were likely to be relatively
sensitive to the 1984 Finance Act were cited and these are
discussed later in the chapter, in the context of the firms'
total investment programmes.   As far as sectoral considerations
were concerned, the typical view was that broad investment
policies were determined in the light of the expected
profitability and growth potential of the firm's activities,
with links rarely being made between the underlying strategic
considerations and tax effects.

   Each sector had its own particular concerns.   Printers were
under intense competitive pressure to reduce unit costs and
increase quality by adopting new technology;   technological
discovery is often the driving force behind investment in the
electronic components sector, with speed of introducing new
products regarded as essential for success.   Manufacturers of
data processing products face shortening product lives and what
is perceived as the increasing ubiquity and aggression of the
industry leader.   The mechanical handling sector was still
recovering from severe recession and the effects of import
penetration in many product areas.   Interviewees in non energy
extraction placed great emphasis on the importance of mineral
reserves to the future continuation and profitability of their
extraction, working and downstream activities, and some thought
the proposed changes in the tax treatment of such reserves
would be more important than the effects of the 1984 Budget.
Recent increases in government regulation were of overriding
concern to pharmaceutical companies and many of the road
hauliers, particularly the smaller firms, complained about
increasing regulation, road tax and safety restrictions, as
well as the effect of the 1984 Finance Act on investment in the
very competitive general haulage section of the market.   Some
increase in demand in specialist contract work was expected,
with the tax changes making own account haulage operations less
attractive.

OTHER FINDINGS

Impact of government grants

Table 10.5
Direct effect of government grant aid on project decisions

Availability and effect of grants	Number of cases
Aid vital to the decision to go ahead in the UK	3
Aid significant to some aspect of project decision	5
Aid a windfall gain	4
Not grant aided	48
Total	60

A number of interviewees believed that government grants of various types had a far more important influence than tax considerations on the firm's past investment programmes generally, and grants were seen as particularly significant by some of the large, relatively footloose, multinationals in the sample. The importance attached to government grants is exemplified in several of the projects studied and Table 10.5 summarises the significance of selective aid according to the direct effect of the subsidy received, ignoring possible indirect liquidity effects of past assistance on funding ability.

. Three large, foreign owned multinationals considered selective aid vital to their decision to make the investments discussed in the UK. Two of these firms had decided to invest and the grants available in Britain determined the project's location. First, the UK subsidiary of a major European based pharmaceutical company was attracted to build a manufacturing plant costing well over £20 million in the UK by regional development grants and other selective financial assistance (case 35). The second example, a decision by a major US multinational in the data processing industry to produce an updated product in Britain, was again dependent on the package

of grants and aid received (case 1).   These covered half the
capital cost of the £3 million investment and resulted in an
estimated payback on the investment of less than three years.
The accelerated capital allowances were not considered
important and the interviewees were quite convinced that the
grants had been 'absolutely the winning feature' in bringing
this investment to Britain.   The third company was the UK
subsidiary of a Californian based semiconductor producer which
had built up its European base in a UK assisted area in the
1970's;   a subsidy under the microelectronics support scheme
was thought vital in gaining the US headquarter's approval for
the proposed investment to build up the design function in
Britain (case 11).

   Government aid was significant in five cases, of which two
involved the decision to invest in Britain, rather than
alternative locations.   Grants received by a major
pharmaceutical company for siting a large research and
development facility in Britain reinforced the effect of 100
per cent capital allowances, for which this type of investment
is still eligible under the post 1986 tax system (case 37).   In
case 12, formal project approval was made dependent on
obtaining a technology grant, although it is unlikely the grant
was critical, in view of the other advantages of the project.
Similarly, the decision by an important UK based electronic
component manufacturer to site a packaging plant in a regional
development area in the UK rather than abroad, was influenced
by regional grants, although the investment was largely for
strategic reasons (case 15).   A small private electronics firm
suffering from capital rationing was able to accelerate its
purchase of a new computer due to the grant received (case 18).
A technology grant was also described as 'quite a factor' in
the decision by a major printer to purchase and develop the
basic technology required to update the printing facilities of
one of its subsidiaries (case 44).

   In four cases, the effect of government aid was of marginal
significance to the investment studied, although not
necessarily to the firm's investment generally.   Two major
pharmaceutical firms stressed the overall importance of
regional development grants and both said that they were being
withdrawn just when the firm would most need them, in view of
declining profitability in their UK operations.   Both of their
projects received regional aid but this was not significant in
the decisions, in one major expansionary investment because the
returns were well within the group's payback criteria without
the grants (case 41), and in another, much smaller, programme
because of the significance of the cost savings involved (case
38).   The investment in a colour press which was partly funded
through grant aid but evaluated as a 'stand alone' decision

(case 47) would probably have proceeded in the absence of financial help. Finally, a private firm producing electronic components would have gone ahead with a major programme of expansion without grant aid but successfully applied for subsidies (case 17). The lengthy application procedure delayed the start of this project by a few months at a time when conditions were ripe for immediate investment but, despite this, the grant aid was still felt worthwhile.

Considerable concern was expressed in a number of firms about the changes to regional development grants after November 1985. There is an enormous literature dealing with the impact of regional policy, both on firms' investment decisions and from the economy's standpoint. A number of studies have questioned its effectiveness (e.g. Marquand, 1980) particularly in periods of slow economic growth and high general unemployment, with sub regional black spots assuming greater importance. It was against this background that the recent government policy changes were made. These cases illustrate the different effects grants can have on individual investments but an assessment of their overall impact was beyond the scope of this study.

Effect of projects

One of the intentions of the 1984 tax reform, as stated in the 1984 Budget speech, was to 'encourage the search for investment projects with a genuinely worthwhile return and discourage uneconomic investment', in contrast to the old system which 'encourages low yielding or uneconomic investment at the expense of jobs'. Although there is some evidence of relatively low net rates of return on manufacturing investment, especially before 1980, the reasons for this, and particularly the importance of investment incentives in encouraging marginal investments, are a matter of dispute (Sargent and Scott, 1986).

In order to provide some evidence at the micro level, this study investigated how far those projects which would have been affected if the post 1986 system of tax had applied at the time the decision was taken, tended to be relatively low yielding, or had particular characteristics in terms of their employment effects and use of technology. It is very difficult to estimate the impact of individual projects from the economy's standpoint and the evidence mainly relates to the expected and actual effects of the projects on the individual firms. As such a small number of projects appeared sensitive to the tax reform, any indications of relative quality would, in any case, be very tentative.

Table 10.6
Project returns anticipated

Type of evaluation	Return anticipated	Number of cases
Pre tax		
Payback (years)	2 - 3	4
	Under 2 years	4
ROC/IROR (%)	10 - 20	2
	20 - 30	3
	Above 30	2
Post tax		
Payback (years)	2 - 3	2
IROR (%)	15 - 20	2
	21 - 30	5
	Above 30	6
Total		30

The expected returns from the thirty investment projects for
which a quantitative evaluation of returns was carried out and
the results disclosed are summarised in Table 10.6, in terms of
the main criterion used to assess each project. No formal
evaluation was applied in twenty-two cases and in a further
eight, which were formally appraised, the results were not
disclosed.   In some cases, the anticipated returns were
revealed at the interviews but are not included in the
published case studies for confidentiality reasons.

A variety of methods were used to calculate the payback and
internal rate of return. The returns were usually calculated
on the basis of nominal cash flows and, where payback was used
as the main criterion, the estimate tended to be based on the
undiscounted cash flows. The treatment of interest and tax in
post tax appraisals varied substantially. Differences in the
basis of the calculations mean that the returns anticipated
from particular investments are not always directly comparable
and, of course, the riskiness of individual projects will vary.
This means that   Table 10.6 only gives a broad view of the
perceived attractiveness of the different investments, rather
than a precise indication of likely comparative returns.

The table suggests that most projects were expected to have

fairly rapid paybacks and high rates of return. Although in some instances, the returns appeared marginal compared with the firm's actual targets, unquantified benefits often played a part in project acceptance. As discussed earlier, none of the tax regime sensitive investments were formally evaluated in a payback or internal rate of return framework. In seven of these, likely returns were not quantified at all, whereas the two expansionary investments were assessed on the ability of post tax returns to repay borrowings, but the precise figures were not disclosed (cases 26 and 60).

Turning now to some of the other characteristics of these investments, twenty-six projects introduced technology significantly more advanced than previously used in the company. Two of these were in the subsample of tax accelerated investments (cases 8 and 23), so the effect of the pre 1984 tax system was to encourage slightly earlier introduction than would have occurred under the post 1986 tax system. Twenty-three of the expansionary investments were expected to increase employment in the firm itself; most had no immediate manpower implications but there were nine which were expected to lead to a reduction in the firm's labour force. Of the nine tax sensitive investments, five replacement investments had no direct impact on the firm's employment (cases 23, 32, 54, 58 and 59). Four expansionary investments were expected to increase employment (cases 8, 26, 57 and 60) although the planned increase was minimal, except in case 8, where the manufacture of new products at an additional site was anticipated.

Very few firms, even among the larger ones studied, carried out formal post investment audits as a matter of routine; in other firms, the interviewees were asked to comment informally on the investment's performance. Of the forty-four projects where sufficient time had elapsed since completion of the project to allow assessment, seven were described as disappointing in various ways. Six of these projects did not perform as well as expected mainly because the anticipated sales were not forthcoming, including two of the tax accelerated investments. In case 8, forecasts of the market for a new product proved over optimistic, but the company's chairman was convinced that inadequate forecasts, rather than the accelerated equipment purchase, were responsible for subsequent losses. The other disappointing accelerated replacement was technically troublesome and, here, the tax driven haste to make the contract was considered partly responsible (case 32). Only one case where expectations were not fulfilled involved grant sensitivity (case 15) and, in this instance, a very severe downturn in the demand for a particular type of electronic component resulted in the project being mothballed before it was completed.

Five tax accelerated road haulage investments feature among the thirty-six cases where expectations were fulfilled. One of the two expansionary investments was needed within nine months of its purchase, as anticipated (case 57) and the other was regarded as a successful purchase (case 60). The remaining investments concerned the early replacement of vehicles. As a vehicle is used, there is a fall in the average capital cost per mile but the average maintenance cost per mile increases. An optimal point is reached, as a vehicle gets older, when the capital cost savings of keeping it any longer fall below the additional maintenance costs. Where the tax system by subsidising capital costs, induced companies to replace vehicles before this point would otherwise have been reached, the decision may be viewed as distorting choice, leading to subsidised capital expenditure being substituted for maintenance expenditure before this would otherwise be worthwhile.

OTHER FINDINGS

Tax sensitivity of other investment decisions

Table 10.7
Effect of the tax system on other investment decisions

Type of effect	Number of firms
On timing only	14*
On extent of capital expenditure	8
On multinational decisions to locate in the UK	4
On entry into sectors or acquisitions	4
No effect	26
Total	56

*8 firms identified a timing effect and another effect

Each participant was asked what impact, if any, the pre 1984 tax system (compared with the post 1986 provisions) had on the nature, scale and timing of the firm's investment programmes since 1979, apart from in the project selected for detailed study. As Table 10.7 shows, in almost half of the sample no effect was recognised or appeared likely on examination of the firm's circumstances and investment procedures. More than one-third, however, thought that the fine timing of some of their past investment had been affected by tax consideratins, and in sixteen cases, an impact on the level, direction or location of capital investment was revealed. This appears to suggest a greater sensitivity to tax than emerged from the study of individual investments, in common with the findings in some earlier studies, which have found a difference between answers to questions about investment policy in general and about specific cases. In view of this, the possible reasons for the different responses here were carefully examined.

The pre 1984 capital allowances and the rates were thought to have increased total investment (compared with its likely level under the post 1986 system) by eight firms. Six of these (cases 25/26, 32, 54, 57/58, 59 and 60) had accelerated, enlarged or approved the specific project because of the pre 1984 capital allowances and the regular impact of taxation in this way would have increased their total fixed capital expenditure prior to 1984. In two other firms where a tax based timing change had been made in the decision studied (cases 8 and 23) such adjustments were sufficiently rare and the extent so limited that the effect on total investment was insignificant.

In case 22, the interviewee was convinced that the tax system had stimulated the group's investment before 1984, but felt it would be impossible to identify a project where the tax incentives were demonstrably critical. The pre 1984 tax treatment of capital expenditures was described as creating a 'climate' within the group which was favourable to the sponsorship of investment proposals, but the group's pre tax evaluation procedures did not allow such incentives to be visibly significant.

The UK finance director of the multinational enterprise studied in case 38 believed that the pre 1984 fiscal environment had significantly increased the UK subsidiary's ability to finance some of its strong growth in capital formation from internally generated funds, on which the average tax rate had been well below 35 per cent. It was possible that, if marginal projects had to be funded from the corporate 'pot' worldwide, some might not have been sanctioned. The specific small cost saving investment examined in detail was, however, thought unlikely to have been affected even if funding, as well as approval from head office had been necessary.

In twenty-two firms, including five where the extent of

investment had been increased by the regularity of tax based timing decisions, the pre 1984 tax provisions had occasionally influenced the timing of some of their past investment. In several of these, the nature of the project studied meant it was impervious to tax considerations but the interviewees stated that, when the opportunity arose, the timing of smaller, less important investments might sometimes be altered to maximise the tax benefit (e.g. case 29). Some firms occasionally invested at the year end to minimise the tax bill but the specific investment studied was scheduled according to 'commercial' rather than tax criteria (e.g. case 56). The timing of two investments in the electronic components sector had been determined by the dates at which grants had been received, unlike firms' other investments (cases 17 and 18).

Particular types of investment were highlighted by some of the respondents as being especially sensitive to tax considerations. The interviewees in two recently established, small, high technology companies believed that 100 per cent allowances were important to the decision by the groups involved to set these firms up (cases 6 and 16), although they were not critical to their later investments. One of these respondents emphasised the benefit of free depreciation in postponing tax, enabling reinvestment of all operating surpluses, while the other highlighted the earlier flow of returns to shareholders which the postponement of tax facilitated. The interviewees stressed, however, that once in these high technology businesses, rapid investment was essential anyway in order to survive.

Two large UK groups with considerable surplus ACT had found this a disincentive both to further investment overseas, which might give rise to unuseable double taxation relief, and to acquisitions in the UK of firms with limited taxable capacity (cases 28 and 29). The interviewees pointed to recent major acquisitions by their groups which had an important element of 'tax fit', providing substantial taxable capacity which would benefit from the ACT. The 1984 Finance Act was regarded as virtually removing the long term problem of surplus ACT and thus the disincentive to invest abroad.

The tax reform was also seen as affecting the attraction of the UK as an investment location, but views on the net effect of the loss of allowances and low tax rates were mixed. In cases 2 and 3, the lower corporation tax rates were seen as making the UK a generally more attractive investment location whereas the interviewee in case 31 regarded the loss of first year allowances as outweighing the lower rates. In case 40, the ability to offset capital start up costs against other income at a rate of 52 per cent was a significant, but not

critical, factor in bringing the investment in a slowly
maturing project to the UK. The interviewee commented that,
for this type of project, the UK would now be a less tax
efficient location. However, none of the participants were
able to give details of any specific case where the 1986 tax
change would have resulted in an investment which had been
located in Britain under the pre 1984 tax system being
rejected, or vice versa. Selective financial assistance was
often regarded as more important and this could readily be
illustrated with reference to individual examples.

Although there are various reasons why the apparent impact of
tax on individual firm's investment programmes, as seen through
fieldwork, and for the economy as a whole, identified through
aggregate investment functions, need not coincide (as discussed
in Chapter 2), it is of interest to compare the results of the
present study with the parallel econometric work carried out by
Levis with Thanassoulas, as part of the wider programme of
research into the effects of the 1984 Finance Act.

Their work relied mainly on the neoclassical approach and, in
common with earlier studies, met with formidable modelling and
measurement problems, which were particularly acute after the
liquidity crisis of 1979. Nevertheless, their results suggest
that government tax policy has influenced past investment and
the effect of the new tax system will be to decrease
investment, although the overall impact is likely to be fairly
limited:

> As a direct consequence of the tax changes the level
> of fixed investment by industrial and commercial
> companies could in the long term be reduced by as much
> as 4%, in comparison to what it would have been under
> the tax system and economic circumstances prevailing
> before the 1984 Budget (Levis and Morgan, 1985, p.ii)

The conclusion that investment may well be reduced as a result
of the tax changes, but by a relatively small amount, accords
with the indications of likely change provided by the case
study evidence.

Effect of the transitional arrangements

Aggregate statistics show a substantial upsurge in investment
in the year following the Budget announcement, part of which is
usually attributed to the effect of the phased tax change.
Thirty-three firms and subsidiaries in the sample had altered
their investment programme noticably to take advantage of the
1984/85 transitional arrangements (as seen in Table 10.8). The
usual response was to accelerate planned investment rather than

to carry out additional investment which would not otherwise have gone ahead. Typically investment was pulled forward by no more than two to three months to meet the March 1985 deadline and, in many cases, the amounts involved were small relative to the firm's total investment. All were aware of the possible advantages of speeding investment and subsidiaries had often received written instructions from head office to accelerate their expenditure. One interviewee commented that this was 'easier to say than to do', a remark which was echoed in many other firms.

Table 10.8
Reaction to the March 1985 transitional arrangements

Reaction	Number of firms
Slight acceleration	18
Significant acceleration	15
Nil or negligible	23
Total	56

A number of constraints on the ability to alter investment plans substantially were mentioned both by those who had been able to benefit to some extent from the transitional and arrangements and others who had not. These included the difficulties of financing early investment, the problems of speeding up large projects, particularly those with long lead times or involving multidisciplinary teams, the need to ensure the right equipment was acquired and the time taken to alter internal budgets.

The attitude of customers was also significant in some cases and was commented on particularly by firms in data processing and mechanical handling, as well as by a major road haulage contractor (case 53). While some firms merely noted the pressure for early delivery (e.g. cases 3 and 19), in others the benefits of accelerating expenditure had been discussed in detail with potential clients. Indeed, one data processing company described this as a very important part of sales policy in the quarter ending 31 March 1985 (case 1). In five of the cases where investment was being accelerated in the transitional period, the November 1985 reduction in regional assistance, rather than tax changes, provided the major impetus (cases 15, 22, 31, 39 and 41).

More companies reported an acceleration of investment to take advantage of the transitional arrangements in the year ending March 1985 than felt their pre 1984 investment programmes in general, if not the specific project, had been affected by tax considerations. The effect of the transitional arrangements may have been easier for managers to identify and remember, as the investments affected were current and investment schedules which had been established before the 1984 Budget announcements often had to be changed. However, the incentive to bring investment forward was greater for many firms in the first year of the transition than previously at the firm's year end, and would have been particularly strong for companies with a March year end.

The transitional arrangements were usually seen as speeding up investment which would have taken place anyway but in one firm, where expenditure had been accelerated quite significantly, it was noted that the timing adjustment might in practice lead to a once and for all increase in capital expenditure, in view of the momentum of investment within the group (case 2). The transitional arrangements certainly resulted in increased expenditure in two small firms studied. One was a small private printing firm which would not have diversified into colour printing without the benefit of the 75 per cent allowances on the new colour press and the prospect of reduced rates of corporation tax on the future profits (case 50). The other was an unincorporated road haulier who described his perception of the short term effect of the 1984 Budget as 'expand, even if you don't want to, or pay tax and reduce in size' and invested accordingly, in the year ending March 1985, to prevent taxable income reaching higher tax brackets in future years (case 59). In firms where investment behaviour was virtually unaffected by the transitional arrangements, the main reasons included tax losses, cash shortages or the nature of the firm's investment programme; in some, a major investment had just occurred before the Budget announcement while others planned very little investment in the immediate future anyway.

Depooling arrangements

As the March 1985 announcement of depooling arrangements for short life assets occurred while the fieldwork was in progress, reactions were only sought for a subsample of the companies. Firms in non energy extraction, in particular, regarded the change as unimportant, in view of the long life of the main assets involved in mining and quarrying and their low disposal value. Others had not yet had sufficient time to give a considered response but the 'administrative headache' of keeping track of each individual asset for which the depooling election was made was generally felt to dilute, if not outweigh, any tax advantages, except possibly where leasing was concerned.

In the detailed guidance issued in January 1986, in response to representations about various problems anticipated with the proposed depooling scheme, the Inland Revenue accepted that it may be impractical for individual capital allowance computations to be maintained for every short life asset, especially where very large numbers are held. Alternative arrangements for short life assets costing similar amounts, which cannot be individually identified, were set out and it was suggested that similar procedures might also be applied where separately identifiable short life assets are acquired in large numbers (Inland Revenue, 1986).

11 Conclusions

There is no doubt that the pre 1984 system of corporate taxation and investment incentives was in need of reform. Numerous fiscal allowances had been progressively extended mainly to encourage the various types of fixed investment which were seen, at the time, as especially important to the economy. The effect of rapid inflation on firms' liquidity in the 1970's was another reason for the ad hoc adjustments.

The operation of this system had become very complex by the late 1970's and its potential effects very discriminatory, often in unintended directions and to an unanticipated extent. Indeed, the government held the old tax system partly responsible for encouraging low productivity investment in manufacturing at the expense of jobs and believed it had contributed significantly to the poor performance of British industry compared with its competitors.

The main aim of the reform announced in the 1984 Budget was to remove some of the distortions and to institute a simpler system, within which firms would be encouraged to make their investment decisions on the basis of future market assessments, rather than tax assessments. The system certainly is simpler than the one it replaces, but the actual effect of the old system on past investment and the likely implications of the new provisions have been a matter of considerable debate.

This book set out to shed some light on the impact fiscal

incentives actually had on investment decisions in recent years and on the possible consequences for individual firms of the shift from a high tax, high allowance system to a low tax, low allowance system. The research focused on the effect that the new provisions would have had on specific investments between 1979 and 1984 if they had applied when these decisions were being taken. In order to concentrate on the effects of removing 100 per cent allowances on certain types of fixed investment, particularly in plant and machinery, it was assumed that some relief would still have been available on stockholdings in years of high inflation. Of course, any future rise in the rate of inflation beyond the low levels currently forecast could have a severe impact on the business sector, as firms are now almost totally unprotected against inflation with the abolition of stock relief under the new tax system.

The results illustrate that over the five years prior to March 1984, limited taxable capacity and unutilised ACT reduced the direct incentive of 100 per cent capital allowances for many firms and restricted any indirect benefit through lower tax payments. Although some firms had used lease finance as a tax efficient source of finance, as well as for other reasons, the tax benefits obtained in this way never appeared critical to the approval of the investments studied. The approval, scale and timing of fifty-one of the sixty projects seemed unlikely to have been affected if the post 1986 tax system of allowances on fixed investment and tax rates had been in operation at the time. Considerations other than the tax benefits of investment generally dominated these decisions.

Nine of the sample would have been directly sensitive to the changes in the tax environment: of these, only one project would have been abandoned completely; this investment was critically dependent on the 100 per cent building allowances available on small industrial buildings and, without this tax relief, the firm would have been unable to meet a realistic repayment schedule on the loan. The scale of two investments would have been reduced without the benefit of the 100 per cent allowances on plant and machinery, and the timing of a further six investments was accelerated to reduce tax payments.

In six of the projects which would have been directly sensitive to the tax changes, the indirect effect of the pre 1984 tax system also appeared to have had an important influence, by enhancing the firm's ability to fund the projects studied. The wider possible second round effects, through the impact on customer demand in producer goods industries, for example, were not generally recognised by those interviewed and proved very difficult to assess.

Previous work indicates that managers may believe their firm's total investment rather more sensitive to tax considerations that can easily be identified with reference to particular cases. There was evidence that a small minority of the sample would have reduced the scale of their total investment under the post 1986 tax regime; these were usually firms where the approval, scale or timing of the specific project had also been critically dependent on the capital allowances available at the time. An effect on the timing of investment again appeared more common but, as such timing changes were rare and generally involved relatively small equipment purchases, their impact on the firms' total capital expenditure programmes seemed negligible. However, this study provided no evidence that additional investment would have been undertaken if the post 1986 tax regime had applied earlier, especially as the firms likely to benefit most in terms of reduced tax payments were highly profitable and had not been subject to capital constraints.

Conclusions based on a limited number of cases are necessarily tentative, but decisions by small firms appeared particularly sensitive to the loss of 100 per cent allowances and four of the small firms, including the two unincorporated businesses, would have altered the specific decision studied under the post 1986 tax provisions. Subsequent discussions with managers in several leading accountancy firms also suggested a widespread tendency for tax driven investment decisions by small, owner managed firms.

Of course, the individual value of investment by such businesses tends to be relatively small and none of the projects costing over £1 million would have been affected by the proposed changes in the tax system, although several were dependent on government grants. The relative tax sensitivity of the small firms sampled contrasts with the recent conclusions reached by Alam and Stafford (1985), but this may be because much smaller firms were included in the present study than in the database from which their sample was drawn. The adverse effect of the removal of initial allowances on the financing ability of small firms is worth stressing, as it runs counter to recent government attempts to foster the small firm sector and aid the financing of such firms.

The only difference in the sensitivity of the individual sectors studied to the tax changes was the marked impact on the road haulage industry, where the decisions of four of the nine firms would have been affected by the post 1986 tax system. This partly reflects the predominance of small firms and unincorporated businesses paying tax at personal rates in road haulage; these already operate on tight margins in very competitive circumstances. It is interesting to note that some major hauliers believed the tax changes would be likely to have a favourable impact on them as the reduction in allowances was expected to make own account operations less attractive, increasing the amount of work contracted out to large haulage specialists.

The apparent sensitivity of some commercial vehicle purchases to year end tax considerations is supported by the behaviour of aggregate vehicle registrations which tend to peak in March, close to many firms' year ends, as well as at the change of registration in August. Short life assets (such as vehicles) would, in theory, be particularly affected by the reduction in allowances announced in the 1984 Budget and depooling provisions were later proposed in recognition of this problem. Many of those interviewed after the relaxation for short life assets was announced in the 1985 Budget thought the potential tax benefit of electing to follow depooling procedures would be outweighed by the administrative costs involved.

One of the stated aims of the 1984 tax reform was to encourage higher yielding investment. Some highly profitable projects will benefit in terms of their post tax yield, but it is not clear how these will be encouraged under the new system. It seems likely that such highly profitable projects would have been relatively attractive even under the old system and would have been undertaken anyway.

The Treasury also suggested that some of the less profitable projects, which would have gone ahead in earlier years, would now be rejected as a result of the stiffer hurdles applied in investment appraisal. Although the cost of capital and hence required returns would theoretically rise for fully tax paying firms, it appears that this will be of limited significance, as only a minority of large companies were paying tax at full marginal rates previously. The cost of capital is likely to fall where rapid utilisation of ACT is expected, as well as in other firms moving to positions of higher tax payment as a result of the 1984 Finance Act. The case study evidence on how investments are actually appraised also casts doubt on the likely impact of these effects in practice.

The relationship between the estimated returns and the criteria against which the projects were assessed was expected to give an indication of the anticipated yield from the firm's standpoint and allow a comparison between tax sensitive and other investments. However, many projects, including most of the tax sensitive ones, were not formally evaluated. Where returns were evaluated, the methods varied considerably, particularly in the treatment of interest and the tax assumptions made in post tax appraisals. Sometimes the tax reliefs were carried forward within the project and in other evaluations they were treated as being 'sold' to the group; the rate at which tax was applied often did not correspond to the effective rate of tax payment.

When the results of any precise evaluations were judged against well defined hurdle rates, these were usually well above any conceivable target based strictly on the cost of capital. The adoption of high round figure targets was largely explained in terms of risk and uncertainty, particularly in expansionary investments, which meant successful projects were seen as needing to earn additional profit to finance the inevitable failures. The use of sensitivity analysis, even when there was no precisely defined target, provides some evidence of risk analysis being regarded as more important than precise assessment of minimum required returns. In addition, various non financial resources limiting investment were often cited, such as in-house engineering capability, management time or labour goodwill, and the setting of high financial targets was seen as helping to limit the acceptance of new projects to the level of these scarce resources.

The investment in firms which were found to be most sensitive to the tax changes did not appear to have any particular characteristics in terms of employment effects and it seems doubtful that the change in the structure of tax will have a major impact on decisions concerning relative factor proportions. Instead, it is more likely that firms will continue to invest in plant and machinery because their success, and even survival in some high technology sectors, is seen as dependant on introducing new machines.

Although the tax reform may not live up to the high expectations of those who introduced it, the evidence of this study suggests that the changes were a move in the right direction. The elaborate structure of investment incentives was not operating effectively in the years just before the tax changes, although it seems unlikely that they played a major part in leading to the poor performance of manufacturing industry. In the future, the scale of expenditure on assets previously eligible for 100 per cent allowances may fall in some instances and be less hasty than before, particularly where small firms and small items are concerned. Even assuming the system remains unaltered, as was the Chancellor's intention, the full effects of the reform will not however be seen until the 1990's; much will then depend on the prevailing economic circumstances, particularly the level of inflation.

Bibliography

Alam, K F and Stafford, L W T, (1985), 'Tax Incentives and Investment Policy: a Survey Report on the United Kingdom Manufacturing Industry', Managerial and Decision Economics, Vol.6, No.1.

BACMI (1985), Statistical Year Book, British Aggregate Construction Materials Industries, London.

Boatwright, B D and Eaton, J R, (1972), 'The Estimation of Investment Functions for Manufacturing Industry in the United Kingdom', Economica, 39.

Corner, D C and William, Alan, (1965), 'The Sensitivity of Businesses to Initial and Investment Allowances', Economica.

Devereux, M P and Mayer, C P, (1984), Corporation Tax: The Impact of the 1984 Budget, Institute of Fiscal Studies, June.

Eisner, R, (1957), 'Interview and other Survey Techniques and the Study of Investment' in NBER, Problems of Capital Formation, Princeton University Press.

Federation of British Industries, (1960), 'Memoranda of Evidence submitted to the Committee on the Working of the Monetary System', Memoranda, Vol.2, HMSO, London.

Feldstein, M S and Flemming, J S, (1971), 'Tax Policy, Corporate Saving and Investment Behaviour in Britain', Review of Economic Studies, 38.

George, K D and Hills, P V, (1968), Productivity and Capital Expenditure in Retailing, Cambridge University Press.

Greenwell, W and Co, (1984), Monetary Bulletin, April, London.

Hart, H and Prussman, D, (1964), 'A Report of the Survey of

Management Accounting Techniques in the South East Coastal Region', unpublished but the results appear, in part, in Scientific Business, November.

Hay, D A and Morris, D J, (1979), Industrial Economics, Oxford University Press.

HMSO, (1970), Investment Incentives, Cmnd 4516, London.

HMSO, (1982), Green Paper on Corporation Tax, Cmnd 8456, London.

HMSO, (1984), Fourth Report from the Treasury and Civil Service Committee. The 1984 Budget, London.

Inland Revenue, (1985), Mine and Oil Wells Allowance: A Consultative Document, London, July.

Inland Revenue, (1986), Capital Allowances: Machinery and Plant: Short Life Assets, Press Release, London, January.

King, M A and Fullerton, D, eds., (1984), The Taxation of Income from Capital, A Comparative Study of the United States, the United Kingdom, Sweden and West Germany, Chicago University Press.

Levis, M and Morgan, E J, with O'Loan, D and Thanassoulas, G, (1986), The 1984 Budget: Effects on Corporation Tax and Investment, Discussion Paper No.67, University of Bath, November.

Lund, P J, (1975), 'The Econometric Assessment of the Impact of Investment Incentives', in Whiting, A (ed.), The Economics of Industrial Subsidies, HMSO, London.

Marquand, J, (1980), Measuring the Effects and Costs of Regional Incentives, Government Economic Service Working Paper No.32, Department of Industry, February.

Mayer, C P and Morris, C N, (1982), A Disaggregated Model of the UK Corporate Tax System, Working Paper No.33, Institute of Fiscal Studies, London.

McKintosh, A, (1963), The Development of Firms, Cambridge University Press.

Melliss, C L and Richardson, P W, (1976), 'The Value of Investment Incentives for Manufacturing Industry 1946-74', in Whiting, A (ed.) The Economics of Industrial Subsidies, HMSO, London.

Morgan, E J, (1986), 'Stimulating Investment: Government Incentives and the Financial Leasing Industry', in Hall, G (ed.), European Industrial Policy, Croom Helm, Kent.

Nedo, (1983), Prospects for the Mechanical Handling Industry, Report to the National Economic Development Council, July.

Pike, R H, (1983), 'A Review of Recent Trends in Formal Capital Budgeting Processes', Accounting and Business Research, Summer.

Rockley, L E, (1973), Investment for Profitability: An Analysis of the Policies and Practies of UK and International Companies, Business Books, London.

Sargent, J R and Scott, M F, (1986), 'Investment and the Tax System in the UK', Midland Bank Review, Spring.

215

Sumner, M, (1984), The Treasury View of Corporate Taxation, University of Sussex, Discussion Paper.

Tomkins, C R, Lowe, J F and Morgan, E J, (1979), An Economic Analysis of the Financial Leasing Industry, Saxon House.

APPENDIX

Appendix 1.1

The direct effect of the tax system by sector and firm size

| | No quantified evaluation | | Pre tax | | Post tax evaluation | | | Total |
	Taxation and leasing ignored or insignificant	Taxation critical	Evaluation ignoring leasing	Comfortably above target	As high under new system	Lower under not critical	New system critical	number of firms
a) By sector								
Data processing	2	1	3	2	-	1	-	9
Electronic components	3	-	3	1	1	1	-	9
Mechanical handling	3	1	3	-	-	-	1	8
Non energy extraction	3	1	2	1	1	-	-	8
Pharmaceuticals	-	-	3	2	2	1	-	8
Printing	1	-	3	1	2	1	-	8
Road haulage	3	4	1	-	1	-	1	10
Total	15	7	18	7	7	4	2	60
b) By employment size								
1 - 99	7	3	1	-	-	-	2	13
100 - 499	3	2	1	-	1	-	-	7
500 - 4999	2	2	2	1	1	2	-	10
5000 +	3	-	14	6	5	2	-	30
Total	15	7	18	7	7	4	2	60

Appendix 1.2

Indirect effect of the tax system on liquidity by sector and firm size

a) By sector	Liquidity improved significantly by old system		Liquidity similar or better under new system			Total number of cases
	Specific invest. Signific. aided	Specific invest. Not signific. aided	Low profits little leasing	Surplus Act	High profits Vis-a-vis FYA	
Data processing	-	-	5	-	4	9
Electronic components	-	3	5	1	-	9
Mechanical handling	1	2	1	-	4	8
Non energy extraction	1	-	3	2	2	8
Pharmaceuticals	-	1	2	2	3	8
Printing	-	2	4	1	1	8
Road haulage	4	-	3	1	2	10
Total	6	8	23	7	15	60
b) By employment size						
1 - 99	5	1	5	-	2	13
100 - 499	1	2	5	-	-	7
500 - 4999	-	3	5	-	2	10
5000 +	-	2	9	7	12	30
Total	6	8	23	7	16	60